Too Much Too Young

Too Much Too Young explores the relationship between popular music, age and gender, examining the role of youth and youthfulness through a series of themed case studies. Sheila Whiteley begins by investigating the exploitation of young artists such as Brenda Lee and Michael Jackson, offering a psychoanalytic reading of the relationship between child star and oppressive manager, and looks at the current glut of boy- and girl-bands and solo performers in the mould of Britney Spears, to examine the continuing fatal fascination of stardom for adolescents.

Whiteley then considers the reception of female singer-songwriters Kate Bush, Tori Amos and Björk, whose 'little girl' voices and characterisation by the media suggest a girlish femininity which is often at odds with the intentions of their musical output. She then moves on to explore the rock/pop divide as it affects the image of male performers, considering why male stars usually fall into the category of 'wild boys' such as Jim Morrison and Jimi Hendrix, or 'nice boys' such as Cliff Richard, The Monkees and Wham! Whiteley ends by asking what happens to artists when they begin to age; why death has bestowed iconic status upon rock musicians; and why the manipulation of youthfulness has been integral to the careers of pop artists such as Kylie Minogue and Cher.

Sheila Whiteley is Chair of Popular Music at the University of Salford.

Too Much Too Young

Popular music, age and gender

Sheila Whiteley

Routledge
Taylor & Francis Group

LONDON AND NEW YORK

First published 2005
by Routledge
2 Park Square, Milton Park, Abingdon, Oxon OX14 4RN

Simultaneously published in the USA and Canada
by Routledge
270 Madison Ave., New York, NY 10016, USA

Routledge is an imprint of the Taylor & Francis Group

Typeset in Goudy by
Taylor & Francis Books Ltd
Printed and bound in Great Britain by
TJ International Ltd, Padstow, Cornwall

British Library Cataloguing in Publication Data
A catalogue record for this book is available from the British
Library

Library of Congress Cataloging in Publication Data
A catalog record for this book has been requested

ISBN 0–415–31029–6 (hbk)
ISBN 0–415–31028–8 (pbk)

Too Much Too Young is dedicated to the memory of my father, Maurice Eivind Astrup who loved and supported me through the good times and the not-so-good times. I will always love you.

Contents

Illustrations

Acknowledgements

As ever, thanks to my family, daughters Lucinda, Bryony, Anni, and grandchildren, Alex, Luisa, Bella, Daniel and James, for their love and support; my partner Graham, for his help with transcriptions, listening and responding to my ideas with unfailing enthusiasm; my cat Milli, for sitting beside me and purring; and the team at Routledge including Kate Ahl, Aileen Irwin and Nick Shah for his cover design. In particular, I'd like to single out Rebecca Barden and Julene Knox who have shared my ordeals over copyright and seem me through to eventual publication. One year on, it was worth it! Thank you.

Björk

Bow Wow Wow

'I Want Candy' written by Bob Feldman/Gerald Goldstein/Richard Gottehrer/ Bert Berns lyrics reproduced by kind permission of Sony/ATV Music Publishing.

Kate Bush

'Wuthering Heights' (*The Kick Inside* 1978) Words and music by Kate Bush © 1977, Reproduced by permission of Kate Bush trading as Noble & Brite, London WC2H 0QY.

'Room For The Life' (*The Kick Inside* 1978) © 1978, Reproduced by permission of Kate Bush trading as Noble & Brite, London WC2H 0QY.'Feel It' (*The Kick Inside* 1978) EMI

'Feel It' (*The Kick Inside* 1978) Words and music by Kate Bush © 1978, Reproduced by permission of Kate Bush trading as Noble & Brite, London WC2H 0QY.'Feel It' (*The Kick Inside* 1978) EMI

'Sat In Your lap' (*The Dreaming* 1982) Words and music by Kate Bush © 1982, Reproduced by permission of Kate Bush trading as Noble & Brite, London WC2H 0QY.

'The Dreaming' (*The Dreaming* 1982) Words and music by Kate Bush © 1982, Reproduced by permission of Kate Bush trading as Noble & Brite, London WC2H 0QY.

'Get Out Of My House' (*The Dreaming* 1982) Words and music by Kate Bush © 1982, Reproduced by permission of Kate Bush trading as Noble & Brite, London WC2H 0QY.

'Running Up That Hill' (*Hounds of Love*, 1985) Words and music by Kate Bush © 1985, Reproduced by permission of Kate Bush trading as Noble & Brite, London WC2H 0QY.

'Waking the Witch' (*Hounds of Love* 1985) Words and music by Kate Bush © 1985, Reproduced by permission of Kate Bush trading as Noble & Brite, London WC2H 0QY.

'Lily' (*The Red Shoes* 1993) Words and music by Kate Bush © 1985, Reproduced by permission of Kate Bush trading as Noble & Brite, London WC2H 0QY.

'Constellation of the Heart' (*The Red Shoes* 1993) Words and music by Kate Bush © 1985, Reproduced by permission of Kate Bush trading as Noble & Brite, London WC2H 0QY.

'Eat the Music' (*The Red Shoes* 1993) Words and music by Kate Bush © 1993, Reproduced by permission of Kate Bush trading as Noble & Brite, London WC2H 0QY.

Angela Carter
Extracts from The Magic Toyshop, 1981. London: Virago, and The Bloody Chamber, 1979. London: Penguin Books. Copyright © Angela Carter 1967. Reproduced by permission of Estate of Angela Carter c/o Rogers, Coleridge & White Ltd, 20 Powis Mews, London W11 1JN.

Great White
'On Your Knees'
Words and Music by Don Dokken, Jack Russell, Mark Kendall, Gary Holland and Loren Black
Copyright © 1984 IRVING MUSIC, INC and WHITE VIXEN SONGS
All Rights Controlled and Administered by IRVING MUSIC, INC
All Rights Reserved Used by Permission

Brenda Lee
'Dynamite'
Words by Tom Glazer
Music by Mort Garson
Copyright © 1957 Skidmore Music Co. Inc and Songs Music Inc.
Copyright Renewed.
International Copyright Secured All Rights Reserved
Used by Permission

Jim Morrison
'Light My Fire'
Words and music by the Doors
Copyright © 1967 Doors Music Co.
Copyright Renewed
All Rights Reserved Used by Permission

'Riders on The Storm'
Words and music by the Doors
Copyright © 1971 Doors Music Co.
Copyright Renewed
All Rights Reserved Used by Permission

'The End'
Words and music by the Doors

'Celebration of The Lizard'
Words and Music by The Doors

Extracts from *The American Night: The Writings of Jim Morrison* by Jim Morrision (Viking, 1991) copyright © Wilderness Publications, 1990:
6 lines from 'An American Prayer' (p3)
4 lines from 'A Wake' (p 62)
4 lines from 'Always A Playground Instructor' (p 124)
Reproduced by permission of Penguin Books Ltd.

Judas Priest

'Eat Me Alive' Words and Music by Glen Tipton, Robert Halford and Kenneth Downing.

Rolling Stones
'Some Girls' (*Some Girls* 1978) Words and Music by Mick Jagger and Keith Richards.

Introduction

In June 1957 Brenda Lee, 'the little girl with grown up reactions' released her single 'Dynamite'. Recorded when she was 13 years old, her vocal delivery abounds with an overtly physical and self-conscious sexual energy that belies her age. What makes her 'sexy' is the sense of 'knowingness' behind what might appear to be innocent lyrics, the erotic pause before a punch line pregnant with innuendo – 'one hour of love tonight just knocks me out like dynamite', with the inference of post-orgasmic exhaustion. I was 16 when the song was released and thought little about the exploitation of young vocalists. Rather, I wondered how someone so young could be so confident, so popular. She obviously possessed that special 'something' that singled her out as 'star' potential, a quality shared by such other young performers as Helen Shapiro who, as a 14-year-old school girl scored her first UK Top 3 hit with 'Don't Treat Me Like A Child' and whose deep intonation again belied her age. My reaction, then, was more likely to have been 'Lucky them!' rather than 'sexploitation'. With age and experience – not least the legacy of feminism and feminist theory and its concern with child abuse – I am more cynical. The erotic potential and appeal of children, not least the attraction of what can be described as an adult performance by a child, continues to exert a questionable appeal. In the profit-driven world of advertising, fashion and music, the image and culture of the young are appropriated for the high pleasure quotient they evoke. Youthful appeal and sexual allure are marketable commodities and are consumed today not simply by teens and adults but equally by the growing market of tweenies, the 8–10 year-olds who make up the majority fan base for girl and boy bands. Fame, however, comes at a cost and as Dr Michelle Elliott of the Children's Charity Kidscape states: 'We have found that with most child stars their journey into adulthood isn't successful. Children need to be children' (Le Vay, 2003, 6).

My initial concern, when researching *Too Much Too Young*, was to examine the problems concerning the exploitation of young musicians. Not least, I wanted to explore the relationship between image, age and musical performance (choice of songs, vocal style) that situated the artist as problematic, as inviting questionable pleasures in their audience. This, in turn, necessitated an understanding of the concept and definition of 'child' and the extent to which this is considered a socially constructed condition rather than one that can be defined objectively with reference to chronological age. My reading here was informed both by sociological texts and, more specifically, the writings of Marina Warner (1994a and 1994b), Angela Carter (1979, 1981, 2000) and Sarah Maitland (1993). Here I found a shared interest in mythology and fairytale, subjects that have interested me for many years, not least for the ways in which they highlight the significance of dialogics and the understanding that 'meaning is situated both socially and historically, that it works through dialogue – echoes, traces, contrasts, responses – both with previous discursive moments and, at the same time, with addressees real or imagined' (Middleton, 2000, 13).

As Middleton observes, the concept of dialogic exchange provides a particular insight into intertextuality and how meaning in popular music is produced at many different levels. A textual analysis of lyrics and musical style provides one important methodological trajectory, but meaning is also produced through dialogue within the textures, voices and structures; between producers and addressees; between discourses, musical and other. Add to this a concern with sexuality and gender, the singing style, the visual gesture, the image and, significantly, the ideological interests that support dominant interpretations, and it is apparent that how one 'tells' the story is crucial to its interpretation. In effect, the story told is one among many, and while musical analysis, and research into historical and cultural data remain important, meaning is always at issue. There is no one scientifically true account of the music, but rather a sense of *collective complicity*: Is this story plausible, (Middleton 2000, 13–14) is my interpretation plausible?

While the concept of dialogic exchange is most apparent in the relationship of rock to the Dionysian cult of excess, it became increasingly apparent that artists such as Kate Bush explored and celebrated female archetypes and iconography, drawing on mythology, history, literature, Arthurian legend and Jungian psychology for provisional identities, using femininity as a cipher of masks and poses. Stereotyped for her 'little girl' voice and characterised as singing with the insatiability of a child who has not yet learnt to curb her voracious desires, it became apparent that childlikeness (and its associations with simplicity and guilelessness) and childishness (in adults, often construed as emotionally immature and prone to petulant outbursts) was associated with girlish femininity, a characteristic shared by Tori Amos and Björk.

My interest in the exploitation of child stars was thus extended to a more general concern with the stereotyping of 'Little Girls' and the ways in which images have a fundamental influence on our preconceptions regarding the nature of women. To an extent, this can be accounted for by the artist's personal vocal style. As Simon Frith observes, 'femininity, as vocal performance, centres around gendered emotions' (1988, 155), and the yelps, howls and screams of anguish that have been described as constituting childish outburst, coupled with a characterisation by the media as childlike, winsome and otherworldly, are both contributory factors in identifying Bush, Amos and Björk as archetypal

'Little Girls'. It is apparent, however, that all three artists possess quite remark-able vocal ranges, of which 'childlike' is but one, and that their vocal delivery relates primarily to their artistic role as storytellers, looking before and after, referring to past events and wisdom, and envisaging the future in light of these interpretations. Again, it is this sense of dialogics that draws into association mythological imagery, the erotic imagination and the feminine within. 'Little Girls', then, is a problematic concept in its relation to image, identity and musical delivery, reflecting the different ways of culturally defining women within a history of what is meant by femininity, and how mythology has articu-lated a cultural sense of what it is to be a woman 'through a celebration of sexuality in both its joyous and darkest manifestations' (McEwan in Carter, 1979, back cover).

The tensions between the erotic (from the Greek *eros*, love or the creative principle) and the thanatic (from the Greek *thanatos*, death or the destructive principle) have been important to my discussion of 'Little Girls' and 'Little Boys'. Not least, the flights of fantasy that inform, for example, Jim Morrison's Oedipal psychodrama 'The End' (1967) relate both to the mythological and to the liberation of passions that result in death and rebirth. This emphasis on the thanatic is also present in Tori Amos's *a capella* account of her rape in 'Me And A Gun', and in Kate Bush's 'Waking the Witch' (1985) which explores the fate of a young woman condemned as 'guilty, guilty, guilty' through fractured elec-tronic sounds and imagery which evoke the horror of exorcism and torture. This sense of violence as spectacle can be traced in classical mythology, in biblical texts, in the chronicles of history; its legitimisation through state and religion can be found in the continuing history of prostitution, rape, 'foot binding, suttee, purdah, clitoridectomy, witch-burning and gynecology' (Tong, 1992, 5), as well as in the rites of passage that can accompany a boy's journey into adult-hood where some form of mutilation (including circumcision and/or tribal scarring) accompanies manhood. For the artist, it relates to the ways in which fiction and fantasy inform the imaginary and the actual concerns of life, and how fear, terror and outrage can be recast and reclaimed. The inner and outer, the mythologised monster, the martyred corpse and the raped woman are thus drawn together through the telling of the story, which in turn becomes both a text of inspiration and a text of sado-masochism.

The 'telling of the story', then, is crucial to its interpretation and advertise-ments, and mainstream films, videos and popular music promos reflect the slippery divide between pulp romance and soft-core and beyond. Research into slasher movies, whereby scenes of extreme violence are juxtaposed with some sort of erotic prelude, reveals a curious comparability with, for example, the storytelling tactics of Boccaccio's *Decameron* or, more overtly, the Marquis de Sade. 'The speed and ease with which one's feelings can be transformed from sensuality into viciousness may surprise even those quite conversant with the links between sexual and violent urges' (Maslin, 1982, 2). It is also a ploy in heavy metal, where themes often centre around fantasy, death, 'black' or satanic subjects, and where power chords, intense hard-driven beats and an emphasis on violence create a mood of aggressive sexuality:

Gut-wrenching frenzy
That deranges every joint
I'm gonna force you at gun point
To eat me alive...

(Judas Priest, 'Eat Me Alive')

The distinction between love of life (*eros*) and love of death (*thanatos*) is problematic. Both evoke and celebrate sensuality – the erotic its joyous, the thanatic its darkest manifestations. Both work in the imagination, but it is arguably the case that the liberation of passions can lead to 'refinements of pleasure, of ecstasies of perception, of courtesies and reciprocities undreamed' (Byatt, 1997, 204), and hence to the liberation of those passions which take pleasure in the hurt of others. Within human nature, the worship of Death and the worship of Beauty and Pleasure are not necessarily distinct. The one can have an uneasy and perverse relationship to the other. Indeed, it is difficult not to surmise that 'shameful things, shameful secrets, desires suppressed with violence (which) are kept secret and separate ... fester in body and brain' (Byatt, 1997, 65). You cannot unsee what you have seen. You cannot unhear what you have heard.

As A.S. Byatt writes:

(we) are children of a time and culture which mistrusted love, 'in love', romantic love, romance *in toto*, and which nevertherless in revenge proliferated sexual language, linguistic sexuality, analysis, dissection, deconstruction, exposure ... (We are) theoretically knowing: ... (we know) about phallocracy and peniseid, punctuation, puncturing and penetration, about polymorphous and polysemous perversity, orality, good and bad breasts, clitoral tumescence, vehicle persecution, the fluids, the solids, the metaphors for these, the systems of desire and damage, infantile greed and oppression and transgression, the iconography of the cervis and the imagery of the expanding and contracting body, desired, attacked, consumed, feared.

(1991, 423)

The ritualisation of the thanatic and its relationship to rites of passage provided a particular trajectory for my discussion of 'Little Boys' and rock culture. Whereas women musicians have had to 'find their own voices', investing both their identity and experience in their music, stressing individuality rather than lineage, estrangement rather than belonging, 'Little Boys' are burdened by the legacy of the founding members of generic dynasties. While this is most apparent in rock, it is nevertheless evident that each genre carries with it particular conventions based both on image and musical characteristics (including performance style) and that these impose a particular, and often constraining, framework. Age, it seems, is particularly relevant here, and, for the rock genre, it carries with it a mythology built on excess which is realised either metaphorically or in reality, by death. In contrast, 'nice boys' are doomed to be the quintessential 'boy-next-door', unthreatening, romantic and uncontaminated by the Dionysian addiction to drugs, drink and sexual excess. Or so they say.

The question is thus raised as to who controls the destiny of young stars and why these destructive frameworks continue to dictate the rules of the game. What happens to popular music's old girls and old boys when they exit the fast lane of superstardom, and how can death become such an exploitable commodity?

Analysis of musical examples

The artists included in *Too Much Too Young* were selected primarily for their significance in opening out the principal debates in the three main sections of my book. A secondary consideration concerned accessibility, i.e. whether their recordings are still available. As a reader, I know there is nothing more irritating than being guided towards a particular book or recording and finding it no longer available. As all of my case studies refer to particular songs and/or albums, this criteria has been important. However, it is perhaps an indication of their perceived value that the artists under discussion continue to assume an important presence in popular music. This is evidenced by the remastering of albums as CDs, which has meant that early tracks by, for example, Brenda Lee, have provided both old and new fans with access to 'Little Miss Dynamite'.

In general, my interpretative approach situates the analysis of the music itself within a cultural-critical framework that responds to, and engages with, a wide range of literature. The case studies themselves are situated within a social and historical context and in relation to popular music styles and genres. This is, I believe, significant. An analysis of rock, for example, will privilege certain stylistic elements, not least the role of lead and rhythm guitar, and the synergy between bass and drums. In contrast, ballads (which draw on folk song, drawing room, Tin Pan Alley and light opera) 'are focused texturally on certain types of flowing, long-breathed lyricism and tend to use sophisticated chains of harmonies (rather than the repeated cycles of simple chord-sequences that are characteristic of up-tempo pop songs and Punk)'. Even so, within this broad commonality, it is possible to 'distinguish "rock ballads", "country ballads", "soul ballads", "pop ballads", all of which bring with them "genre synecdoches" (defined as from inside one musical style to elements of another, thence to the genre of which the second style is part) and "style indicators"' (Middleton, 1997, 37). Group singing, for example, is significant within boy and girl groups and this is reflected in, for example, call-and-response, familiar from black musical traditions, or in the close harmony of fifties vocal groups and nineties

boy bands, or in a varied mixture of the two, as in the Beatles.[1] What is significant here is that the stylistic identity of a genre can mutate over time, not least
in today's musical climate of increasing hybridity.

While my musical analysis is sensitive to both stylistic and generic conventions, I am also concerned with the unique elements of an artist's style and the
ways in which s/he engages with the musical parameters of melody, harmony,
rhythm, texture, form and, where important, production. I am also concerned
with the ways in which a singer expresses a particular perspective through the
narrative of the lyrics, the vocabulary used, and how this relates to the vocal
gesture and melodic phrasing. The formal details of the musical analysis are
opened out by a more interpretative focus which relates the lyrics to their
dramatic function as in, for example, the tensions between the singer's voice
and the supporting musical texture, and to the broader context of, for example,
personal trauma in many of the songs by Tori Amos, or the literary and mythological references in songs by Kate Bush and Jim Morrison. My analysis here is
centred largely on extramusical meanings which relate to the concept of
'dialogics – echoes, traces, contrasts, responses – both with previous discursive
moments and, at the same time, with addressees real or imagined' (Middleton,
2000, 13), as discussed previously. This means that 'its signifying stream … is
always multivoiced' and that 'meanings are produced through dialogue at many
levels' (Middleton, 2000, 13). There is, then, no fixed or absolute meaning
when interpreting the songs under discussion, but biographies of the artists
suggest that my readings are relevant to the points raised.

An overview of the book

Too Much Too Young has three main sections. Part I, Nursery Crymes,[2] explores
the problems surrounding the eroticising of the child star. Prefaced by a discussion of the condition of childhood and the conceptualisation of innocence that
underpins the contemporary paradox of both containing child sexuality and
accepting its exploitation through, for example, the media, my first case study is
based on Brenda Lee. Nicknamed 'Little Miss Dynamite' when she first began
recording for Decca at the age of eleven, her status as a pre-pubescent child
whose sexually potent songs inferred an implicit maturity and her marketed
image of a 'little girl with grown up reactions', the delivery of her songs was
arguably at odds with her actual image of a diminutive, curly-haired child.

My discussion of Brenda Lee is opened out by reference to other representations of eroticised children, from the nineteenth century through to the present
day. This includes a discussion of Lewis Carroll, whose fascination, and
suppressed desire, for the innocent world of the child was equalled only by his
desire to 'escape from the improper implications of passion introduced into his
world by the adult women around him' (Dijkstra, 1986, 189). His photography
of 'adorable little girls in the full innocence of their nudity' (Dijkstra, 1986,
189) included Alice Liddell, the real Alice whose fictional adventures were

chronicled in *Alice in Wonderland* and *Alice Through the Looking Glass*. My discussion of child sexuality in fine art and the reality of child prostitution in the nineteenth century is then given a more contemporary focus in the debates surrounding Vladimir Nabokov's *Lolita*.(1959) As Jeremy Irons (who played Humbert Humbert in Adrian Lynes' film of the book) explains : 'Its power comes from moments when you want the love between the man and the girl to succeed, when their happiness seems untouchable' (Hasted, 1998, 4). It is evident, however, that *Lolita* skirts a thin line between pornography and so-called 'art' movies in that it both provokes debate, forcing the viewer to reassess his relation to his own sexuality, while engaging with libidinous fantasy.

Today, there is a curious silence from progressive and other radical cultural workers about the ways in which children and sex are portrayed in films, advertising and media culture in general (Giroux, 1998, 47). While such images are not necessarily pornographic, they can nevertheless invite questionable pleasures in their audience. And this, I believe, is the problem surrounding the careers of young artists such as Brenda Lee.

My second case study concerns the career of Michael Jackson, arguably the most visible of all child stars mutated by fame. His 40 years as a performer has seen his transition from a child star to a childlike star who continues to embody the Peter Pan qualities associated with the boy who refuses the pathway to adulthood. Dominated by two father-figures, Joseph Jackson (his real-life father) and Berry Gordy (the boss of Tamla Motown), his perverse personality and increasingly mask-like features problematise his Afro-American origins through a blanched and overly-taut skin, so suggesting an attempt to abolish both masculinity and any resemblance to his abusive father.

My analysis of Jackson draws on Freud, most specifically his identification of the *phallic* stage and the boy child's attempt to resolve the Oedipus complex, and Lacan's discussion of sexuality as structured around the primary symbol of cultural authority. It is here that Jackson's confused metemorphoses, his attempts to achieve an idealised image, a totality out of its disparate parts, can be interpreted both as a challenge to the omnipotent phantom of his father and as a contemporary realisation of the story of 'The Picture of Dorian Gray'. Gray's face, like the mask that is now Jackson's face, is illusory. The story expresses a will to stay forever young. The concept of metamorphoses and masquerade is further explored through Michael Jackson's video and single, 'Thriller'. This is opened out through a critical appraisal of Kobena Mercer's seminal article 'Monster metaphors: notes on Michael Jackson's Thriller' (1991). Jackson's metamorphosis into a wolf is related to Angela Carter's short stories in *The Bloody Chamber* (1979), and it is suggested that his mutation relates to his own identification with animals (rather than adult humans, as exemplified in his extensive collection of animals at his home 'Neverland') and to the injured childlike man behind the mask whose desire to remain ever-young has led increasingly to his problematic association with children. His second metamorphosis into a zombie, relates his transformation to an allegory of the parasitic, the non-stop media investigations into his image that led, increasingly, to his retreat into the fantasy-world of 'Neverland'. In summary, it is argued that Jackson remains a childlike star, living in a make-believe world, a small, seemingly vulnerable person who affirms the 'connection with that childhood Eden in which the Lost Boys are still living, defying the death of the child within' (Warner, 1994b, 43).

While Jackson was seemingly incapable of resolving the Oedipal complex, Jim Morrison (my third case study) confronts his desire to 'kill the father' and 'fuck the mother' in his chilling Oedipal psychodrama 'The End'. Like Jackson, Morrison was profoundly alienated from his father, and his feeling of estrangement was informed not only by his identification with the Beat poet Jack Kerouac, the writer William Burroughs and the philosopher Norman O. Brown, but also by his growing reliance on LSD, which, in 1965, was both plentiful and legal in California. As the Oedipal myth reveals, the only way for a son to achieve power is to rid himself of the father, and the song provides a primal and emotive evocation of Morrison's urge to separate himself from his past in order to control his present and future.

While Joseph Jackson and George Morrison provide two examples of the effects of extreme paternal authority, my fourth case study explores the destructive drives inherent in Malcolm McLaren's manipulative management of Annabella Lwin, the 14-year-old lead singer of the 1980s pop group, Bow Wow Wow. Here, my discussion is opened out with reference to McLaren's earlier management of the Sex Pistols, his proposed promotional film for the Slits, and his early draft script for *The Great Rock 'n' Roll Swindle* (a collaboration with Julian Temple on the story of the Sex Pistols). McLaren's management of Bow Wow Wow had involved a transformation of lead singer Annabella, who was photographed semi-nude on an album-sleeve pastiche of Manet's *Dejeuner sur l'Herbe* (see Part I for copy of the sleeve). His aim was to project her as an embodiment of exotic, under-age sex. Her image relates her not only to past inscriptions of black and other ethnic groups within colonial and post-colonial discourse but, as I explain, the continuing problem of the child within pornography and prostitution. McLaren's exploitation of Annabella is, then, highly problematic, and reflects what Simon Reynolds describes as his five-year transition from 'a neo-Situationist agent provocateur to a dirty old man' (Reynolds and Press, 1995, 42).

As my chapter argues, while research demonstrates that young audiences (including 8–10 year olds) have an active engagement with popular music whereby their own gendered identities can be both explored and negotiated (Bloustein, 1999b, Baker 2002), the problems of mis-use remain, not least those concerning overly-exploitative record companies, and 'Nursery Crymes' concludes with a brief survey of other child stars who have suffered under the patriarchal dictates of music management. In particular, I draw attention to the ways in which looks and image continue to dominate the careers of would-be pop idols, and the continuing fatal attraction of stardom for adolescent wannabes.

Part II deals with the stereotyping of 'Little Girls' and the ways in which images have a fundamental influence on our preconceptions regarding the nature of women. I begin with a consideration of the term 'girl' and how it has been inscribed within different genres of popular music. While the specifics of genres are context-dependent, it is apparent that the conceptualisation of 'girl' is inscribed within the common sense of stereotype and cliché. Thus, while the misogynistic of heavy rock/metal inscribes 'girl' as an unproblematic sex object, the more romantic evocations of, for example, the Beatles, relate more to the traditional attributes of femininity: empathy, supportiveness, gentleness, tenderness and unselfishness. Both extremes remind us that the codes we live by (not least those concerning sex/sexuality/gender) are neither natural nor innocent, and that terms such as 'girl' are grounded in the common sense of everyday discourse where they emerge as a site of contradiction, conflict and tension.

My three case studies explore a specific example of the inscription of 'Little Girl' within popular music discourse. Here, my earlier discussion of 'little girls with grown up reactions' shifts to women whose 'little-girl voices' and characterisation by the media as winsome and otherworldly suggests a girlish femininity which is often at odds with the intentions of their musical output. My three case studies, Kate Bush, Tori Amos and Björk explore the conceptualisation of their girlish femininity and, hence, the preconceptions concerning the nature of 'little girls'. What my analysis demonstrates is that all three artists possess quite remarkable vocal ranges, of which the 'childlike' is but one, and that their vocal delivery relates primarily to their artistic roles as storytellers.

My discussion of Kate Bush begins with a detailed analysis of her first single, 'Wuthering Heights' (1978), the promo for her debut album, *The Kick Inside*. Its impact is undoubtedly due to the ethereal quality of the vocal, which resonates with the dementia of Cathy, the star-crossed heroine of Emily Brontë's gothic novel. In particular, the seemingly unnaturally high register of Bush's vocal line, which assumes both childlike qualities in its purity of tone and an underlying eroticism in its sinuous melodic contours and obsessive vocalised femininity, provides the first indication of her ability to create a new kind of feminised language in popular music. Bush's struggle with femininity is explored further in my discussion of her second album, *Lionheart*, where I return to the conceptualisation of Peter Pan earlier explored in my analysis of Michael Jackson. For Jackson, his identification with Peter Pan relates to his refusal to grow up, his desire to remain in the fantastic world of 'Neverland'. For Bush, the groundedness of being a girl, the reality of a future where the fun has been taken out of life and where understanding comes with age, is challenged by the recognition that freedom comes with retaining and exploring childlike dreams and refusing domesticity, as embodied in the 'full eyes' but 'empty face' in her mirror image. To free herself of the image of the eroticised girl pop artist that dominated her reviews she has to fly, and the imaginary provides a way of transcending the conflicts of gender and the constrictions of being 'EMI's daughter'. Childhood fantasy, however, has to be tempered with reality. The music business was, and largely remains, a man's world and 'to fly' an artist has to be capable of using her own physicality as a resource and to redefine herself against the limitations of femininity. Her solution was to take more control over her career, forming her own publishing and management companies (Kate Bush Music and Novercia) with herself as managing director and her family on the board of directors.

Never For Ever (1980), her first Number One album, was co-produced by Bush and John Kelly. She also wrote and arranged the songs, performing vocals, piano and harmonies, and is pictured on the album sleeve with a multitude of flying creatures and mythological beasts, flying bat-like on the back cover which was conceived and photographed by her brother, John Carder Bush. The songs cover the vocal spectrum characteristic of Bush: the childlike embodied in 'The Infant Kiss' and 'Army Dreamers', the punk-driven dementia (comparable to the Banshee-like screams of Siouxsie Sioux) of 'Violin', and the dramatic poignancy of 'Breathing' with its Floyd-like outro. To an extent, the album provides a retrospective on her compositional output to date in its rich melodicism and sense of drama. *The Dreaming*, released two years later in 1982, is altogether different, heavily percussive and fraught with a wild, angry emotion. It was her 'she's gone mad'[3] album but while it was her least successful in the UK, it attracted attention in America where it was hailed as a musical tour de force.

After a two-year hiatus, Bush released *Hounds of Love* (1985), a work that is arguably her greatest to date. The gap between her albums was recognised by fans and critics alike as a sign of creative effort and praise of her ability to produce as well as to write her own music is reflected in reviews by, for example, *Digital Audio*. Across pop history, recordings are characterised by their sound quality and 'artists and producers have enjoyed considerable scope for personal expression and experimentation when composing and recording music in the studio' (Negus, 1992, 91). All genres have their conventions, but with the significance given to the voice – which most explicitly expresses a performer's personality and aurally signals their presence within the music – it is not too surprising that Bush should become obsessive in producing a sound quality that was comparable to the dramatic conception of her own vocal qualities and range. *Hounds of Love* is characterised not only by its expansive and dramatic sense of soundscaping, but equally by its sculpting of individual sound moments. Whereas *The Dreaming* suggested an obsessively over-produced album, *Hounds of Love* evidences Bush's ability to transform the emotional content of the songs into a well-balanced whole, showcasing her skills as both a competent engineer and as someone who has a mastery of synthesisers and sequencers, so demonstrating an ability to both draw on established techniques while exploring the possibilities offered by new technologies. The result was a well-crafted album, which revealed her strengths not only as a writer and singer but, most crucially for a woman, as a producer. Above all, it is sensual in its erotic play on sounds and images that both transform and situate the lyrics and vocal line within an often metaphysical and otherworldly soundscape.

Her follow-up album, *The Sensual World* (1989), provided further opportunity for evocative and unusual arrangements and choice of instrumentation and is considered Bush's most explicitly female-identified statement. This is reflected, most specifically in the title track, which traces feminine speech back to Molly Bloom's soliloquy from the close of James Joyce's *Ulysses*. Contextualised by uillean pipes, fiddle and bouzouki, the non-verbal is explored through exotic and sensuous textures which link the chaos of the inner world to the feminine of Nature. *The Red Shoes* (1993) is, at the time of writing, Kate Bush's last recorded album and evokes a sense of nostalgia. 'Moments of Pleasure' draws on memories of 'Wuthering Heights' in its soaring 'Just being alive/It can really hurt'. 'You're the One' again has a reflexive nod backwards to 'Wuthering Heights' in the melodic line 'She's no good for you baby', a comparable vocal tone, 'Take me up to the top of the city', and high vocal register, 'And I don't mind if it's dangerous'. Above all, the album sets out what appeared to be a personal agenda, the 'Song of Solomon' juxtaposes the ecstatic of love (I'll be your Rose of Sharon, Lilly of the Valley) against the realistic 'Don't want your bullshit, just want your sexuality'; the 'why should I love you (of all the people in the world)', and the not wanting to leave of 'You're the One'.

Bush's 'errant individualism' (O'Brien, 1995, 188) has placed her at the forefront of the singer-songwriter tradition. More specifically, she exemplifies one of only a few female performers who have fulfilled the role of composer and producer, so allowing her flights of erotic fantasy full rein. Her compositions address both the specific subjugation and revitalisation of women's experience, drawing on the tensions between representation and its relationship to history, ideology and culture; marginalisation and its impact on cultural self-expression; and the urge to create and articulate personal perspectives and points of view. Not least, her construction of images and the different ways of culturally defining women reflects both a history of what is meant by femininity, and the ways in which mythology and fairytale have articulated a cultural sense of what it is to be a women. Her music, then, can be characterised as both a strategy of difference and a strategy of defiance, and its otherworldly imagery and neo-gothic sound was, for many years, one of the few alternatives to girl pop.

While my discussion of Kate Bush has been informed by the mythological, my second case study, Tori Amos, deals with personal experience at its most extreme. I begin with an analysis of 'Me And A Gun' and 'Silent All These Years' from her debut album, *Little Earthquakes* (1992). Both explore painful memories, working through feelings of victimisation and so giving vent to the pent-up negativity that characterises victims of rape. Her performance can thus be interpreted as both personal catharsis and as a way of identifying Amos as part of the continuing history of women who have negotiated the problems surrounding violence and oppression. This sense of dialogics is equally evident in her second album, *Under the Pink* (1994), which reflects on the emotional violence between women, rather than between the sexes, the 'pecking order, which men don't usually see' (St. Michael, 1996, 88). This is most evident in 'The Waitress', where dissonant electronic effects and reverse samples on cymbal effect a dramatic underpinning for her declamatory 'I want to kill', and the issues surrounding victimisation and retribution in 'Cornflake Girl'. There is also a continuing tussle with the metaphysical, this time God rather than his Son, in the promo from the album. Characterised as self-centred and, perhaps, a little crazy, the sense of a Christian, 'westernised' God is extended in the accompanying video where live rats crawl over Amos's body, and where large snakes symbolically evoke the perverse communion between Eve and the devil. Religion, hypocrisy and rejection are explored further in 'Icicle', through a challenging composition that confronts female autoeroticism. In doing so, Amos provides a feminised account of the ways in which women are sexualised, victimised and ultimately disabled by the moral imperatives of the church, and where her body (and those of countless women before her) becomes a battlefield in the fight for liberation.

Among the final tracks on the album, 'Space Dog' and 'Anastasia', provide a showcase for Amos's virtuoso piano playing and evoke the epic drama of the Romantic tone poem. While they evidence her ability to orchestrate, to develop ideas and stretch her abilities as a composer, they lack the sense of intimacy and spontaneity of her more evocative songs. They also raise questions of 'just how long does a little girl remain a little girl'. My discussion of *Boys for Pele* (1996) opens out this debate through an analysis of 'Hey Jupiter', which reflects on the emotions surrounding relationships, while demonstrating that Amos's self-characterisation has moved to a more mature, but equally tempestuous femininity. This sense of a personal journey is extended in *from the choirgirl hotel* (1998) in tracks that partly explore the traumas surrounding her miscarriage and the problems surrounding drug addiction.

Amos's ability to sculpt her music around the lyrics, to work with varied textures and to explore her personal development through songs which relate to the full colour spectrum of her transition from 'little girl' to woman relates strongly to her underlying strength of purpose. It is a characteristic that is shared by Björk, my third case study, yet it seems that the press have consistently paid more attention to her appearance, her wildness and her elfin image than to a serious consideration of her quite exceptional musical talent. To an extent this is not surprising. Björk has always looked unconventional, different, and has played on her image across her musical career, from the Icelandic elf characteristic of her early techno days, through to the bleached hair and self-styled kookie image of 1996, and beyond to the exotic of the geisha on *Homogenic* (1997), and the emergent swan-like figure of *Vespertine* (2001). My analysis of Björk explores this transition in relation to her music, drawing particular attention to the ways in which she uses the flexibility of her vocal range, from the mischief of her often quirky delivery, through to the poetic and melodically eloquent.

I begin with a discussion of *Debut* (1993), for which she teamed up with Nellee Hooper (producer) and Marius De Vries (programmer) to produce an album which resonated with the House-inflected imagination of the early 1990s. The album is authoritative in its contemporary feel, and the repetitive grooves and often seamless rhythms of the tracks allow Björk a certain indulgence in her vocal delivery, which is often rhythmically erratic. At the same time, it provides a particular insight into her idiosyncratic shaping of words, the concentration on the syllabic quality of sounds, the upward yodels, and the emphasis on individual consonants and vowels. In common with both Bush and Amos, Björk has a personalised feel for language which often relates to her state of mind when writing, and which moves from aggression through to a defencelessness associated with her 'little girl' voice. Her broken English is also used to good effect in opening out a sense of aloneness and linguistic frustration, attributable both to her move to England and her subsequent tours abroad. It seems, however, that there is an underlying knowingness about her seemingly childlike delivery. Her tone often conceals a hidden chuckle, while her occasional growling 'rrr's' confirm her identity as exotically different, as in the classic House feel of track 4, 'There's More To Life Than This'. Above all, Björk's love of words seems to resonate with her multifaceted personality, whether this is hardcore industrial or the poetic eloquence of 'Venus As A Boy', where there is an almost tactile and voluptuous quality to the vocal, evocative of the beauty of sexual awakening. Björk, then, is a quintessential storyteller and her ability to colour her vocal inflections serves, primarily, to open out the narrative and to situate the listener within her chosen environments.

Post (1995) was even more successful than *Debut*, and showed little real shift in direction, so reflecting once again the chart potential of techno beats and House. While they both contributed to Björk's acclaim as an international artist, her success also draws attention to the problems associated with stardom. Not least, the suicide by fan Ricardo Lopez, and the bomb posted by him to her home address in London, changed her life. In particular, she was concerned that her son, Sindri was, like her, vulnerable to attack and this darkening mood is reflected in *Homogenic* (1997). In particular, the album resonates with the volatile emotional states associated with trauma and breakups (her relationship with drum 'n' bass artist, Goldie). At the same time, there is a new sense of maturity in the mesmeric quality of the songs which provides a personal insight into 'what it is to be a woman', and this is complimented by the adventurous arrangements, not least the lush, sweeping sounds of the Icelandic String Quartet. Above all, the album is dark and introspective, albeit ending with a feeling of rebirth on the final track, 'love is all around you'. It seems, from her latest album, *Vespertine* (2001), that the romantic prevails and that the growls, shrieks and hard techno beats of the past are gone. In their place is a new sense of control which allows the 'little girl' vocal to soar effortlessly into a newly found freedom of expression.

While 'Little Girls' have their own problems in terms of stereotyping, 'Little Boys' have to negotiate the imperatives of history where each genre has its own traditions, both in terms of music and image. Part III contextualises these problems with reference to two principal examples, the 'wild boys' of rock vs the 'nice boys' of pop, and why their prevailing codes continue to exercise a sense of who belongs and who is excluded. I begin, once again, with a discussion of the problems surrounding definition, this time the historical evolution of cultural and musical criteria which effectively control what is/is not acceptable within the stylistic conventions of respective musical genres. This is given a specific focus in the distinctions surrounding rock/pop and the ways in which the connotations of boy/boyish, lad/laddish are constituted within rock 'n' roll, 1960s rock and pop, 1970s punk and the ironic use of cliché and convention in 1980s pop and beyond. Finally, I consider rites of passage and the relationship to masculinity, before ending with a detailed case study of Jim Morrison and Jimi Hendrix.

As discussed previously in 'Nursery Crymes', Jim Morrison's psychodrama 'The End' has a particular relevance to rock mythology, and here I develop my discussion of the Oedipal with reference to his birth as the lizard king of rock. For his fans, Morrison's persona is linked to Dionysus. He was a man who acknowledged no restraints, rules or laws, and his continuing significance is reflected in the countless pilgrimages to his Paris grave in the Père Lachaise cemetery where such graffiti as 'Jim Morrison is God' are now perpetuated by a third generation of fans. Morrison was the first rock icon to interpret his life in Messianic terms, and this sense of self-omnipotence is traced through such songs as 'The Celebration of the Lizard', 'Celebration' and 'Crawling King Snake'.

Morrison's identification with the thanatic is also significant, and the association between sex, murder and revolution relates to his personal identification as shaman/lizard king, situating the worship of the penis[4] within a love of excess and self-destruction, 'death and my cock'. Musically, this is anchored within a hallucinogenic frame of reference and Morrison's personal experience of LSD. This is discussed with reference to 'Light My Fire', where the initial sentiments of the song are transformed into a transcendent love/death ritual, and 'Riders on the Storm'. Morrison's commitment to death as the ultimate form of sexual excess is reflected in the rock creed of live fast and die young, and his death, at the age of 27, contributed to his recognition as God. It is obvious, however, that his death was largely the result of the pressures of superstardom and the demands of countless public performances. These pressures were also shared by my second case study, Jimi Hendrix, who, like Morrison, died at the aged 27.

Hendrix continues to top the polls for 'best lead guitarist' and his status as a rock musician is without precedent. Like Morrison, his compositions and performance were underpinned by hallucinogenic experience: 'he *played* the sound of LSD' (Ellis, 1995, 201–2). My analysis here includes 'Purple Haze' and 'Love or Confusion' from his 1967 album, *Are You Experienced*. Again, there is a strong relationship between hallucinogenics and sexuality, and this is discussed both in relation to his performances and his attitude towards women. It is, however, his extraordinary sense of musicianship that is most significant to his continuing status as God. He single-handedly shifted the whole course of guitar playing and in doing so created a legacy which continues to dominate the course of rock and rock fusion, and which has crossed over into jazz through his work with Miles Davis.

The deaths of Morrison and Hendrix, and their resultant status as 'gods', has informed the whole trajectory of rock culture, as evidenced in my discussion of such iconic figures as Kurt Cobain and the cult of dead heroes. It is argued that self-destruction, whether drug-related, suicide or the result of severe risk taking, is curiously related to the excesses of a rock 'n' roll life style and that 'two hundred years of Romanticism have established the conventions of driving on the road to excess' (Pattison, 1987, 125). Not surprisingly, the rocker is always in the fast lane. In contrast, 'nice boys' retain a sense of naïve purity, and my next case study explores the ways in which pop idols are presented to their audience, their performance and their image. More specifically, while their repertoire can cross over to such phallocentric genres of rock, it is tempered by performance codes which signify enjoyment and fun rather than control and power and, as such, is effectively castrated.

I begin with a discussion of Cliff Richard, the UK's first pop idol. Initially associated with rock 'n' roll and a Presley-inflected performance style, his appeal as a middle-of-the-road performer was more dependent upon his boyish good looks and his ability as a vocalist. His enigmatic sexuality and his emerging persona as the eternal 'Bachelor Boy' was powerful in establishing both a straight and gay fan base, and this was extended by his appearance in films, summer seasons and regular TV slots. His determination to remain a performer also presages the change in career of two other pop idols, David Cassidy and Robbie Williams. My discussion of pop stars also includes a brief analysis of The Monkees, a group of fun-loving individuals who engaged in a string of band-related adventures in the American TV series of the same name. Their million-selling debut album and attendant singles, 'Last Train to Clarksville' and 'I'm A Believer' challenged the popularity of the Beatles and provided an important precedent for the successful marketing of future manufactured groups. My case studies also draw attention to the importance of age and personality, as exemplified in the career of the Bay City Rollers who were acclaimed as the biggest phenomenon to hit the UK pop music scene since the Beatles. However, it is evident that their success was largely due to their astute management and a succession of carefully chosen singles that enabled the group to reach the heights of stardom. Their somewhat unsavoury end also provided another lesson for the managers and members of would-be pop groups: 'Nice Boys' must live up to their image as clean-living.

This is demonstrated in the history of Wham!, the most successful teen-oriented group of the 1980s, whose founder member George Michael was finally outed in 1998 after years of denial that he was, in fact, a closet gay. What is important to the successful marketing of boy groups is that homoerotic connotations are contained and that the spectacle of male desire remains simply one of male-to-male looking, as evidenced in videos by Wham!, Boyzone and Westlife. It is also obvious that boy groups, like the single pop idol, have to be young (between the ages of 18 and 25, although many are younger), clean living, attractive and heterosexual[5] if they are to retain their position within teen and pre-teen culture. Finally, I move to a consideration of pop idols and the contemporary importance of reality television. Today, it appears that the manufactured pop star is no longer a figure of contempt for the majority audience. The unprecedented success of *Pop Idol* winner Will Young and runner-up Gareth Gates confirms for their fans that it was their adulation which created the stars who have earned the accolade 'pop idol'. Clearly this is only part of the story. The 'zombies' earlier described in 'Nursery Crymes' continue to gain most, so demonstrating once again that titles such as pop idol reflect, at best, a hollow crown.

If rock stars ideally die aged 27, and the appropriate age for a pop star is between 18 and 25, what happens to those who survive and wish to continue their careers in popular music? As my discussion so far indicates, age is critical to the identity of both performers and musical genres, but while my analysis of the 'wild boys' of rock draws attention to the significance of those who died young and who were subsequently venerated as gods, it is apparent that nostalgia continues to exert a strong presence, as evidenced in the increasing number of Golden Oldies in the album charts and musicals that capitalise on past glories. Even so, the continuing emphasis on youth does raise the question of what happens to those who have exited from the fast lane of superstardom: is there life after death, and what strategies are involved in resurrecting and redefining careers that are all too often built on image? These questions are explored further in the Postscript to *Too Much Too Young*, with particular reference to Elvis Presley, guitar heroes, the singer-songwriter tradition and such ageing pop idols as Cher, Madonna and Kylie Minogue.

Too Much Too Young provides a particular insight into the relationship between popular music, age and gender, but it is also evident that images have a fundamental influence on the development of our preconceptions concerning the popular arts. As such, I would conclude with an anecdote, one concerning my personal identity as a woman in popular music. In July 2000 I was promoted to Chair of Popular Music at Salford University and in the months that followed I experienced a great deal of media attention that related directly both to my job and my personal identity. On the one hand there was the accolade – that popular music is now recognised as a well-established academic discipline, as worthy of study, incontrovertibly evidenced by the increasing number of courses worldwide both in further and higher education. An accolade, too, for

Salford University in promoting the significance of popular music through the creation of the first personal chair in the UK. No problem overall, then, with the concept 'Professor of Popular Music' itself. Rather, interviewers were more interested in my personal identity, my image, my age, and the fact that I am a grandmother.

And so, from the onset, the headlines: 'Grandmother becomes first Professor of Popular Music'. Photos wanted the image authenticated: situating me either in a recording studio, next to an electric guitar, or posing kitten-like on my bed surrounded by my favourite LPs and CDs – you know, 'like you would have done as a teenager'. I was written up as Jim Morrison's lover – a slight confusion here as the interviewer had asked me what sort of music attracted me in the 1960s. Like the many women about whom I have written, from Janis Joplin and Joni Mitchell, through to Kate Bush, Tori Amos and Björk, the same fixation arises – image and, wherever possible, sensationalism. I wonder whether the same fate would surround a male professor of physics who was in his late fifties? Still, there have been pay-offs – appearing on the TV programme *Ready Steady Cook*; commenting on why it seems that only males can be lead guitarists for the Channel 4 TV series *Top Ten*; talking to indomitable politicians such as Britain's Edwina Curry, and discussing the rise of pop idols and reality television for the BBC . However, I do have to ask myself, is it because of my background as a popular musicologist, or is it something to do with being a woman in what still seems to be a male domain: which is the real attraction?

Part I

Nursery Crymes

> The summer she was fifteen, Melanie discovered she was made of flesh and blood. O, my America, my new found land. She embarked on a tranced voyage, exploring the whole of herself, clambering her own mountain ranges, penetrating the moist richness of her secret valleys, a physiological Cortez da Gama or Mungo Park. For hours she stared at herself, naked, in the mirror of her wardrobe; she would follow with her finger the elegant structure of her rib-cage, where the heart fluttered under the flesh like a bird under a blanket, and she would draw down the long line from breast-bone to navel (which was a mysterious cavern or grotto), and she would rasp her palms against her bud-wing shoulder blades. And then she would writhe about, clasping herself, laughing, sometimes doing cart-wheels and handstands out of sheer exhilaration at the supple surprise of herself now she was no longer a little girl.
>
> (Carter, 1981, 1)

Childhood, as many writers have observed, is a socially constructed condition rather than one that can be defined objectively through reference to chronological age, and its tenuous boundaries vary both historically and culturally. The United Nations, for example, defines a child as someone under 18 years of age, whereas in Great Britain a child is defined as under 14 in criminal law and under 16 for some Acts of Parliament. While such definitions obscure the significance of adolescence and youth – the betwixt and between – and, in certain circumstances, gender (such as a difference in the age of consent for practising homosexuals), they nevertheless place childhood tangential to adulthood, as something different both in terms of legal status and experience.

The social passage from the status of a child to a woman, a child to a man, can be considered as embodying both biological change and social experience. Menstruation, for example, is widely accepted as a powerful sign from the body that the girl has become a woman; sex gives her more experience, hence she becomes more adult. The final transition comes with giving birth, with rearing a child. While such definitions are problematic in their direct association of the effects of female biology on woman's self-perception, status and function, not least her assumed heterosexuality (the concept of 'natural order' and the institutionalising of motherhood under patriarchy), the concept of bodily change and its relationship to personal identity is important. Not least it invites a discussion of *inside* – a person's consciously or self-consciously held image of himself or herself – and *outside* – their status within social groups and society.

She was too thin for a Titian or a Renoir but she contrived a pale, smug Cranach Venus with a bit of net curtain wound round her head and the necklace of cultured pearls they gave her when she was confirmed at her throat. After she read *Lady Chatterley's Lover*, she secretly picked forget-me-nots and stuck them in her pubic hair. ... All this went on behind a locked door in her pastel, innocent bedroom, with Edward Bear (swollen stomach concealing striped pyjamas) beadily regarding her from the pillow. ... This is what Melanie did the summer she was fifteen ...

(Carter, 1981, 1)

Angela Carter's vivid descriptions of what might be termed Melanie's 'awakening conscience' is curiously similar to Britney Spears' photo shoot for the May 1999 edition of *Rolling Stone*. Dressed in a black polka-dot bra and white boy-leg knickers, Spears was pictured laying on pink satin sheets, phone in one hand, Teletubby in the other, while the cover announced: 'Barely legal: Britney Spears – inside the bedroom of a teen dream'. (Koha 1999, 47) Both take place in the bedroom, still the prime site of girls' consumption of pop music; both highlight the distinction between childlikeness (the presence of Edward Bear and his association with the golden age of innocence, Teletubbies and their appeal to the under-fives); both reflect considered choices in the construction of (self) representation (Bloustien, 1996: 27); both are situated within the intimate world of the imagination; both are about teenagers. For Melanie, it is her active fantasy life, her make-believe play which draws on the erotic potential of her fifteen-year old body; for Britney it seems more a ploy of her record company who are reported to have 'orchestrated a sophisticated guessing game about her level of sexual awareness, alternating apple-pie wholesomeness with brazen acts of sexual provocation, which led to a global obsession with the question of Britney's virginity. One minute she's the bashful girl next door who swears allegiance to her mum, God and the flag, the next she is writhing on stage in a bikini with a python between her legs.' (McCormack, 2002). The principal distinction, then, is between the private world of Melanie's bedroom and the public arena of marketing. Britney Spears embodies 'a chastity that is not chastity, a performative pretense' (Baker, 207), but nevertheless one that engages with the active imagination of her young fans. 'Her song lyrics and dance performances are quintessentially anti-virginity. Her famous belly button, her open-air substitute vulva, is the center of her public sexuality. Together with her smile and her thrust out breasts, Britney Spears' midriff is a calculated sex substitute: sexual purity meets pure sex,' (Lockard, 2001) 'the eroticised images [are] struggled over in attempt to understand what older girlhood entailed and the potential for this to be redefined.' (Baker, 2002, 196)

There is, then, an observable tension between what might be termed an image of imagined childhood and the hidden and problematic perversity of child sexuality that characterises much of contemporary thinking[1] about the *separate* and potentially *problematic* nature of children. Not least, they do not know the difference between good and evil, only between nice and nasty. S/he is good if s/he does not do anything bad. The ideal of children thus focuses on their innocence, their playfulness, their direct access to the world of make-believe which, in turn, connects them to the black and white ethical world of fable and fairytale. It is, however, this conceptualisation of innocence that underpins the contemporary paradox of both containing child sexuality and accepting its exploitation through, for example, the media. On the one hand, legal measures such as the Children's Act have highlighted the need to take account of their personal experiences, whether this is concerned with family, incest, rape, or choice of parent within divorce proceedings. Conversely, children have been used increasingly as visible points of identification within the field of marketing, as both commodities and consumers. At its most extreme, this privatisation of the child as an economic unit in the circulation of money and desire is evidenced in the rapid increase in networked child pornography. In both instances, however, it can be argued that the child simply reflects and embodies adult desires and dreams; that the cult of consumerism, like the cult of pornography, is a manifestation of the adult mind. What draws together the barely disguised kiddie porn of contemporary advertising, fashion, music promos, popular satanist films and the paedophilic imagery of the Internet is the preoccupation with children as objects of desire: they are what we have made them.

While it is accepted that the contemporary investment in childhood innocence – that there is a proper 'childlike way' for children to be and behave – is counter-balanced by the empirical evidence of delinquency, the institutionalisation of childhood as different from the world of the adult is significant. On the one hand it accounts for the horror surrounding James Bulger's death, which was heightened by the age of his murderers. As Marina Warner observes: 'their trial revealed a brutal absence of pity for them as children. It was conducted as if they were adults – not because they had behaved with adult consciousness but because they had betrayed an abstract myth about children's proper childlikeness' (1994b, 35). While the Bulger case, like that of Mary Bell, is an extreme example of children's cruelty to children, the depiction of the child as transgressive, as enjoying acts of sado-masochism, has long been evident in such books as William Golding's *Lord of the Flies*, Henry James's *The Turn of the Screw* and Iain Banks's *The Wasp Factory*. They reflect Freud's conceptualisation of the polymorphous perversity of children who have not yet learnt the dual concepts of cruelty and pity. In a social sense, no child is yet fully human. Doing good/doing bad both imply a social context of action, a whole system of social relations.

Childhood, then, is perceived as innocent and yet potentially transgressive, magical yet vulnerable, as evidenced in the spate of such satanic horror movies as *The Omen* and *The Exorcist*. At a more heroic level, the child as protagonist, as actively enjoying and killing monsters, is reflected in such films as *Jurassic Park*; outwitting grownups or solving problems accounts for the unprecedented popularity of the child magician in the *Harry Potter* series which, in August 2001, held three of the top ten places in British soft-back fiction and which attracted an unprecedented child audience when released as a movie in November 2001. Within popular music, the child star is omnipresent in the seemingly endless girl and boy groups where identification with the age 8–10 market equally involves merchandise and look-alike clothing – examples are the bandanna and sweat-bands favoured by young rappers such as Eminem, and the devil-red leathers of Britney Spears, whose grooming by Jive Records and extensive promotion paid off when her debut album and single 'Baby One More Time' topped the American charts at the start of 1999. She was seventeen, and the last teenage superstar of the millennium. Dressed in schoolgirl uniform, Spears was arguably marketed for her 'jail bait' image.

> Put a 40-year-old in a vamped-up school uniform and she's saucily sexy, do it at 25 and she's looking hot. At 16 the same outfit is perfectly legal, but six months earlier, fertile and blooming into womanhood, and you're delving into the realms of perversion. At 15 a girl has most of the attributes which will make her desirable as a woman, but to recognise her sexuality as taboo - who wouldn't be confused?
>
> (Black, Francis)

As R & B artist Aaliyah[2] mused at the tender age of 15, 'Age Ain't Nothing But A Number'. While this is arguably true, the uneasy relationship between childhood as *innocent* and childhood as *knowing* continues to inform the tensions surrounding the erotic potential of the young body.

How children and young adults *use* popular music is one side of the debate. 'Today, stars like Madonna and Cher don't figure in pre-teen discussions, rather it is the young bodies of female pop stars that they are drawn to, and it is the thin, lithe and tight body as sported by such popstars as Pink, Britney Spears and Christina Aguilera that are significant. Fat bodies symbolise a failure to achieve an ideally feminine self.' (Baker, 2002, 117) Similarly, musical choice is a statement of cultural identity and girls under the age of 14 now account for at least half of all recording purchases. (Dubecki 2000; Eliezer 2001) Those who do not have the means to purchase pop music rely on recording songs off the radio. Research also indicates that it is around the age of nine that children begin to prefer Top 40 music rather than other kinds. Do we see that as a problem and, if so, what is the solution?

Clearly our answer depends very much on whether we see the young as cultural dupes or as actively making sense of their own identities. 'Inherent in this process of identification is the girls' exploration of their developing sexuality. Their sexualised musical play is often shown to be in direct contrast to contemporary Western discourses of childhood which position very young girls as asexual.' (Baker, 2002, 42) It is also apparent that young girls use popular music and its associated images to negotiate their gendered identities within their micro-worlds, and that rather than being cultural dupes, music is used to explore and challenge where they 'fit' in terms of other social forces. In particular, the girls' play with popular music highlights their attempts to grasp meanings of what it is to be a pre-teenage/teenage girl – i.e. no longer 'kids' – and a culturally legitimate sexual being through using 'everyday' technology in particularly creative and gendered ways. Not least, they are selective in their choice of pop idol, in their choice of songs, in their discussion of style, their rejection of 'too much make-up', and overly-sexual images. Rather than being simply a fun-making activity, pop music, dancing and the exploration of images 'is much more about an expression of cultural identity which, in its very embodiment, represents an attempt to make sense of "the real me" of the emerging self'. (Baker 2002, 98-9) As adults we may be concerned that the emerging self is overly influenced by the marketing of such stars as Britney Spears, S Club Juniors and Atomic Kitten, but are we simply singling out pop from the continual bombardment of images that dominate contemporary life – those that range from war and man's inhumanity to man, to those associated with the shifting fashions of advertising or, indeed, children's television? And is it really so much different from our own experiences, our own discovery of pop and rock?

What is obvious to me, is that popular music has all too often been the scapegoat of public morals – from early rock 'n' roll through to the eroticised bodies of contemporary manufactured pop idols. Children have always engaged in dressing-up, play and performance, not least dance. It enables them a particular access to both individual and group identity. As Gerry Bloustein observes, 'the teenybop culture allows girls to "break open" and "explore" familial, cultural and societal discourses, to "test, explore and challenge" the symbolic boundaries of age, gender, ethnicity and cultural identity and to keep uncertainty in check'. (Bloustein, 1999b, 83) Thus while generalisations cannot obviously be made (and research into the 8–10 year old's experiencing of pop music is still at an embryonic stage, not least in the field of emerging masculinities and the young male audience), it would seem that their prime concern is the critiquing of images, particularly those concerning the body as presented to them by pop stars. Their's is not so much a passive relationship with commercially-produced popular music. Rather, they have an active engagement whereby their own gendered identities can be both explored and played-out. In other words, it seems that the young know how to *use* pop. The problems of *mis-use*, however, remain, not least those concerning overly-exploitative record companies, and the fact 'that with most child stars their journey into adulthood isn't successful. Children need to be children, and that time being a child is invaluable'. (Le Vay, 2001, 6) There is also the added problem that record companies are increasingly recognising the economic potential of paedo-pop and that this is fuelling both their marketing strategies and my concern for the exploitation of young bodies and the resultant voyeurism associated with the paeodophilic gaze.

Little Miss Dynamite

The exploitative play on innocence vs knowingness has a long history within popular music. In the 1950s, Brenda Lee (born Brenda Mae Tarpley, December 11, 1944 in Lithonia, Georgia, USA, and nicknamed 'Little Miss Dynamite' when she began recording for Decca at the age of 11) was quickly heralded as 'the little girl with grown up reactions'.[3] Billed as being nine years old, her first single, a revival of Hank William's 'Jambalaya', provides an initial indication of the adult dynamic of her vocal delivery, albeit that its innocuous lyrics offer little opportunity for the more sensual delivery associated with her later hits. Rather, it provided a unique marketing opportunity to exploit her as a child prodigy, a novelty performer, a factor which equally helped in ensuring the success of her million-selling single 'Rockin' Around the Christmas Tree'. While such songs are indicative of Lee's authoritative and charismatic performing ability, it is interesting to note that her producer, Owen Bradley, also worked with the country & western diva Patsy Cline, and that his role in shaping both Lee's musical output and the delivery of the songs – not least his trademark studio style – contributed towards the development of a vocal style which projected a sexual maturity which was arguably at odds with the image of a diminutive, curly-haired child. By 1957, the release of such sexually-loaded songs as 'Let's Jump the Broomstick' and 'Speak To Me Pretty' ensured that Brenda Lee's ability to slide between a husky, intimate delivery and what has been described as 'raucous lust' (Larkin, 1999, 754) attracted a growing following on the country/rockabilly scene. It equally ensured a profitable but arguably misogynistc marketing strategy: a pre-pubescent girl whose sexually potent songs inferred an implicit maturity, so situating her as fantasy nymphet.

Brenda Lee's nickname 'Little Miss Dynamite', with its connotations of a sexually-charged single woman, came to the fore in the 1957 single 'Dynamite'. Recorded when she was 13 years old, her explosive potential is linked to the sexual dynamism of her lover 'when you kiss, it's dynamite', 'when you hug me all the time, I just explode like dynamite'.

In common with all rockabilly songs of the 1950s, the rhythm of the song is 'nervously up-tempo, accented on the off-beat … with a kind of thinness and manic energy' (Guralnick, 1989, 68) and a clean, uncluttered sound. The double-time feel, with the quaver after-beats on kit, and accompaniment on electric guitar, double bass and tenor sax., is accentuated by the doo-wop-a-doo backing vocals and handclaps. While this is arguably formulaic and imitative of many rockabilly songs of the period (Elvis Presley, Carl Perkins, Gene Vincent, Eddie Cochrane), Lee's vocal delivery dominates, the urgency and attack of her voice propelling the lyrics.

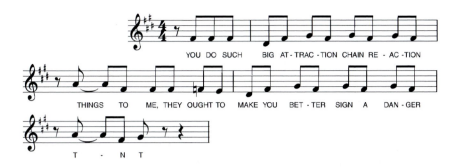

Transcription 1

There is also the promise of physical intimacy, 'Love me right, Hey baby let's make history tonight'. The effect of the vocal nuance is undeniably erotic. Lee carries the story line, the melody, to its conclusion with a reiterated 'you're dyna-mite'. At the same time, she provides a point of identification for the listener as she shapes the context of the words, stretching vowels, delaying outcome, accenting key words of action ('do'), so heightening the sexual innuendo:

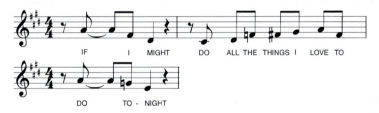

Transcription 2

Not least, her repeated focus on the underlying dynamic shape of the key signi-fier of her volatile emotional state – 'dynamite' – which appears eleven times in this three-minute single, both reveals and confirms her own publicly mediated personality as Little Miss Dynamite.

While the song can be enjoyed simply as an up-beat rockabilly single, it never-theless presents the listener with a paradox. 'Dynamite' is full of sexual innuendo yet, as Lee observed: 'When I listen to the rock songs I sang, not knowing what the words must've meant, I was singing them like I knew'. 'I wanted to get into trouble, but there was no way' (Tucker, 1989, 280) – for parental intercession kept her publicly salacious but privately demure. In retrospect, this strategy is intriguing. If one accepts the argument that Lee is innocently erotic, that as a child she cannot arouse desire, then the sexuality in her songs, the lusty grain of her voice, creates an underlying unease. At best, her expressions of desire cannot be taken seriously as the irreconcilability of her physical appearance, her childlikeness (pre-pubescent and freckle-faced) and the sexually-charged lyrics would signal a moral impasse. For some, the solution was to displace her childlike appearance and 'certain portions of the public were convinced that Lee was a midget. Others took the singer's physical appearance at face value, disregarding her affective maturity' (Sanjek, 1997, 150). Either way, there is the suggestion that it would be wrong to take her expression of desire seriously, that the taboo against acknowledging her sexuality necessitated either a kitsch admiration of Lee as cute and sexually inactive or an acknowledgement of the listeners' own predatory instincts.

While songs such as 'Dynamite', 'One Teenager to Another' (1957) and 'Ain't That Love' (1957) situate Lee as paradoxical, the success of songs such as 'One Step At A Time' (which went to number 15 on the Country Charts), the 1960 Top 40 hit 'Sweet Nothin's' (No. 4) and the controversial 'I'm Sorry' (No. 1) most reflect the tensions between Lee's adult delivery, her appearance and the socially prescribed innocence of her actual age.

'I'm Sorry' can only be described as 'adult' in its mode of address. Presaged by a sweetly sentimental string introduction, the 12/8 feel of the song is enhanced by piano triplets and bass to evoke the classic mood of a country ballad, where the 'I know I done you wrong' is firmly contextualised by a coherent and stable framework that valorises romance, love and loss. Above all, such clichés as 'love was blind', 'I was too blind to see' relate to the topos of sincerity: speaking only when you have something truthful to say. In particular, the voice 'becomes a metaphor of truth and authenticity, a source of self present "living" speech … an intimate link between sound and sense, an inward and immediate realisation of meaning which yields itself up without reserve to perfect, transparent understanding' (Moi, 1985, 107). Lee was 15 when 'I'm Sorry' was released, and the implied 'knowingness' of the ballad provoked some discussion that it was too 'adult' for a child to sing. However, once again the troubling discrepancy between her actual age and the affective maturity of her vocal delivery was conveniently put to one side, and the song sold over ten million copies.

Lee's vocals come across as both truthful and mature, and coupled with her ability to deliver more up-beat songs with a range of vocal gestures ranging from a soft purr to a panting which can only be described as sexually loaded, there is ample evidence to support her description as 'the little girl with grown up reactions'. What makes her delivery 'sexy' is arguably the sense of 'knowingness' behind what might appear to be innocent lyrics, the erotic pause before a punchline pregnant with innuendo: '...one hour of love tonight just knocks me out like dynamite' ('Dynamite'), with its inference of post-orgasmic exhaustion. It is this sense of a 'hole' in the musical texture that aligns her delivery of songs with the pornographic, the irreconcilability of physical attractiveness and sexuality with a pre-sexual child. As Angela Carter argues: 'for a text to be pornographic there has to be an imaginary "hole", a gap just the right size for the reader to insert his prick into' (Carter, 2000, 16). Pornography's 'principal and most humanly significant function is that of arousing sexual excitement … ' It engages at a non-intellectual, *sensa-*

tional level with personal desire but always throws the listener back on his own resources (Carter, 2000, 14). Pornographic literature (and, by analogy the musical text) has a gap left in it on purpose so that the listener may, in imagination, step inside it, albeit that the fantastic gratification promised by the text is illusory. It engages the listener in the most intimate fashion ('do all the things I love to … do tonight') before it leaves him to his own resources. In effect, then, the imaginary 'gap', the space between the notes, becomes a masturbatory hole into which the listener can insert the erect penis.

While I am not suggesting that Lee attracted an audience of paedophiles, the fact that she exhibited an often-uncomfortable world-weary and overtly physical self-conscious sexuality that belied her actual age does create a certain unease. What her songs promised was not the reality of her body, 'but rather an unfulfilled promise of which the unfulfillment is a consolation rather than a regret. So she retains her virginity even if she is raped by a thousand eyes twice nightly' (Carter, 2000, 67). What is sold, then, is her image. The listener is not dealing with real flesh, but with a simulacrum which has the power to arouse, but not, in itself, to assuage desire. As David Sanjek observes, 'Her early success reminds one that the public was, perhaps, most comfortable with a female phenomenon when they could distance themselves from it by reducing the phenomenon to a caricature. Brenda Lee's youth prohibited anyone from taking her expressions of desire seriously … she exaggerated female sexuality to the point that it was effectively neutralised' (1997, 151).

While Sanjek's interpretation is reassuring, it is interesting to note that Brenda Lee's popularity was at its height in 1960. 'I'm Sorry' was followed by four more Top 40 hits, including a second No. 1 with 'I Want To Be Wanted'. Over the next few years she continued to release heartbreak ballads such as 'All Alone Am I', 'Losing You', 'I Wonder' and 'As Usual' (each entering the Top 20 in 1963) as well as playing an acting role in the children's fantasy movie *The Two Little Bears*, but by the end of 1964 her principal success lay in yet another Christmas novelty song 'Christmas Will be Just Another Lonely Day'. Only minor hits followed and in Europe Brenda Lee remained mostly a memory – despite Coast to Coast's hit revival of 'Let's Jump the Broomstick' and a high placing for 1980's *Little Miss Dynamite* greatest hits collections.[4] How does one account, then, for the unprecedented popularity of the *child* star, Brenda Lee ?

Clearly, novelty acts which feature child protégés have always had a strong appeal, and here one can include not only such ingénues as Shirley Temple, whose 'cutie' performance of 'The Good Ship Lollipop' was arguably a paedophile's dream, but equally the young Mozart, and his sister Nanerl, whose performances attracted public acclaim across Europe. The attraction of what can be described as an adult performance by a child – and its association with a prodigious or monstrous talent – centres the argument once again on what is considered natural/un-natural and the tensions inherent in innocence/knowingness, purity/sin. Brenda Lee, 'the little girl with grown up reactions' is certainly no isolated case.

The appeal of the eroticised child during the nineteenth century, for example, is well documented in the volume of paintings which straddle a fine line between sentimentalism and obscenity. Not least, the seeming obsession with the child's naked body – whether in the seemingly innocent portrayal of *The Little Girl's Room* by Swedish artist Carl Larsson, or the more eroticised depictions of toddlers by such artists as Leon Perrault (*Bacchus as a Child*), Bruno Piglhein (*Christmas Morning*) and Matthew Maris's *Butterflies*, where a reclining little girl with flowers in her hair, a pair of butterflies in the air above her and an extremely knowing glance in her eyes, reflects a disturbing alliance between fine art and child pornography.[5] The portrayal of purity, it would seem, equally titillated thoughts of sin; the pre-pubescent or pubescent child, 'mysteriously slumbering in deceptive serenity', also embodied the 'prurient certainty of carnal knowledge, the shadow of evil, that hovers threateningly behind the young girl in Edvard Munch's familiar painting *Puberty*' (Dijkstra, 1986, 191–3). What these paintings offered to the viewer is a fantasy of love, a carnal knowledge, without fear of reprisal.

The sexual gratification offered by the sleeping child is also evident in the trade in young girls during the mid-nineteenth century. Pretty young girls from poor families were procured, kidnapped off the streets or bought as prospective maids and served up as dainty morsels for the rich. The price for a virgin was around £13, a sound investment for the wealthy when venereal disease and, in particular, syphilis, was rife. Virginity, then, was a realisable asset, a levying of the maiden tribute, and drowsed by a dose of laudanum and chloroform, the child was sound asleep when violated. The sleeping child was, then, far more than a *sujet d'art* and it is easy to speculate about the voyeuristic value of such paintings to the Victorian paedophile. Overt pornography, however, remained under cover and it was the more explicit form of child exploitation that became the focus of concern for nineteenth-century reformers. It is interesting to note, however, that although child prostitution was recognised by such crusaders as the Salvation Army and middle-class reformers such as Josephine Butler as an unacceptable exploitation of the poor, the Criminal Law Amendment Act to raise the Age of Consent for Girls to 16 was rigorously opposed by aristocratic Members of Parliament and the House of Lords who saw it as a direct challenge to male privilege – not least the deflowering of virgins was seen as a safe rite of passage for their sons who might otherwise be at risk from venereal disease.[6]

While the portrayal of child sexuality in fine art and the reality of child prostitution provide two insights into the erotic potential of children, so situating eroticism as the pornography of the elite, it is apparent that the forbidden nature of sexual relationships with minors exercises an unusually tenuous hold over the imagination. Flaubert, for example, gave his Saint Anthony a nightmare vision of 'a beautiful dusky child amid the sands, which revealed itself to me as the spirit of fornication' (Dijkstra, 1986, 195). The Rev. Charles Dodgson, better known as Lewis Carroll, was also tormented by his fascination, and suppressed desire, for children. As an early photography buff, he began to take photos of children, including Alice Liddell (of *Alice in Wonderland* and *Alice Through The Looking Glass*). 'Naked children are so perfectly pure and lovely', he explained to his friend Harry Furniss (*Confessions of a Caricaturist*, 1, 106). He also glued a tiny picture of Alice Liddell at the end of one of his telescopes, 'as if to fix the line which closes *Through the Looking Glass*:

> Still she haunts me, phantomwise
>
> Alice moving under skies
>
> Never seen by waking eyes ...
>
> Life, what is it, but a dream
>
> Warner, 2002, 189

Carroll's photographs of nude pre-pubescent girls (boys did not, it seem, appeal to him) were mostly destroyed by Carroll before he died. Those that remain show children posed as adult nymphs. As Bram Dijkstra observes: 'It all seemed very pure, this exploration of the soft vulnerability of childhood, very "ideal" – but it is obvious that these men were playing with the fire that turns innocence into sin' (1986, 189). It is an experience that is at its most explicit in Nabokov's *Lolita*, in which a 40-year-old man, continually haunted by his first sexual experience as a young teenager with a girl who died four months later from typhoid, is emotionally revitalised by the sight of the 12-year-old Lolita,

> light of my life, fire of my loins. My sin, my soul. Lo-lee-ta: the tip of the tongue taking a trip of three steps down the palate to tap, at three, on the teeth. Lo. Lee. Ta. She was Lo, plain Lo, in the morning, standing four feet ten in one sock. She was Dolly at school. She was Dolores on the dotted line. But in my arms she was always Lolita.
>
> (Nabokov, 1959, 11)

The power of the book – and indeed the filmed versions by Stanley Kubrick and, more recently, Adrian Lyne – lies in its seductiveness. 'Its power comes from moments when you want the love between the man and the girl to succeed, when their happiness seems untouchable' (Hasted, 1998, 4). However, as Jeremy Irons (who plays Humbert Humbert in the Lyne film) explains: 'There has to be a moment when the audience thinks, "God, this is great !" It has to be sexy, they have to see what's attractive to Humbert, what's attractive to Lolita, before the shit hits the fan. The film taints you, it doesn't let you be distant' (Hasted, 1998, 4). Irons's comments on teenage sexuality have been condemned by many, but his views evidence the struggle with doubt that characterises many discussions on under-age sex. 'I think we all contain within us the murderer, the rapist, the paedophile. I don't think that a man who feels attracted to a 14-year old has anything inherently wrong with him. I think it's just an animal feeling. In our society, he's not allowed to act on it. I think that is absolutely right. But I think we have to understand ourselves, we have to recognise what we're made up of. My character Humbert Humbert is a monster, because he's harming a child. But he's also quite like-able. He's not someone who you can say, "that is the sort of person I could never be"' (Hasted, 1998, 4).

Irons's performance of Humbert certainly confirms the 'quite likeable'. Indeed, it could be argued that Lolita is projected as the instigator of desire, that the seeming 'knowingness' behind her early flirtations with Humbert, her overt challenge to her mother's mature sexuality, and her subsequent manipulative bargaining (the recognition that Humbert will reward her with money and indulge her more childlike taste for chocolate ice-cream sodas and bubblegum – 'I earned that money' – and which is heightened by her revelation that she never loved him) imply a precocious sexual awareness which transcends the 'innocence' of her years. '"Okay", said Lolita, "here is where we start". ... Suffice to say that not a trace of modesty did I perceive in this beautiful hardly formed young girl whom modern co-education, juvenile mores, the campfire racket and so forth had utterly and hopelessly depraved ... It was she who seduced me' (Nabokov, 1959, 131–2). As Humbert muses: 'a normal man, given a photo of a group of schoolgirls and asked to point out the loveliest among them will not necessarily identify the nymphet. You have to be an artist, a madman full of shame and melancholy to recognise the little deadly demon among the others'. 'I was in a paradise whose skies were the colour of hell-flames, but a paradise still'.[7]

While the fantasy and reality surrounding the eroticised child, like the repressions and taboos that govern our experience of sex and sexuality, are historically formed (and in other culture's Lolita's precocious sexuality would be sufficient to ensure her passage to womanhood), in today's society, where 'paedophiles are glimpsed like vampires on the edge of every frenzied British town' (Hasted, 1998, 4) Irons's comments – and indeed his portrayal of love for a child who is, herself, unconscious of her fantastic power, 'the perilous magic of nymphets' (Nabokov, 1959, 132) – are as problematic as Humbert's blissful awakening in Lolita's arms. We, the audience, see Lolita through his eyes and, as such, become engaged in the tortured realisation of his tainted love. In contrast, what we perceive as a 'real' paedophile, the lecherous Clare Quilty, serves to confirm the caricature of a monster who actively procures young girls and whose monstrous behaviour involves a liking for both snuff movies and executions. He, surely, is the villain, the archetypal paedophile who society actively condemns, or so the film leads us to believe. His is the face we should fear.[8]

Arguably, the portrayal of under-age sex is problematic. On the one hand we can empathise with the young lovers in *Romeo and Juliet* while questioning and even condemning the love of Humbert Humbert for Lolita. Clearly films, like novels, can actively engage the sympathy of the viewer/reader. This is part of the stock in trade of the skilful writer or director – and *Lolita* skirts a thin line between pornography and so-termed 'art' movies in that it both provokes debate, forcing the viewer to reassess his relation to his own sexuality, while engaging with libidinous fantasy. Reality, however, is a different matter and today, the World Wide Web has become the focus of concern as it allows for a seemingly unstoppable licentious trafficking in both child pornography and child prostitution. In August 2001 the Federal Authorities in Washington announced the arrest of 100 people linked to a multimillion-dollar child pornography operation on the Internet where children as young as four were offered for various forms of sexual exploitation (Johnson, 2001, 1). As the FBI confirmed, this was only the tip of the iceberg. The Soham murders of Holly Wells and Jessica Chapman provide one chilling example of the paeodophile's attraction to young children and the lengths taken to avoid the scrutiny of those in authority, and each week new arrests confirm the scale of the problem. The images of eroticised stars and the chat-rooms associated with their websites thus provoke concern – not least when one considers the age of their fans – but while paedophiles provide the most extreme example of child abuse, it is becoming disconcertingly apparent that there is no such thing as 'the innocent eye' in contemporary society. Films, books, art, the media and popular music continue to have an ambivalent attitude towards both representations of children-as-adults and adults-as-children (as evidenced, for example, in the current craze for flirty girl glamour: 'If it's pink and/or fluffy, then life probably isn't complete without one'[9] within the imperatives of a free market and global economy). In the profit-driven world of advertising, fashion and music, the image and culture of the young are appropriated for the high pleasure quotient they evoke. Youthful allure and sexual titillation are marketable commodities and are consumed today not simply by teens and adults but equally the growing market of tweenies, the 8–10 year olds who make up the majority fan base for girl and boy bands. Today, with the constant exposure of a seemingly unstoppable trade in paedophilic imagery and www sites that offer horrendous excursions into child pornography, the young pop stars – and indeed the fans who engage with their networks – are tantalising bait.

The displays of sexuality by such artists as Britney Spears, Christina Aguilera and Atomic Kitten, and their negotiation by young female fans, thus raise significant problems. As writer/journalist Lucy O'Brien rightly observes, 'Creating the fuckable fantasy woman has long been a preoccupation of pop music, especially now the medium has become so visible' (1995, 231) and the struggle to understand what 'being a teenager' entails is one that conflates uneasily with the tensions inherent in innocence/experience discussed earlier. More specifically, 'there is a massive denial located within the culture ... which eroticises little girls and then massively denies the eroticization, laying desire at the door of perverts,' (Walkerdine, 1993, p. 19) a fact tacitly accepted by major recording companies who call such teenybop songs, paedopop. As Henry

Giroux observes, 'As the right wing wages war against sex education, condom distribution in schools, sex on the internet, and video stores that carry pornographic films, there is a curious silence from progressive and other radical cultural workers about the ways in which children and sex are portrayed in films, advertising and media culture in general' (1998, 47). The erotic codes, while ostensibly directed at a young audience are thus tainted by a paedophilic discourse and, as Kitzinger tellingly observes, 'pornography leaves little doubt that innocence is a sexual commodity.' (1997, 168)

As my discussion so far shows, while images of children are not necessarily pornographic, they can nevertheless invite questionable pleasures in their audience. And this, I believe, is the problem surrounding the careers of young artists such as Brenda Lee.

It is also interesting to note the way in which Lee's legacy as Little Miss Dynamite informed the recent publicity surrounding Niomi Mclean-Daley whose debut album, *A Little Deeper* (2002), won the 2002 Mercury Music prize. Her single 'Dy-na-Mi-Tee' has also achieved significant chart success and Ms Dynamite (as she is now called) has been hailed as the new queen of British hip-hop soul. The source of her power lies in her background as 'a sad adolescent ... "When I was supposed to be a child," she says, "I had the responsibilities of an adult" and at 15, while still at school, she left home ... "All I ever used to do was smoke and drink, smoke and drink ... go to school, come back, have a drink ... I actually felt suicidal"' (Cairns, 2002, 6). Her album reflects many of the problems she confronted, and draws on a childhood of jotting down words, making up rhymes to amuse her friends and, crucially, bottling up the anger she felt. The result is a mix of hip hop, ragga, soul grooves and lyrics which attack wife-beaters, drug-dealers, black-on-black violence and feckless former lovers. While there is clearly a world of difference between Ms and Little Miss Dynamite both lyrically and musically, the connotations remain in that she has a similarly powerful voice while looking young and vulnerable. With her sights on the American R & B scene, success depends on the blessings of big-name producers, Salaam Remi (who has worked with Nas, D'Angelo and the Fugees) and P Diddy's beatmaster, Punch and, as such, she remains susceptible to the machinations of the music industry. Only time will tell whether she will take her place beside such artists as Lauryn Hill, Erkyka Badu and Angie Stone. As Cairns observes, 'she embodies a whole lifetime of warring human impulses and emotions – a lot to bear for anybody, let only a prodigiously talented but enduringly insecure 21-year old' (2002, 7).

While my discussion so far has focused largely on issues surrounding eroticism and the young girl, it is clearly the case that the sexploitation of the young is not gender-biased. The 14-year-old Lil Bow Wow (Shad Moss) is but one of the new wave of super-talented teens and his debut hip hop album went platinum on both sides of the Atlantic. Discovered at the age of 6 by Snoop Dog, and having memorised the entire works of NWA (Niggers With Attitude) when only age 4, his pre-pubescent fame has made him an idol for young children across the world. As Lulu Le Vay writes: 'Aside from LBW, the sweeping wave of teen stardom has lately witnessed many fresh additions. Puff Daddy's gyrating Britney-inspired protégés Dream (aged 14–16) smashed the US charts with their debut single 'He Loves U Not' … Meanwhile, black Billie Piper wannabe Lisa Roxanne, also 14, has been signed to Palm Pictures for a whopping £1m … Over the last few years, the pre-adult thirst for fame has become ever more insatiable … Teen-read *Bliss* has seen sales rise since it relaunched last July (2000) with its tag "the magazine that made you famous". And in February 2001, 13m people tuned in to see the final five out of 3,000 hopefuls strike gold in *Popstars*' (Le Vay, 2001, 6). The follow-up, *Pop Idol* (October/ November 2001) attracted 5,000 contestants, the majority of whom appeared to be weaned on karaoke and girl/group, boy/group dance routines. Again, the programme attracted large audiences who voted on the final 50 contestants over a month-long schedule. Predictably, the winner, Will Young, was stereotypically attractive – as well as a good performer. His subsequent revelation of his gay sexuality did not seem to jeopardise the sales of his debut single, albeit that it is unlikely that he will become an idol for the 8–10-year-old market – 'someone mum and dad would approve of'. Parents would find explanations too problematic, albeit that a large proportion of his fan base are the mums themselves.

However, the programme had lead to debates as to whether a somewhat 'fat' lad could achieve his aim and become the winner of *Pop Idol*. For the curious, the answer is 'No!' but one year on, the accolade of being number one Pop Idol was won by Michelle McManus, a bubbly and decidely overweight Scottish contestant. Meanwhile, the winning student of Fame Academy was an upfront lesbian, Alex Parks, the mainstream audience vote suggesting that sexuality – provided it is attractively packaged – is no longer an issue. Whether this is due to the flirtation with bi-sexuality and gay culture that characterised much of the early 1990s and which was given a particular frisson in the 2003 Eurovision Song Contest with Tatu's lesbian kiss, is a matter of conjecture. What was evident was Alex's believability – she had a great stage presence and was approachable and friendly to her fans.

Again, it may be that I have become increasingly cynical over the years, but given the existing research into the pre-teen and teenage market, I think Alex's personality – which is arguably stronger than her vocal ability – was an important contributory factor in the marketing strategy. Returning briefly to the Russian duo, Tatu, it is interesting to note that their manager at the time was a trained psychiatrist who was fully aware of the role of pop music in young people's lives. It is one way in which they learn about their developing bodies, their desires, their dreams. But what if the young person is gay or a lesbian? Given the heteronormative make-up of popular music, there is clearly a market for songs which provide insights into gay identities, that suggest 'I am not alone.' Tatu have sold remarkably well; Will Young's latest album moved rapidly to the top of the charts, and Alex, I think, will also provide an important role model for young audiences. She's fun, she comes from a supportive family, she's successful but, at the same time, she's not extraordinary, so being a lesbian is nothing extraordinary. Today, it may even be a unique selling point. Potentially, then, Alex should do well, and the reality is that a short-term return in investment is what everyone is looking for right now, not least because many record companies are merging.

As Peter Robinson wrote in *The Observer Music Monthly* (October 2003), the music industry is not a charity. Launching a new pop act is a high risk exercise. You have to record an album, which can cost anywhere between £200,000 and £500,000. It'll be paid for out of the band's advance – but it's still money the label will have stumped up. Factor in a video at a cost of between £70,000 and £150,000, as well as marketing and advertising costs, schools tours and the price of keeping a band in distressed jeans for a year of 'development' and the project will easily run up bills of over a million pounds before a single record is in the shops. If the first single doesn't sell, chances are the band (or, in Alex's or Michelle's case, the singer) will be dropped.' (p.26)

While the dictum 'you're only as good as your last single' accounts for the rapid turnover of young pop bands, the sexploitation of the young is long-standing. Lena Zavaroni died at the age of 36 having developed an eating disorder aged 13 when her agent told her she was too fat (she died weighing three-and-a-half stone). Musical Youth, a Birmingham boy band aged between 10 and 15, shot to fame with their first release, 'Pass the Dutchie' (1982), a classic reggae song about smoking marijuana originally sung by Mighty Diamond. The original 'Pass the Kouchi' (cannabis) had been changed to 'Pass the Dutchie' (cooking pot), but nevertheless the accompanying video, which was partly set in a court house, was censored. Three years later the band split as interest in the group failed. Singer Dennis Seaton had a breakdown, bass player Patrick Waite died while awaiting a court appearance on drug charges in 1993. Their fate is not dissimilar to that of Judy Garland whose neurotic addiction to alcohol and pills were the legacy of her years as a child star in Hollywood. Exposure to fame is always problematic, but with the young it is doubly so, and even those who survive tend to bear the scars. As Dr Michelle Elliott, of children's charity Kidscape, states: 'We have found that with most child stars that their journey into adulthood isn't successful, children need to be children, and that time being a child is invaluable' (Le Vay, 2001, 6).

The boy behind the mask

Of all child stars mutated by fame, Michael Jackson is arguably the most visible. His 40 years as a performer has seen the transition from a child star to a child-like star who continues to embody the Peter Pan qualities associated with the boy who refuses the pathway to adulthood. Arguably, it is the spectre of an overly dominant father who has caused the persona to remain imprisoned within a mask that curiously resembles both his sister, Janet and soul diva Diana

Ross (the sharp retroussé nose and overly feminised features) while simultaneously problematising his Afro-American origins through a blanched and
overly-taut skin. Meanwhile, the more recent problems concerning allegations
of child abuse are causing global ripples of unease. If found guilty – and lawyers
met on February 13, 2004 to discuss the date of Jackson's preliminary hearing –
he could face up to twenty years in jail.

Michael Jackson (born 29 August, 1958, Gary, Indiana, USA) first hit the
headlines at the age of 4 as one of the founder members of the family vocal
group, The Jackson Five (Jackie, Tito, Jermaine, Michael and Marlon).
Modelling his vocal style and dance routines on James Brown, his onstage
performance demonstrated an absolute self-confidence that belied his years,
and he soon became the group's lead vocalist and frontman. The success of
The Jackson Five had been masterminded by their father, Joseph (a guitarist
with Chicago group, The Falcons), who had fostered the boys' musical interest
by buying them second-hand instruments, insisting that each should become
proficient on at least one. It was, however, their vocal abilities that most
clearly signalled a marketable asset. Having won a talent show at Roosevelt
High School and several regional competitions, their father launched them on
to the neighbouring Chicago gig circuit where they sang material borrowed
mainly from The Temptations and The Miracles. A benefit concert for the
Mayor of Gary, Richard Hatcher, attracted the attention of Tamla Motown
impresario Berry Gordy and in 1968 they signed to Motown Records; their
early releases 'I Want You Back' and 'I'll Be There' demonstrating a remarkable
maturity of delivery.

While the 'manufactured' boy band is recognised as a legacy of the 1990s,[10]
the success of The Valentines, Cadillacs and, in particular, The Moonglows –
a vocal group, fostered by their mentor DJ Alan Freed, whose performances
signalled the emergence of R & B from its black subculture into mainstream
rock 'n' roll teen culture – suggests a parallel for the emerging vocal doo wop
groups of the 1950s. Not least, the potential offered by an emerging teen
culture, the attraction of songs geared to a lifestyle distinct from that of their
parents (encapsulated by such early rock 'n' roll songs as Chuck Berry's
'Maybelline', 'Sweet Little Sixteen' and 'School Days'), and the success of
young performers such as Elvis Presley and Buddy Holly, triggered a recognition that commercial success lay in producing performers whose youthful and
sexy image matched the content of their songs. For Tamla Motown boss Berry
Gordy, this equally implied targeting a white crossover market, and the
Corporation's (Berry Gordy, Fonso Mizell, Freddy Perren and Deke Richards)
skilful manipulation of the performance style – stripping it of its implicit
ghetto inflections whilst retaining a zestful and soul-inflected delivery – and
the signing of young, commercially inexperienced and hence exploitable
talent, resulted in a stable of artists which included The Miracles, The Four
Tops, The Temptations, Marvin Gaye and Stevie Wonder, as well as girl
groups The Marvelettes, The Chantelles and The Supremes. It is, then, no

surprise to see The Miracles (Smokey Robinson, Emerson Rogers, Bobby Rogers, Ronnie White and Warren 'Pete' Moore) and The Temptations (Eddie Kendricks, Paul Williams, Melvin Franklin, Eldridge Bryant – subsequently replaced in 1963 by David Ruffin – and Otis Williams) singled out by their father as vocal role models for the young Jackson Five. Their string of hits during the late 1950s/early 1960s indicated that the commercial potential of five young, black brothers lay in their ability to deliver up-beat, close-harmony pop whilst capitalising on their youthful appeal through well-staged performances. It was an opportunity that arguably underpinned the over-zealous ambition of Joe Jackson, whose brutal abuse of his young son, Michael, led both to a pathological loathing by Michael of his father and to a life-long obsession with a lost childhood.

While I would agree with feminist theorists of Freud and Lacan that

- psychoanalysis is based on an epistemological impossibility by professing to interpret what it cannot by definition understand, since the unconscious act is not immediately accessible to knowledge; and
- that it lays too much emphasis on the conservative identification that sexual identifications can only be understood by returning it to foundational events that occurred extremely early in childhood'

(Bristow, 1997, 98)

they nevertheless provide some interpretative, albeit bleak, insights into Jackson's problematic sexuality and his dysfunctional attitude towards his father. Not least, his too-early socialisation and entry into the external world of show business under the extreme dictates of both Joe Jackson and Berry Gordy (arguably another father-figure representing the extremes of patriarchal control) suggests both a problematic constraint on his childhood and a need to adjust, by the age of 4, to an all-too adult world. More specifically, the expectations imposed upon his mind and body during the course of his development as a child – the mimicking of James Brown (whose raw and uninhibited performance style earned him the sobriquet 'The Godfather of Soul') vs the need to be white ('"Listen. Diana Ross didn't become a star by being black. She became one by being popular. As far as I'm concerned the Jackson 5 aren't Black either. So let's have none of that black stuff", said Berry Gordy' [Taraborrelli, 1992, 98]) – arguably created an inner conflict that has manifested itself in both a racial and sexual ambiguity. As Kobena Mercer observes, he is 'neither child nor man, not clearly either black or white, and with an androgynous image that is neither masculine nor feminine' (1991, 304). For other commentators, not least in Martin Bashir's report 'Living With Michael Jackson' (ITV, February 3, 2003), Jackson's perverse personality and image is attributable to his childhood experiences, and questions were raised as to whether his plastic surgery did not simply abolish blackness, but also masculinity, and, in particular, any resemblance to his hated father.

According to Freud, it is during the *phallic* stage, when the 3- or 4-year-old discovers the pleasurable potential of the genitals, that he either resolves or fails to resolve the so-called Oedipus and castration complexes. While the boy's Oedipus complex stems from his first and natural attachment to the mother, the recognition of the father as a rival for her attentions leads to a primary urge to kill him. However, as Freud points out, this desire is short-lived because the boy has good reason to fear his father. Having seen either his mother or another woman naked, he speculates that they have been castrated and fears that his father will also castrate him should he dare to act on his desires for his mother. It is a fear that is curiously paralleled in the punitive *Struwwelpeter*, where the terrifying scissor man punishes young children for being naughty, and was used by Victorian parents to actively discourage masturbation. For Freud, however, the child's fear of castration is psychological: it causes the boy child to withdraw from his mother and to begin to develop what is termed a superego.

As Rosemary Tong explains, 'To the degree that the superego is the internalisation by the son of the father's values, it is a patriarchal, social conscience. Boys who successfully resolve the Oedipus and castration complexes ... learn how to submit themselves to the authority of the fathers ... Were it not for the(se) traumas ... boys would never grow up to be men who are willing to tow the party line ...' (1997, 141). However, as Nancy Chodorow points out 'since boys have so little control over their relationship with fathers, this can encourage them to create this control within an imaginary realm, since they cannot experience it in a living relation' (in Seidler, 1995, 99). It is the identification of the 'imaginary' that seems best to encapsulate the problematic and paradoxical image of the mature Jackson. The transition from a cuddly child star to 'a boy sprite who won't grow up ... epitomises the intense, risky paradoxical allure of the Peter Pan myth. He leaps and dances and sings "I'm Bad", gives his estate the name 'Neverland', (and) draws the passionate worship of millions of children' (Warner, 1994b, 43). He is a childlike star, living in a make-believe world, a small, seemingly vulnerable person who affirms the 'connection with that childhood Eden in which the Lost Boys are still living, defying the death of the child within' (Warner, 1994b, 42).

In one sense, Jackson's retention of an imaginary childhood can be curiously associated with Freud's identification of the phallic stage (the pleasurable potential of the genitals and the associated fear of castration). His constant clutching of his crotch while dancing, for example, is explained by Michael Jackson in his 1993 interview with Oprah Winfrey as 'unintentional'. Rather, 'he does what the music compels him to do'. It is like the indiscriminate masturbatory play that characterises early genital awareness, a compulsively sexual yet protective gesture which focuses fear of loss and, perhaps, a continuing fear of the father who so traumatised his early childhood.

The tension surrounding the urge to restore and relive what should have been a 'normal' childhood, and the pull between change and development, has been described as 'a vacillating rhythm' whereby psychic energies try to achieve a particular aim while conserving an 'earlier state', rushing forward yet being constantly jerked back to a certain point to make a fresh start (Bristow, 1997, 121). Although Freud's observations relate most specifically to their convergence in heterosexual sex where the perpetuation of life rests upon the momentary death of orgasm (Freud, 1920, 36), the compulsion to repeat is equally observable in the way in which young children want stories to be told and retold, over and over again. It is an obsession that equally characterises Jackson's love of dressing up, 'the staging of an appearance-as-disappearance within a strategy of continuous masquerade of erotic metamorphoses' (Roland Barthes in Gaines and Herzog, 1990, 238). As Jackson explains, 'I love it so much. It's escape. It's fun. It's just neat to become another thing, another person. Especially when you really believe and it's not like acting' (Warhol and Colacello, 1982). It is a statement that draws attention to three key words – escape, another thing, another person, through an underlying strategy based on masquerade.

Telling stories of all kinds is the primary way that human beings have endeavoured to make sense of themselves and their social world, and Jackson's media portrayal as a figure trapped in an eternal childhood, surrounded by toys and pet animals, isolated from the traumas of the real world, was consolidated by his portrayal of the Scarecrow in the 1978 film *The Wiz* (a remake of *The Wizard of Oz*), his narration of an album based on the 1982 fantasy film, *ET – The Extra-Terrestrial*[11], and his 1985 role in *Captain Eo*, a short film laden with special effects, shown only at the Disneyworld Amusement Park. All three encapsulate the black and white ethical world of fairytales, and this sense of doing good/doing bad also dominates the fantasy world of Jackson's epic solo albums and videos: *Thriller* (1982), *Bad* (1987) and *HIStory – Past, Present and Future – Book 1* (1995), in which Jackson, dressed in Christ-like white robes and surrounded by, among others, worshipping children and a Rabbi, recalls his earlier acclaim as the Messiah by a group of Jehovah's witnesses.

Jackson's seeming obsession with being perceived as 'good' (so conforming to the doing good/doing bad world of childhood and the avoidance of punishment) is evident in, for example, 'Smooth Criminal' (1987), where his white gangsta-style costume situates him as different from those who wear the symbolic 'black' of the criminal class; in 'Beat It' (1982) where the lines 'don't be a macho man' underpin his personal dislike of violence whilst hinting at his earlier child abuse by an overly dominant and 'macho' father; and the 'I'm not like other guys' and the girl's reply 'Of course not. That's why I love you' of *Thriller* (1983), which implies both a love for her fictional boyfriend (who saves her from the monsters of the horror movie) and for Michael Jackson, the 'real' superstar. However, as discussed earlier, the 'real' and the 'imaginary' Michael Jackson are equally conjectural. Both rely on the manipulation of an image whereby identity is held at bay, revealing it to be no more than a mask, a complex masquerade which complicates both his gendered and ethnic identity.

Magic expresses itself above all in shape-shifting and metamorphosis; and in mythology and fairytales, the quest for love entails a quest for recognition of the self which challenges the barriers of conventional expectation. As such, transformations comment on the oppressive narrowness of the prevailing canon of beauty, and for Michael Jackson involves both the projection of a sexual and racial ambiguity which problematise dominant representations of black male sexuality. The transition from the cute little boy, through to the trendy teenager with an exaggerated Afro (symbolic of Black Pride and its cultural association with soul), to the short, curly wet-look hairstyle associated with the release of his first solo album *Off The Wall* (1979), arguably reflects Berry Gordy's conviction that an artist who came across as 'too black' (with the implicit assumption that this could suggest a political alliance with the Black Power Movement) would alienate a white audience. Three years later, with the release of *Thriller* (1982) his appearance seemed to have changed further. The curls dangling over his eyes affected a sense of 'cool'; his nose was smaller and more pointed. *Bad* (1987) was accompanied by a further change, with his skin appearing lighter, and by 1992, with the release of *Dangerous*, his facial bone structure and skin colour emphasised his increasingly androgynous appearance.

While it is accepted that Jackson both responded to, and set, fashion trends (for example, in his adoption of white socks, a black Fedora and single glove on his right hand), his increasingly 'white' and feminised appearance equally suggests both a reaction to the associated brutishness of his black father – a disavowal of his roots – and a growing self-awareness of his power as nurturant mediator, as implied in the 1982 single and video 'Billie Jean', where the accompanying video portrayed Jackson as a master of dance, a magician who could transform life, and a shadowy figure who lived outside the everyday world. In the 1983 rock classic 'Beat It', Jackson mediates between two rival gangs, bringing them together through a choreographed dance evocative of *West Side Story*. It was also the first black record to receive rotation airplay on the MTV video station. Finally, Jackson adopts his messiah-like role in the 1985 Africa benefit single 'We Are The World', and his 1991 release 'Heal the World'.

Physical change and metamorphosis seem inextricably linked both to Jackson's self-definition and to his staged and video performances. It is here that the concept of masquerade and its expression through metamorphosis are most evident. *Thriller* (Jackson's second album with Quincy Jones) and its promotional singles won Jackson seven Grammies, establishing him both as the 'King of Pop' and the master of special effects. It is, however, the 'Thriller' single and its promotional videos that show most clearly the significance of metamorphosis and its potential meaning within Jackson's personal life.

Kobena Mercer's perceptive analysis of *Thriller* (1991, 300–16) discusses the two principal metamorphoses – the werewolf and the zombie – which, it is argued, evidence the horror fascination with sexuality whereby gender identity is codified in terms that revolve around the symbolic presence of the monster. As the wolf, Jackson's transformation from the 'boy-next-door' implies a move into a more rapacious masculinity, one which is more bestial, predatory and aggressive. The powerful effect of the metamorphosis is due largely to it taking place in 'real' time (thus effecting a similar fascination to that experienced in the 1984 film of Angela Carter's *Company of Wolves*). Its horrifying effect, however, is intensified by the visual mutation of Jackson's face. The mask (as *The Making of Michael Jackson's Thriller* [1984] shows) is designed and constructed 'through a series of transparent cells, each with details of the animal features (which) are gradually superimposed on a publicity image of Jackson from the cover of *Rolling Stone* magazine'. The effect is a 'confusion of roles Jackson is playing (boyfriend/star)' and a violation, by the mask, of the image of the star himself. 'The squeaks, cries and other wordless sounds which emanate from his throat as he grips his stomach grotesquely mimic the sounds which are the stylistic trademarks of Jackson's voice'; while 'the pallor of his complexion, the eerie sight of his skull beneath the wet-look curls', draws attention to the artificiality of his own image (Mercer, 1991, 312–13).

Mercer's analysis of the metamorphosis – that it can be seen as an accelerated allegory of the morphological development of Jackson's facial features – from child to adult, from boyfriend to monster, from star to superstar – is persuasive. However, it is suggested that while the werewolf is traditionally an object of horror, Angela Carter's short story 'The Company of Wolves' (1979) – in common with her interpretations of the traditional fairytales 'The Tiger's Bride' and 'The Courtship of Mr Lyon', of 'Beauty and the Beast' – demonstrate more the erotic tenderness that lies beneath the animal pelt:

> See ! Sweet and sound she sleeps in granny's bed, between the paws of the tender wolf.
>
> (1979, 118)

> He dragged himself closer and closer to me, until I felt the harsh velvet of his head against my hand, then a tongue, abrasive as sandpaper. 'He will lick the skin off me !' And each stroke of his tongue ripped off skin after successive skin, all the skins of a life in the world, and left behind a nascent patina of shining hairs ... my beautiful fur.
>
> (1979, 67)

> When her lips touched the meat-hook claws, they drew back into their pads ... Her tears fell on his face like snow and, under their soft transformation, the bones showed through the pelt, the flesh through the wide tawny brow. And then it was no longer a lion in her arms but a man.
>
> (1979, 51)

Jackson's metamorphosis into the wolf, then, suggests both a reply to the media's increasing fixation on his image, and a hint that behind any apparent mutation lies what is, in effect, an injured childlike man. It is also an affirmation of his belief that animals are better friends than their human counterparts

– a belief that is confirmed by his own commitment to wildlife and implicit in the tiger cub, draped over his knee on the sleeve to the *Thriller* LP.

His second metamorphosis into a zombie, the undead corpse with a ghostly pallor who engages in a funky dance routine, implies for Mercer that 'as star Jackson only comes alive when he is on stage performing' (1991, 312). However, the prefacing of the dance sequence by the lyrics 'Night creatures crawl and the dead start to walk in the masquerade' suggest not only a parody of the horror film (and it is Vincent Price's unmistakable voice that delivers the rap) but equally a confirmation that while the undead are an invention of darkness, they are also provide an allegory for worldly compromise. It is a perception that originates in William Godwin's writings. As one of Rousseau's English disciples and father-in-law of Romantic poet Percy Bysshe Shelley, he condemned those whose social compromises placed restrictions upon their freedom, situating the term 'co-oper-ation' as 'an evil'. His views were later reflected in William Wordsworth's interpretation of the world and worldliness, as tainted by 'the flesh and the devil' and, later, by T.S. Eliot who adds the 'zombie businessman' to the list of the worldly. It is a characteristic that is picked up by rock star Iggy Pop, whose concept of the world as a 'zombie birdhouse' influenced such artists as The Clash ('London Calling') where the zombies of death carry out the orders of the estab-lishment. 'All you zombies hide your faces' thus becomes a condemnation of the stupidity of mankind. It is this sense of the zombie which, I feel, underpins Jackson's parody in 'Thriller'. They are the living dead who possess no energy of their own, accepting whatever mask the world imposes on them. There is, then, a direct analogy with Marc Bolan's sentiments in 'Rip Off',

> I'm a social person,
> I'm the creature in disguise …

where he is obliged to wear one of the masks imposed on him. While one solu-tion is 'the fleetfoot voodoo man' who dabbles in alien possession, Bolan (as rocker) wants only to be self-possessed, to be in control of his own life.[12] The metamorphosis into zombie by Jackson is not so dissimilar. It is also suggests an allegory on the parasitic, the non-stop media investigations into his image that led increasingly to his retreat into the fantasy world of 'Neverland' and his befriending of underprivileged children.

Jackson's multiple masks and metamorphoses, ruses and disguises arguably underline the importance of trueness of heart and toughness of mind evocative of fairytales and mythology, and an emphasis on the inner world as opposed to the outer world. They also suggest a constant retreat back to a turbulent childhood and, more recently, an attempt to come to terms with Joe Jackson's all-powerful presence through his self-portrayal as a Christ-like figure in *HIStory*. As the patri-arch, Joe's demands that his sons were compliant with his authority have a certain congruence with the demanding and jealous God of Judaism (whereby Abraham is commanded to sacrifice his son, Isaac) and Christianity (where the son pays the price for the world's sins by showing total submission to the will of the father). The situation also demonstrates Jackson's continuing problem with 'authority figures' such as the media whose probing demands for interviews had been refused until his 1992 interview with Oprah Winfrey.[13] It would appear that his reluctance was, in retrospect, well-founded. In February 2003, Gavin Arvizo – who has accused Jackson of plying him with wine and sexually abusing him – appeared in Martin Bashir's controversial TV documentary. He had been befriended by Jackson, who had taken a personal interest in his medical case (he has only one kidney and while his cancer is in remission, had been worried about his future). While Jackson is attributing the accusations to family greed, there is little doubt that the case will be the showbiz trial of the century and the popular press are quick to herald 'the boy who could destroy Jacko.' (*Sunday Mirror*, February 15, 2004, p. 4) For his fans worldwide, it is yet another instance of misinterpretation of Jackson's love of young people and his desire to give them an opportunity to enjoy the child-like fantasy world of Neverland.

As Lacan (1997) argues, sexuality is structured around the primary symbol of cultural authority and comprises turbulent, if not destructive, drives whose early formation can at times prove impossible to eradicate in adult life. Not least, the human experience of pleasure is based on the repetition of painful instances when the subject experienced those moments of separation and loss through which his/her subjectivity was constituted in the first place, obliging a re-enactment of those moments, and so situating the subject as a masochistic victim. Michael Jackson's struggle with his personal identity and his seeming desire to return constantly to a childlike world would suggest that his subjectivity is imaginary. As such, it is relevant to examine briefly Lacan's identification of the significance of the mirror stage, whereby a child's first recognition of his/her image requires a projected 'I' that provides at least an image of coherence. Such an image then permits the 'I' to come together from fragmentary parts, to gain some stability no matter how imaginary, in its development. Yet stability is not easily attained and the young child enters a structure of anticipation, since it projects the 'I' it believes itself to be. It is, as Bristow observes, 'a drama which manufactures for the subject, caught up in the lure of spatial identification, the succession of fantasies that extends from a fragmented boy-image to a form of its totality'. Eventually, however, the 'I' adopts 'the armour of an alienating identity ... it must defend itself well, because its fictional direction means it can never coincide with itself' (1997, 86).

Arguably, Jackson's confused metamorphoses, his almost hallucinatory efforts to achieve an idealised image, a totality out of its disparate parts, can be interpreted as both a challenge to the omnipotent phantom of his father and as a contemporary realisation of the story of 'Dorian Gray'. His face, like the mask that is now Jackson's face, is illusory. It expresses a will to stay forever young. The reality, for Michael Jackson, is that of an ageing, arguably damaged childlike star whose face embodies the disturbing androgynety of one who 'wanted more than anything else to be a typical little boy'.[14] The problem for Jackson, however, was that his desire to remain a child involved befriending real children. On December 18, 2003 he was charged with seven counts of sexual abuse and two of giving his accuser, Gavin Arvizo, alcohol. The trial is scheduled for December, 2005.

> What is realised in my history is not the past definite of what was, since it is no more, or even the present perfect of what has been in what I am, but the future anterior of what I shall have been for what I am in the process of becoming.
>
> (Lacan, 1977, 86)

Father ... I want to kill you: the birth of the Lizard King

The pathway to adulthood and the construction of male sexual identity is complex. To become a heterosexual male the boy child's initial desire for his mother results in a sense of competition with the father, resulting in a fear of castration. Because of this the child surrenders the love for his mother, which is transferred to another adult woman. In doing so, he is able to identify with the father and, in time, assume his own place as a father. While this is a symbolic process and an ideal psychoanalytic model, problems can arise. If the boy has been too submissive to the father he must challenge him for the mother's love. Failure to do so will result in an inability to take on the role of the father himself in later life. If, however, the father is attacked excessively, the boy will remain rebellious and infantile and unable to give up his attachment to the mother. As Antony Easthope explains, 'the two possibilities correspond to the two sides of the little boy's sexuality, or rather bisexuality. His heterosexual side seeks the mother and opposes the father. But his homosexual side tries to avoid the father's threat by taking the mother's place and becoming the object of the father's love' (Easthope, 1990, 19).

While my discussion so far has provided particular insights into control figures, Jim Morrison's psychodrama 'The End' provides a primal and emotive evocation of his urge to separate himself from his past in order to control both his present and his future. Here, he was influenced by the neo-Freudian scholar Norman O. Brown, whose argument that 'the death instinct is only reconciled in a life which is not repressed' (in Roszak, 1970, 107) informed his personal philosophy of total freedom, subjective expression and instinctual self-liberation, not least in his emotional outburst, 'Father, I want to kill you. Mother, I want to fuck you'.

Violence as spectacle had a particular resonance in the 1960s, not least in Antonin Artaud's Theatre of Cruelty. It was a theatre of blood, screams and bodily extremities and was based on the concept of 'shattering language in order to shatter life' (Byatt, 1997, 168). Glenda Jackson (now a British Labour Party MP) appeared as Christine Keeler, 'stripped, bathed and ritually clothed as a convict to the recitation of the words of the Keeler court case' (Byatt, 1997, 168). She also featured as a wildly erotic Charlotte Corday in *The Persecution and Assassination of Marat as Performed by the Inmates of Charenton under the Direction of the Marquis de Sade*. The counter culture itself supported the more general concerns of freedom of expression which underpinned such previously censored texts as D.H. Lawrence's *Lady Chatterley's Lover*, Henry Miller's *Tropic of Cancer* and *Tropic of Capricorn* and where the publication of William Burrough's *The Naked Lunch* and *Dead Fingers Talk* (1963) attracted adverse criticism by such notable writers as Dame Edith Sitwell. 'The public canonization of that insignificant, dirty little book *Lady Chatterley's Lover* was a signal to persons who wish to unload the filth in their minds on the British public' (Burroughs, 1988, 213). Another letter to the editor called attention to the way in which 'many writers, critics, publishers and other toilers in literary furrows have fallen into the modern hypocrisy of confusing literature with lechery and vision with voyeurism ... It is not possible to base great art on the sexual organs and the alimentary tract' (Burroughs, 1988, 234).

The influence of such contemporary writers as William Burroughs and Jack Kerouac upon the young Morrison was profound. Like others of his generation he was also inspired by the Beats and French bohemian artists and intelligentsia, most notably the existentialist values of Jean-Paul Sartre, which espoused the primacy of experiences, subjectivity and individuality in social and personal life. Chastity and purity, in particular, were superseded by a more upfront sexuality, and sexual equality oscillated uneasily between such extremes as a general concern to confront the laws surrounding homosexuality, the imposed morality surrounding birth control and abortion, to a joyful endorsement of group sex. In retrospect, it is not really possible to separate Morrison's 'The End' from this wider historical context and to interpret his psychodrama as both violent spectacle and progressive rock theatre. It is also suggested that the association of mythological imagery, the erotic/thanatic imagination, and his ritualised performance provides both a specific insight into the resolution of the Oedipal complex and rites of passage which, in turn, have profoundly influenced the masculine of rock culture – a point I will return to later in Part III, Little Boys.

Jim Morrison (b. James Douglas Morrison, December 8, 1943) was, like one of his heroes, Alexander the Great, profoundly alienated from his father. He had constantly referred to his parents as 'having died' – a practice he discontinued in 1969, explaining that he just didn't want to involve them in the litigation surrounding his on-stage exposure in Miami, Florida. His childhood was similar to many whose fathers are engaged in a naval career, constantly on the move and hence constantly destabilised. His first three years were spent in Clearwater, Florida, where he lived with his grandparents and mother, Clara, whilst his father was on active service in the Pacific; he then moved briefly to Washington, DC, and Albuquerque, New Mexico (where, at the age of 4 he saw the 'Indians scattered all over the highway, bleeding to death', an experience that was later to inspire both his self-perception as a shamanistic figure and 'Ghost Song'). After a further two years in Claremont, LA he then moved to Los Altos in California, before moving back to the general area of San Francisco. The family then followed his father back to Washington where Morrison spent three years at the George Washington High School, developing an interest in writing poetry. Following graduation he went to live with his parents in Clearwater, but after one year at the Junior College he transferred to Florida State University and thence to UCLA (the University of California, Los Angeles) to study cinematography. Here he developed an interest in Aldous Huxley and William Blake and although leaving before completing his course, he met with Ray Manzarek (b. February 12, 1935), before moving to Venice, California to avoid conscription.[15]

As my brief outline of Morrison's childhood shows, his early years were structured entirely around his father's movements,[16] and while Morrison's nomadic existence may well have contributed to his somewhat unstable character, his antipathy to war and his belief that 'Alexander had met his intimidation by being everything his father wasn't: artistic, a thinker, a pupil of Aristotle' (Riordan and Prochnicky, 1991, 35–6) draws into association his own sense of alienation and a comparable hostility towards his own father.[17] He, too, met his intimidation by being everything his father wasn't. Morrison's early addiction to drugs and alcohol, his identification with Beat poet Jack Kerouac and writer William S. Burroughs,[18] his avoidance of conscription, the formation of The Doors (1965) and his growing notoriety as an overtly sexual yet poetic performer, situate him as diametrically opposed to the more bourgeois and intensely patriotic lifestyle of his parents. This sense of difference, of being estranged, was fed by a growing reliance on LSD which, in 1965, was both plentiful and legal in California.

The Doors were named after Aldous Huxley's *Doors of Perception*, which was itself inspired by William Blake's lines 'If the doors of perception were cleansed, everything would appear to man as it is, infinite'. It was a concept that was to underpin much of Morrison's poetry and music, not least his Oedipal confrontation in 'The End'. In January 1966 The Doors had played briefly at the London Fog on Sunset Strip before taking up residency at the Whiskey A-Go-Go. During this period, Morrison composed the majority of the songs later sung by The Doors, using the residency to develop his ideas. Recognising their talent, local rival Arthur Lee ('Love') recommended the band to their own label, Elektra, where they were assigned to producer, Paul A. Rothchild. Rothchild had already seen the band perform at the Whiskey and his relationship with the Doors and, in particular, Jim Morrison was based on a shared love of poetry. 'He was (also) very strong in the studio, knew his jazz, rock 'n' roll and folk music' and his relationship with the band 'was a marriage made in heaven' (Tobler and Doe, 1987, 24) – an accolade reflected in his decision to record 'The End' in its entirety for The Doors' debut album.

Its first performance had been met with outrage, and while Rothchild's visit to the Whiskey preceded Morrison's chilling psychodrama, he would have been well aware of its potential to generate public outrage. As such, his decision to record the song reflects his belief in giving the band their lead when they wanted to go in a new direction. Improvised and partly spoken over a raga-rock framework, the son's awakening, preparation and movements are related to the apocryphal words

> 'Father ... Yes, son? I want to kill you!
> Mother ... I want to ...
> FUUCCCKKK YOOUUU!!'

In common with the Beatles' 'A Day In the Life' (*Sgt. Pepper's Lonely Hearts' Club Band*, July 1967), 'The End' is one of the most, if not the most, controversial, celebrated and analysed album tracks to emerge from the rock stable. In essence, it is a two-verse song, but since its inception it had grown in length and complexity (amounting to some seven minutes on the album). It had been performed live only once, at the Whiskey, some eleven minutes before The Doors were shown the door. Its complexity is explained by producer, Paul Rothchild:

> Jim was fascinated with the concept of death, spiritual death rather than physical death; it's a theme of many of his songs ... there's that amazing Oedipal section, the first big build. Jim screamed there, for obvious reasons, because even for him there were cultural strictures ... but it's more effective, basic, primal, the reason and the motivation. What he was basically suggesting was that we should kill the alien concepts, get back to reality; and that's what the song is all about – the rebirth of personal concepts. Discover, search for your own reality.
>
> (Tobler and Doe, 1987, 24)

There is no doubt that Morrison's seemingly spontaneous outburst is shocking in its confrontational stance. It is equally certain that his extreme expression of lust/hatred was unprecedented at the time, preceding MC5's turbulent 'Kick Out the Jams (Motherfuckers)' (Elektra 1969) by some three years. There is also little doubt that Morrison was 'still on an acid trip (when recording), but it was done during the after-period, the clear light, the reflective part of a trip' (Tobler and Doe, 1987, 33). As such, the dramatised killing of the father, the fucking of the mother, would seem to come from deep within his subconsciousness. However, Morrison's love of dramatic technique and his ability to engage his audience also implies a staging of his emergence as the 'Lizard King' of Rock, the significance of which is discussed on pp. 136–40. As Rothchild's observes (on the producing and engineering of 'The End') :

That half hour when we recorded The End was one of the most beautiful moments I've ever had in a recording studio. I was totally overwhelmed … for this one take I was completely sucked up into it, absolutely audience … it was a magic moment, and it was almost a shock when the song was over. It was like, yeah, that's the end, that's the statement, it can't go any further … the muse did visit the studio that time: and all of us were audience.

(Tobler and Doe, 1987, 33–4)

Thus, while it is tempting to suggest that Morrison's earlier acquaintance with the Classics (Greek and Roman history and mythology) could have led to an internalisation of the Oedipal myth and its seemingly spontaneous re-enactment in 'The End', his sense of the dramatic would suggest more a staged event for his self- proclamation as the sovereign-king of rock. However, as the Oedipus myth demonstrates, the only way for the son to achieve such power is to rid himself of the father and, as already suggested, the existing antipathy does suggest a certain *cri-de-coeur* while providing a focal point for a dramatic proclamation of self-identity. As Rothchild observes: 'Morrison's personal catechism – "kill the father, fuck the mother" – was concerned with over-throwing the law, laying waste to old precepts; while re-connecting with absolute reality, penetrating to the core' (Reynolds and Press, 1995, 125). What was primal was the emotive effect of the words, the rhythmic intensity that drove the 'kill, kill, kill', the 'fuck, fuck, fuck' of the ragga section and which was mixed down almost to the point of inaudibility in Rothchild's original mix.[19]

Morrison's call for an end to the subjugation of the past, his cry for a personal identity, centres around his self-realisation as the hybrid shaman-istic/Dionysian leader of rock culture. His self-proclamation as the Lizard King necessitated the death of the old and the instigation of what the pop journal *Helix* identifies as a 'cunnilingual style with overtones of the Massacre of the Innocents. An electrified sex slaughter. A musical blood-bath ….' It continues, 'their talons, fangs and folded wings are seldom out of view, but if they leave us crotch-raw and exhausted, at least they leave us aware of our aliveness. And of our destiny. The Doors scream into the darkened auditorium what all of us in the underground are whispering more softly in our hearts: we want the world and we want it … NOW!' (*Helix*. Seattle, July 1967 in Roszak, 1970, 109). Arguably, the price of such freedom is to liberate oneself from the past and, for Morrison, this involved a retreat into Oedipal mythology and the annihilation of the father.

The death of the father, the fucking of the mother (the forbidden incestuous first-love) can thus be interpreted as Morrison's emergence as the rebel Dionysian god, the Lizard King – sometimes a devil, sometimes a saint; sometimes an angel, sometimes a demon from hell. *The End* is thus simultaneously both the present and the future: wanting it all, wanting it now. As Morrison wrote in his poem 'An American Prayer':

Let's reinvent the gods, all the myths of the ages
Celebrate symbols from deep elder forests
(Have you forgotten the lessons of the ancient war)

We need great golden copulations

The fathers are cackling in trees of the forest
Our mother is dead in the sea.

'The End' continues to be a controversial song and while other Oedipal psychodramas have followed (not least Iggy Pop's 'Sister Midnight' from his 1977 album *The Idiot*), Morrison's adolescent exhibitionism, his confrontation with the Oedipal wish, provide a particular insight into his urge to separate himself from the past – including the omnipresent father-figure – in order to control his own present and future. As Marina Warner observes:

> Myths and fairytales do not have only begetters, but are reworked from traditions and other sources and crystallised in one form at one time by one teller for one audience, with different listeners in mind … They pass through a mesh of common images and utterance which are grounded in ideas about nature and the supernatural, about destiny and origin.
>
> (Warner, 1994b, xii)

Oedipus is one such myth, but its power is such that it provides a focal point for dramatic self-realisation, whether in Shakespeare's *Hamlet* or in Morrison's 'The End'. Not least it demonstrates the need to 'break on through to the other side', to free oneself of the past (including parental control and/or the limiting strictures of management) if an artist is to take charge of his or her personal destiny.

Monsters and ogres

While Joe Jackson and George Morrison provide two examples of the effects of extreme paternal authority, the legacy of the destructive drives of all-powerful father figures is also evident in the manipulative figure of Malcolm McLaren. Better known for his management of punk group, the Sex Pistols, he was also responsible for masterminding the pornographic imagery associated with Annabella Lwin, the 14-year-old lead singer of 1980s pop group Bow Wow Wow.

Formed in 1980, the group consisted of three former members of Adam and the Ants: David Barbarossa (drums), Matthew Ashman (guitar) and Leigh Gorman (bass). The success of the group had tailed off in 1979 and McLaren had been invited to become their new manager. Although deciding not to change the style of the group, McLaren fired the lead singer, replacing him with his latest protégé, a 14-year-old Anglo-Burmese girl, reputedly discovered singing in a dry cleaner's in Kilburn, London. It was a decision that was arguably based both upon a recognition that the popularity of image-based pop groups was rapidly taking over from the well-established Abba, and McLaren's personal predilection for sado-masochism (as evidenced in his partnership with Vivienne Westwood and their notorious shop SEX). As such, it is probable that the vocal ability of Annabella was perceived as far less significant to her success than her potential for exploiting what McLaren saw as the new post-punk ethos of 'nouveau savagery: cassette piracy, Burundi rhythms, swashbuckling clothes, tribal style and underage sex' (Larkin, 1999, 167). Not least, Annabella Lwin (b. Myant Myant Ae, 1966, Rangoon, Burma) can be seen as 'McLaren's female equivalent of Frankie Lymon – the boy wonder, whose recording of 'Why Do Fools Fall In Love' reached No. 1 in the UK Charts in 1956 and went on to sell two million copies world-wide' (Larkin, 1999, 167). As a 12-year-old with no previous musical experience and a subsequent reputation for under-age sex, he evidenced an example of an ingénue who could be moulded to perfection.[20]

As Simon Reynolds observes, 'the strain of sexism peddled by Malcolm McLaren has been largely ignored' (Reynolds and Press, 1995, 38), and compared with the inventiveness of his management of and publicity for the Sex Pistols (not least their notorious interview with Bill Grundy which triggered the famous lines 'You fucking rotter' from Steve Severin, so bringing the group their initial notoriety), his ideas for managing the all-female group The Slits were characteristically misogynistic. While The Slits (Ari Up, b. Arianna Forster, vocals; Viv Albertine, guitarist; Tessa Pollitt, bass; and Palmolive, ex-drummer with the Raincoats and subsequently replaced by Big in Japan percussionist 'Budgie', Pete Clark) are better known as a feminist punk group whose aggressive and confrontational style expressed what it was to be a woman in the early 1980s,[21] McLaren's concept of female rebellion was more firmly based on the exploitative potential of overt pornographic imagery.

Talking to *Melody Maker*'s Michael Watts in the summer of 1979, McLaren revealed that Chris Blackwell of Island Records had offered him a £100,000 to take on The Slits and make a film with them (with a sound track produced by Eurodisco pioneer Giorgio Moroder). According to Watts,

> McLaren worked out a plot which bears the unmistakable influence of Russ Meyer (the American porn director who was involved in the original unfinished Pistols' movie *Who Killed Bambi?*) They would be four girls, sent to Mexico by a cheap London cabaret agency, who discover that in effect they have been sold into slavery. Their adventures would be sensational. McLaren still gets excited as he outlines his idea: 'The girls, you see, believe in the whole fabulous thing of a rock 'n' roll group going to Mexico and making an experience for themselves. But what I wanted to prove was that when they arrived in Mexico, the only thing that the Mexicans wanted to see was their ass and fanny; they would end up strip-tease dancers, totally fed-up and

worried and being fucked from one end of Mexico to the other. Finally they are married to certain forces in Mexico and become fabulous disco stars'.

(Reynolds and Press, 1995, 38)

While McLaren's projection of The Slits was never realised, his obsession with pornography is evident in his early draft script for *The Great Rock 'n' roll Swindle* (a collaboration with Julian Temple on the story of the Sex Pistols). Although the released version bears little relation to McLaren's vision of guitarist Steve Jones' orgy with 'Jewish princesses in Stanmore (Middlesex)', and which involved Robert Plant and other famous guitarists 'wanking all over them' in their suburban drawing rooms, his manipulative and corrupt attitude towards his protégés is equally evident in his plans for Sid Vicious who had stabbed to death his lover, Nancy Spungen, on October 12, 1978. As Reynolds observes: he 'saw Spungen's death as a springboard for launching Vicious as a global megastar – an uncanny echo of when he was a boutique owner and had thought of turning the Cambridge Rapist into a Pop Star', overprinting a t-shirt with a copy of his mask with the words 'Cambridge Rapist' and adding a small picture of Brian Epstein in the bottom corner. He saw it 'as a gift for bored teenagers' (Reynolds and Press, 1995, 41). Whether McLaren's attitude reflects an underlying irony is a matter of conjecture. His earlier statement that 'buying the Sex Pistols records was never the point of punk', and that he'd prefer a bored teenager to 'play nothing. Kick the TV in, smash his mother … screw his mother' (Interview with *Melody Maker*, in Reynolds and Press, 1995, 39) suggests otherwise. The fascination with incest and the pornographic continued, and after the death of Sid Vicious of an overdose in New York (February 2, 1979) McLaren went to Paris to make porn movies. His return to England and the subsequent management of Bow Wow Wow reflects both his vitriolic misogynism and the aborted Slits project.

McLaren's genius as a promoter – or, as Johnny Thunders, legendary guitarist of the New York Dolls, called him 'the greatest con-man I ever met'[22] – secured a five-figure advance from EMI prior to Bow Wow Wow's debut single 'C30, C60, C90 Go'. In a sense, it was a good bet. The late 1970s had seen the emergence of disco, a highly successful commercial dance style which had been triggered by the huge success of the film and soundtrack to *Saturday Night Fever* (RSO, 1977). Originally associated with US gay bars, its sensual 'whole body rhythm' – associated with the dynamic use of drum machines and synthesisers – had attracted a growing following in the UK. Not least the Bee Gees' reputation as the reinvented gods of disco, their platinum success with *Children Of The World* (RSO 1976) and the attendant single 'You Should Be Dancing', their soundtrack to *Saturday Night Fever* (which sold in excess of thirty million copies), and a staggering run of chart successes – which included 'Stayin' Alive' – suggested a lucrative direction, albeit one that was in direct contrast to the abrasive attitude of punk. What was needed, however, was a more anarchic image and a revitalised live sound which capitalised on the popularity of dance. The opportunity to provide a new image for Adam and the Ants was clearly fortuitous here. The group's incorporation of bondage gear and sado-masochistic imagery into their live acts and repertoire, together with their allegiance to the Sex Pistols was attractive to McLaren. It suggested a willingness both to flaunt convention and to follow McLaren's lead in developing their image. The result was a radical shift in policy and a new look: Native North American (Apache) imagery and piratical garb. However, by January 1980 Barbe, Ashman and Gorman had fallen victim to McLaren's charisma and had abandoned vocalist Stuart Goddard (Adam) to form Bow Wow Wow.[23]

To a certain extent, McLaren's earlier espousal of anarchy, which was evidenced in his earlier association with the Situationists,[24] and promoted through such hits as 'Anarchy in the UK', remains. 'C30 C60 C90 Go!' (written by McLaren and released as a cassette single, unique at the time) is a paean to the illegal delights of home-taping, but instead of the snarled vocals and emphatic four-square rhythms of punk, the song is driven by an African-influenced Burundi rhythm. Its follow-up, the ironically entitled, cassette-only *Your Cassette Pet*, featured eight tracks in EP format, including the bizarre 'Sexy Eiffel Tower'. This time, and in addition to the Burundi influence, the group combined a 1950s-sounding Gretsch guitar, complete with echo and tremolo. Despite attracting a large following on London's underground scene, Bow Wow Wow – like their predecessors, the Sex Pistols – enjoyed only limited success with EMI and McLaren signed them to RCA, enlivening his promotion of the group with a series of publicity stunts which hinted strongly at what might be termed paedophilic pop.

McLaren's promotion of Bow Wow Wow as embodying a new post-punk ethos of 'nouveau savagery' had involved a transformation of lead singer Annabella who was photographed semi-nude on an album-sleeve pastiche of Manet's *Dejeuner sur l'Herbe* (Figure 1). In effect, she had become an embodiment of exotic under-age sex, a point heightened by McLaren's plans for the final part of his marketing package, a magazine called *Chicken*, which he envisaged as 'a junior Playboy for the primitive boy and girl'. As Simon Reynolds observes, 'before the magazine ever got off the ground its editor Fred Vermorel resigned. According to NME he alleged that Annabella had been pressured by McLaren to be photographed nude for the magazine, and that McLaren was introducing a pornographic element into the proceedings, effectively turning what was supposed to be a sort of sexy Smash Hits into "a magazine for adults that features kids as objects". Chicken, for those in the know, is slang for underage boys or paedophile jailbait' (Reynolds and Press, 1995, 41–2).

The projection of the pubescent exotic savage as an object of the paedophilic gaze is hardly new. The glorification of the innocent strength of the noble savage was celebrated by Rousseau in his *Discourse on the Origin of Inequality* (1755) and subsequently informed such novels as Longfellow's

Figure 1   Bow Wow Wow album cover for *See Jungle! Go Join Your Gang, Yeh, City All Over! Go Ape/Crazy!* (RCA 1981)

Hiawatha, D.H. Lawrence's *The Plumed Serpent*, the paintings by Gauguin of his Philippino bride, as well as anthropological texts *The Sexual Lives of Savages* and *Sex and Repression in Savage Society* (B. Malinowski, 1927, 1929), *Coming of Age in Samoa* (Margaret Mead, 1943) and *Triste Tropiques* (Lèvi-Strauss). While the early myth of the primitive, which draws both on innocence and heightened sexuality, is arguably the creation of a Western minority, poets and intellectuals, its hold on the Western imagination has spawned such popular incarnations as Edgar Rice Burrough's *Tarzan*, the comic-book hero Conan the Barbarian and the half-vampire vigilante *Blade*.

For women, their portrayal as 'the sexually available exotic other, without agency, without self-determination, a passive victim, waiting to be inscribed with meaning from those who wish to gaze upon her and name her' (Mirza, 1997, 6) relates not only to the past inscriptions of black and other ethnic groups within colonial and post-colonial discourse, but equally to the continuing problem of the child within pornography and prostitution. As Julia O'Connell Davidson observes, 'any group which represents a source of demand for commercial sex can be assumed to supply a significant number of child sex exploiters, many of whom sexually abuse children ... in a world which, on the one hand, places sexual value on youth and, on the other, forces large numbers of children (either through direct coercion or economic necessity) into working in the sex industry' (1998, 11). An Internet guide to Bangkok, for example, provides an insight into the terrifying powerlessness of bonded prostitutes. 'The hotel girls are usually younger than most other "available" girls in Bangkok, 14- and 15-year-olds being rather common. They are in effect "owned" by the hotel, which means that you can treat them more or less anyway you want – and many men do'.[25] Hotels like this should be a paradise for those of us who are into S&M' (O'Connell Davidson, 1998, 11).

McLaren's proposed exploitation of Annabella is, then, highly suspect and reflects what Reynolds describes as his five-year transition from 'a neo-Situationist agent provocateur to a dirty old man' (Reynolds and Press, 1995, 42). While *Chicken* never materialised, 15-year-old Annabella's semi-naked pose on the sleeve of the debut album, together with McLaren's wild talk of 'paedophiliac pop' was sufficient to ensure a UK Top 10 hit with the single 'Go Wild In The Country', a frenzied, almost animalistic display of sensuous exuberance. With the song's title providing the lyric hook of the chorus, the metric accent on 'wild' and the well-established metaphor of snake/penis (which comes on the first beat of the 5th bar) draws together the sense of abandon characteristic of Bacchanalian sex. Given her age and undeniable sensuality, the breathy vocal against the rhythmic intensity of the drumming, and the inference of available under-age sex promised by the lyrics is engaging. Not least the resolute emphasis on free and gratis sex (as suggested by the lyric line and the multi-tracked vocal) creates a mood of unmitigated wildness that is heightened by the crotchet rest with which the phrase ends, providing a momentary pause for reflection –: 'do you want it ?' – before a banshee-like shriek (comparable to Siouxsie Sioux) lifts the momentum into the next verse. The incessant drumming continues and the party carries on.

Bow Wow Wow released their second album, *Last of the Mohicans* in 1982 and the band's cover version of the Strangeloves/Brian Poole and the Tremeloes 'I Want Candy' hit the Top 10 in England and also enjoyed some success in mainland Europe. The song initially comes across as curious pastiche of Bo Diddley in its rhythmic delivery

Transcription 3

and is characterised by an almost rap-like delivery by Annabella. The overall effect is an audience participation song and, together with the sexual mode of address, invites an exuberant tribal feel analogous to the repertoire of the re-formed Adam and the Ants and, curiously, Gary Glitter whose 'I'm the Leader of the Gang (I Am)' (1980) invites a comparable atavistic response.

It is apparent, however, that McLaren's choice of subject matter ('Giant Baby Sized Thing', 'Sexy Eiffel Tower', 'Go Wild in the Country', 'Mile High Club'), together with the driving sexuality inherent in Annabella's vocal delivery, dominates the sense of Dionysian tribal togetherness which characterises Bow Wow Wow's musical style. This is also evident in Mike Chapman's production of 'When the Going Gets Tough, The Tough Get Going' and the singles 'Do You Wanna Hold Me' and 'The Man Mountain' which provided more chart success. Yet it appeared that McLaren was losing control of his original concept. A second lead singer was briefly recruited, the curiously named Lieutenant Lush. Flaunting a series of flamboyant cross-dressing styles, his joint billing at a concert at London's Rainbow Theatre eclipsed the now familiar figure of Annabella and he was rapidly ousted – only to reappear as Boy George in Culture Club. By 1985 the backing group left and Annabella took a sabbatical, reappearing in 1985 for what was to prove an unsuccessful solo career.[26]

McLaren's exploitation of the young and inexperienced Annabella, and his masterminding of pornographic pop, link him both to Michael Jackson's zombie and the traditional ogre of folk mythology. Like the greedy villains of fairytale, his appetite for the exploitation of the young and inexperienced is disguised by his promise of fame. What he offers is a magical metamorphosis from unknown to star, but the cost of opening the door is a total subjugation to his will.

When will they ever learn ...

Any resolution of the problems surrounding the relationship of popular music stars to the more extreme dictates of management is both problematic and complex. For such superstars as George Michael, former member of the 1980s most commercially successful teen-oriented duo Wham!, the answer to overly dominant managers was to sack them. However, Michael's clash with record label Sony in 1993 and 1994 (estimated to have cost him $7 million) and his claim that his contract had rendered him a 'pop slave' was unsuccessful. By 1995 he managed to free himself from Sony, but only at the cost of $40 million, a buy-out financed by David Geffen's new media empire, DreamWorks, and Virgin Records who were reputed to have paid him an advance of £30 million for his next two albums (Larkin, 1999, 857). For Michael Jackson, it appears that his desire to control his own life was matched by a desire to control the output of two of the most notable composers in the pop world: Paul McCartney and John Lennon. He spent $47.5 million in purchasing the ATV Music Company and in doing so effectively sabotaged his musical relationship with McCartney, which had earlier resulted in the 1982 hit 'The Girl Is Mine' (Larkin, 1999, 664).

Stevie Wonder (b. Steveland Judkins, May 13, 1950, Saginaw, Michigan) provides another example of a child star whose experiences with all-controlling managers led to direct confrontation with his record company, Motown. Signed by Berry Gordy at the age of 11 and placed in the care of writer/producer Clarence Paul, he was initially marketed as 'Little Stevie

Wonder' (the Little was dropped in 1964), multi-instrumentalist and child prodigy. In common with the other major Motown stars, recording material was chosen for him by the label's executives and his early albums failed to exhibit the real sense of musical direction that characterise his own compositions. Rather, they were a mix of conventional soul compositions with pop standards typical of the Motown sound. In 1963 the release of the live recording 'Fingertips' established a certain commercial success but, with his voice breaking, his career was put on hold. He re-emerged in 1965 with 'Uptight (Everything's Alright)' which he co-wrote with Henry Cosby and Sylvia Moy, and for the next six years had an unbroken run of US Top 40 hits. His contract with Motown expired in 1971 and rather than re-signing, Wonder financed the recording of two albums of his own material, pioneering the use of the synthesiser in black music and widening his lyrical concerns to take in both racial problems and spiritual questions. He then used his success to persuade Motown to offer a more open contract which allowed him total artistic control over his music, plus the opportunity to hold the rights to the music published by his own company, Black Bull Music.

Others were not so strong. Berry Gordy was notorious for his control over his artists and his treatments of such teenage groups as The Vandellas, The Marvelettes and The Velvelettes demonstrated a total ruthlessness. Not least his famous charm school (under the tutelage of Maxine Powell) was aimed at smoothing out the 'street' from her girls and those who failed to reach her high standards were dropped – regardless of hit successes. Martha Reeves and the Vandellas, for example, did not have the glitzy superstar quality Gordy was seeking and, like Gladys Knight and the Pips, failed to achieve their potential with Motown. In contrast, while The Supremes became America's most successful group of all times, Gordy was quick to identify Diana Ross as the most marketable asset and her name was given precedence over the other three members. After six years of grooming (and rumours that she and Gordy had romantic links) Ross embarked on her solo career with Motown and released a long series of chart topping singles, including 'Ain't No Mountain High Enough' (1971). She left Motown in 1981, amidst speculation of a romance with Michael Jackson whose career she had helped to guide since 1969.

Parallels can also be drawn with the Scepter recording label and the dependence of The Shirelle's upon their producer, Luther Dixon who, once again, had almost total artistic control over their output, choosing the songs, the arrangements and controlling the sound produced. When he left Scepter in 1962, the Shirelles were obliged to continue recording with the label on a new low-budget production policy and their popularity and sales declined, largely due to poor-quality recordings and arrangements. As one of the most successful girl groups of their time in the USA, they had little financial gain. Moreover, the money they had earned (supposedly held in trust by record label owner Florence Greenberg) was non-existent as all profit had been expended for recording costs, promotion, touring, arrangers' fees and so on.

The majority of early female rockabilly artists also suffered from the despotic arrogance of their producers. As David Sanjek observes: 'Known only to devotees of the genre, they remain ciphers to the general public, faceless reminders of a day and sound gone by. In most cases, their commercial failure and obliteration even from the reputable histories cannot be blamed on technical ineptitude … a number of these figures – Bonnie-Lou, Jo-Ann Campbell, Jean Chapel, Sparkle Moore, Lauri Lee Perkins, as well as Lucille Starr and Bob Reagan to name a few – are examples that might be said to epitomise the also-rans that the record industry dismisses with the flip phrase 'one-hit' wonder' (Sanjek, 1997, 152). Janis Martin, who like many of her peers, began to sing at the young age of 11, provides another chilling example of a singer who suffered under the extremes of management control. In 1958 she had earned the title 'Most Promising Female Vocalist' for her cover version of Roy Orbison's 'Ooby Dooby'. 'Her clean-scrubbed looks and pert appearance, blonde ponytail bobbing as she sang, made her an accessible representative of her generation, neither too aggressive not too sugar coated' (Sanjek, 1997, 154). Her outward appearance, however, belied a more complex private life. She married at 15 and gave birth to a son in 1958 but her new role as teenage mother did not go hand-in-hand with her image of a 'rockin' country gal' and she was dropped by her label, RCA Victor. Like others before her, her commercial credibility depended on her sexuality remaining contained: 'It was quite one thing to sing about high school boyfriends; it was quite another to marry one' (Sanjek, 1997, 154).

It is a lesson that has clearly been learned by Britney Spears (b. 1982, Kentwood, Louisiana, USA), whose image and sexy vocal delivery have made her, at one and the same time, an idol for the tweeny-market and a paedophilic dream. The video promo for 'One More Time' (Jive Records, 1998) – as previously discussed – presents her as the embodiment of the classic schoolgirl fantasy image which, along with baby doll routines, is a mainstay of strip culture: dressed in a school uniform, her shirt tied up to reveal a tanned midriff, a mid thigh length skirt, thigh high socks and hair tied in bunches. Rather than an adult experimenting with role play, she comes across, however, as a young girl expressing her sexuality. As Elizabeth Wilson observes, 'Dress links the biological body to the social being, and public to private. This makes it uneasy territory, since it forces us to recognise that the human body is more than a biological entity. It is an organism in culture, a cultural artifact.' (1985, 2–3) In effect, dress codes create 'drama and interest' for the spectator, and images of Britney wearing hot pants with the word 'baby' inscribed on her bottom, pushing a little girl's bike (too small to ride in reality) whilst looking back seductively towards the camera, in her bedroom in bra and pants – evidence the ways in which clothing animates and constitutes erotic arousal. Not least her public insistence on her virginity (now ousted for a more up-front sexuality) was at odds with her excessive display of staged-sexuality, and it is not insignificant, perhaps, that the piano hook for 'One More Time' is borrowed from Eminem's 'Guilty Conscience', where the second verse focuses on a man who is struggling to decide whether or not to sexually abuse a fifteen year old girl.

Paedopop is clearly big business and Britney's image has been a highly sellable commodity and one that is being copied by such emerging stars as Lisa Roxanne. Discovered singing at a local talent show by Chris Blackwell, the man who signed reggae legend Bob Marley and U2, her debut single 'No Flow' made the Top 20 over the summer of 2001. At present her dream to 'get to the top' and the marketing strategy focused once again on her dual role as pop star/school girl. Wearing a tee-shirt emblazoned with the words 'Daddy, I Want a Party', her image is tantalisingly 'come on' and with her upfront r&b-influenced pop style, there is the hint of the 'little girl with grown up reactions' that earlier characterised Brenda Lee, Lolita, Annabella and Britney Spears.

The promotion of certain images within pop music – not least those of the pubescent girl who successfully blends innocence and knowingness – certainly appears to have had a strong influence on who is chosen for the uncertain pathway to stardom. The secret, it seems, is ensure that the sexually potent content of the songs is balanced by a seemly demeanour, so providing a marketable façade for the ambiguous maturity of pop nymphettes. With 50 years of rock and pop history to draw on, this formula still works. Yet, as Marina Warner points out: 'Children are our copy, in little. In Pol Pot's Cambodia they'll denounce their own families; in the affluent cities of the West, they'll wail for expensive trainers with the right label like their friend's. The one thing that can be said for absolute certain is that they're very quick to learn' (Warner, 1994b, 48). What is clear is that children are no longer chattels. The law has given them the right to make themselves heard in the choices and decision-making about their legal situation, and this includes ridding themselves of interfering parents, whether in the ritualistic nihilation of Jim Morrison, or in pop star Tiffany's dramatic divorce from her mother and father in the late 1980s.

Tiffany (Rene Darwish) provides one of the most famous instances of a pop star who successfully challenged the underlying greed that can motivate parental control. In particular, she is an example of how a talented child can be exploited to provide an income for an otherwise impoverished family. Born into a poor white family, with an alcoholic mother and a svengali-like step-father who engineered her move on to the country circuit at the age of 15, she epitomised the somewhat vacuous, cheerleading young girls who characterised the late 1980s pop scene. Here she met with another manipulative father-figure, producer George Tobin, who sent her out to the US shopping malls, favourite haunt of the 12-year-old girl, to promote her new single 'Don't Call The Police'. Other hits followed, most notably a UK No. 1, 'Could Have Been'. Pursued by a fan, who eventually became 'almost one of the family', and infuriated by her parent's demand for a bigger slice of the pie, Tiffany then took out an injunction against her family. While her successful court case effectively curtailed any future participation in her career, the effect on her private life was traumatic and, like so many before her, she swapped pop for coke, before staging an unsuccessful comeback in the 1990s. Her image, it seems, no longer appealed.

Within the contemporary pop world, looks and image continue to dominate the choice of would-be hopefuls and careful grooming is still an integral part of the packaging process. Pete Waterman has produced a stable of successful stars – including pop princess Kylie Minogue and supergroup Steps. As he observed at a Granada TV Chat Show (December 2000), 'I once took a chance on a young and talented girl whose image simply didn't fit. The group had one hit and I dropped them. They simply didn't work'. Yet the number of young singers who want to be stars continues unabated. The question that arises is who does the pushing: is it the child, the parent or the management?

Controlling and overly ambitious parents are, it seems, constantly lurking behind the scenes. They are to be seen, waiting in the wings, as young hopefuls battle for the position of pop stars or, more recently, *Pop Idol* (ITV's 2001 interactive 'audition' series to discover and create the nation's newest megastar) and *Fame Academy*. Arguably, their children provide an outlet for their own unfulfilled dreams and there is often a curious correlation between the level of desperation and the utter unsuitability of their progeny. Even so, the success of *Popstars* and its progeny Hear'Say has created a compulsive viewing habit, not least among the very young, and an unprecedented number of would-be-stars. 10,000 young people, between the ages of 16 and 26, competed for the number one position and the grooming that would make them the nation's newest idol. The first half of the series *Pop Idol* showed the standard tears-and-embarrassment structure as the judges (Simon Cowell, Nicki Chapman, Pete Waterman and 'Dr' Neil Fox) embarked on the mission to find the nation's next megastar. Geared to cull the 10,000 hopefuls down to a manageable 50 – when the survivors are sent out to face the voting public in a series of live shows – the judge's reactions ranged from the laughing incredulity of 'I don't think you know what a voice is' to brutal frankness, 'You've just answered the audition from Hell'. Pete Waterman's semi-ironic 'Taking out my insurance for the parents' death threats' nevertheless shows their serious investment in their progenies, not least the amount of money they hope will accrue when their offspring inherits the golden fleece that the recording industry has previously bestowed on such megastars as Madonna, Kylie Minogue, George Michael, Robbie Williams and Britney Spears.

The series are highly interactive and Web-friendly – a concept that extends to the range of merchandise we now come to expect from boy groups, girl groups and manufactured pop stars. But this is hardly surprising. As Christine Gledhill rightly observes, 'the star ... (is) the product of mass culture ... a social sign, carrying cultural meanings and ideological values, which expresses the intimacies of individual personality, inviting desire and identification, an emblem of national celebrity, founded on the body, fashion and personal style; a product of capitalism and the ideology of individualism ... a figure consumed for his or her personal life' (1991, xiii). Gledhill's last point is particularly telling. As my discussion has shown, the list of fatalities is significantly large and despite the lessons to be learnt from such stars as Michael Jackson and Anabella, the attraction of stardom continues to exert a fatal fascination for adolescent wannabes. For the majority, however, there is the constant reminder that the world of popular music is about rejection. One-hit wonders are scattered across the killing-fields of the pop industry but early success all too often comes at a price. It can, as John Lennon so tellingly wrote, leave you 'crippled inside'.

To return to my original question,' Who is in the driving seat?' As those on Critics Choice (*Television Guardian*, Saturday October 6, 2001, 83) observed, comparing both our TV viewing habits and the national psyche with the earlier fascination of watching public executions as entertainment, it seems 'we are an audience of sadists revelling in the pathetic capering of terminally deluded fame-seekers'. Perhaps it would be more accurate to pinpoint the zombie-like role of the music business entrepreneurs who continue to live off the vulnerability of the young.

Part II

Little Girls

Introduction

Although the term 'girl' circulates in everyday discourse, its multiple, context-dependent connotations are both complex and contradictory. Definitions, for example, largely identify an age distinction: a girl is a female child, a young woman. There is, at the same time, an implied lack of sexual knowledge. A girl is an unmarried woman, with the underlying assumption that she is a virgin. It is here that the first problem arises. Virginity is not necessarily an attribute of age and, as such, the term 'girl' can also apply to any woman. She can be an old-girl – with the inference of being 'left on the shelf' or, as I argued in Part I, an eroticised child, a little girl with grown up reactions. It is also apparent that the association with virginity traditionally situates the girl within the context of compulsive heterosexuality: what makes a girl is a specific social and biological relation to a boy. Yet, as Simone de Beauvoir critically observed, 'One is not born, but becomes a woman' and feminists would generally agree that girls, like women, are socially constructed rather than biologically given, and that girls become women in very different ways in different social and historical contexts.[1]

The identification of the 'social and historical' provides one useful contextualisation for the analysis of 'girls' within the discourse of popular music. Not least, it highlights both the different connotations of the word 'girl' itself as in, for example, the supportive 'girl talk' in Barbara Bradby's discussion of female backing vocalists in 1960s girl groups (1990, 341–68); in the 1990s' identification of girl power, and riot grrrl culture and, more recently, the emphasis on personal virginity within an otherwise sexually-driven performance by Britney Spears[2] and its comparison with Madonna's 'Like a Virgin' (1984), itself contextualised by her earlier involvement in soft-porn.[3] In contrast, the conflation of girl with babe, baby and mama which has it origins in the blues, informs the sexually knowledgeable exchange between Janis Joplin and her audience in her late 1960s' live performance of 'Tell Mama'.

While the term 'girl' generally implies a heterosexual mode of address within popular music, so implying that there is a radical difference between men and women and that there is a specifically female culture and way of being in the world,[4] the acknowledgement that there is no single 'woman's body' by theorists such as Judith Butler and Mary Russo resonates with k.d. lang's ironic, 'first-strike wit' 'which worked to reveal the constructedness and conservatism of a stable heterosexuality' (Butler in Case, 1990, 265). Not least, the stylistic conventions of country in such songs such as 'Three Days' and 'Big Love' are compromised by a play on multiple, heterogeneous difference and a flamboyant performance style, where the mid-West home-centred connotations of 'gals' ('Big Boned Gals') is undercut by a daring premise of queer affection and desire.[5] More overtly, Skin (Skunk Anansie) both emphasises and explores the subjective experience of female sexuality, relating it both to her experience as a black lesbian in, for example, 'She's My Heroine' (1996), and taking the particular experience of 'womanhood' further with her reference to menstruation in 'Twisted (Everyday Hurts)' (1996).

While the examples cited above provide some discussion of the ways in which 'girl' has been situated within popular music discourse, it is evident that the term itself has particular emphasis within the masculine of rock. The album sleeve for *Some Girls* (Rolling Stones, 1978), for example, might suggest an exploration of subjectivity in its play on transvestism, but the title track, with its stereotypical listing of women as 'girls', Black, White, Chinese, French, Italian, English, American, reads like a catalogue of success stories. Each girl is stereotyped:

> White girls, they're so pretty, but sometimes they drive me mad
> Black girls just like to get fucked all night;
> I just don't have that much jam

and in common with their earlier songs, the girl is objectified as sexual, existing solely for the pleasure of the man. She is a 'Backstreet Girl', a 'Factory Girl', a 'Stupid Girl', 'yesterday's girl' ('Yesterday's Papers'), a 'little girl' ('Heart of Stone', 'The Spider and the Fly') an obsession ('My Obsession') and 'Under My Thumb'.[6] The derogatory of 'girls' is also evident in Bruce Springsteen's songs where 'female characters faithfully recreate the divide between "good-time girl" and wife that is rooted in the western … Women first have to be captured then placed in the home where they come to represent the ambiguous prize of domesticity … "Racing in the Streets" is typical in that the "little girl" is the prize which the hero wins in a race. However, she ends up alone and "crying on the porch of her daddy's house, all her pretty dreams are torn"' (Palmer, 1997, 103). As Gareth Palmer observes, in *The River* (1980), 'an album considered one of his most profound and reflective, Springsteen offers one of the most restricted readings of women to emerge from an adult-rocker in some time. In nine of the twenty tracks women are referred to as "little girls". Further to this, they are seen as hopeless figures in need of men to protect them via marriage, thus perpetuating the male/female divide of patriarchy' (1999, 104).

While it could be argued that heavy rock/heavy metal is the most extreme in its misogynistic treatment of 'girls', as exemplified in such lyrics as:

Takin' what I please
Fallin' on your knees
(...)
Takin' what I choose girl
Never gonna lose

(Great White, 'On Your Knees', 1984)

The most common portrayal in sex-oriented heavy metal is that of sex toys,[7] with the inference that girls want men to control their sexuality and that their role is simply to please. Motley Crue's 'Tonight We Need A Lover' (1985) asks 'will you please us all tonight?' and the woman, 'honey dripping from her pot', serves all four band members, so linking the aphrodisiac of the star (the band's literal and symbolic fame) to that of the groupie who is 'at the bottom of the babe food chain'.[8] Once used, 'this party's over so get the fuck out ... (or) you'll be beaten to a pulp' (Skid Row, 'Get the Fuck Out', 1991). The justification for bruising and rape (in many of the songs by Axl Rose of Guns 'n' Roses, by Skid Row and by Jackyl for example) resides in the realisation that girls are, at heart, 'bad', 'tainted angels', 'such a pretty little whore' and violence is the only way of controlling them. It is a characterisation that leads directly to the beautiful but deadly femme fatale, the black widow who both seduces and threatens and is thus equally deserving of violent treatment. It is a legacy that can be traced back to such groups as the Rolling Stones ('Brown Sugar', 1971, 'Bitch', 1971 and *Black and Blue*, 1976) which is underpinned by Jagger's 'reported contempt for women who have been no more to him than objects of carnal desire'[9] so endowing brutality with personal authenticity.

While the more romantic and sentimentalised femininity associated with the Beatles[10] appears less threatening, it nevertheless provided a commonplace yet fiercely patriarchal basis for constructing appropriate codes for behaviour and identity. As Susan Sontag tellingly observes: 'To be feminine, according to an ordinary definition, is to be attractive, or to do one's best in being attractive and attract' (2000, 18). A successful girl is loved 'Eight Days A Week', she's 'the kind of girl you want so much' ('Girl'), she's 'my little girl' ('Hello Little Girl) and 'waiting at home for me' ('When I Get Home'). The key to being attractive, to being wanted, remains embedded within traditional definitions of femininity. Good girls (with the underlying inference that these are also 'natural' girls) are valued for their gentleness, their supportiveness, their empathy, tenderness and unselfishness, so subscribing to the traditional attributes of femininity. Their reward is the stability of marriage. The distinction earlier noted between the 'little girl' and the 'good-time' girl thus remains: 'my little girl' retains the sweetness of innocence albeit tempered by the promise of sexuality; conversely, the 'good-time' girl, the 'bad' girl is there to be used, so establishing the ideological terrain for the three As of *a*buse, *a*bjection and *a*lienation.

What is apparent so far is that the word 'girl' is problematic. It circulates not only in everyday discourse, but equally in the discourse of popular music, and while its connotations are context-dependent and often imprecise, meaning relies heavily on the common sense of stereotype and cliché. It is primarily for this reason that the challenge made by k.d. lang is so effective. Her early down-home songs of romance, love and loss are disturbed by her self-presentation as 'raucously female', which, in turn, contrasted with her musical persona, her more knowing butch identity. Conversely, female artists within metal have all too often embraced the abjection of the 'girl'. 'To love you is a death wish' ('Die for Me Only', 1983), 'I was a virgin, you were the steel ... you must find plea-sure in cruelty' ('Stiletto', 1990), 'I get a little taste of his venom, I feel it in my veins, I cannot break the chains, I'm in heaven' ('Ripper', 1990). While Lita Ford's songs take on the definitions of 'girl' as embodied in sex-metal, including the deadly femme fatale, many all-female metal bands appropriate the violence for themselves, taking on the role of the dangerous woman as in Cycle Sluts's 'By the Balls' (1991) and Phantom Blue's 'Loved Ya to Pieces' (1993), songs which often reflect back on their brutalisation when girls. The result is an affir-mation of the unproblematic rock sex-object, or the tomboy rocker who celebrates her own sexuality, so reappropriating the codes of metal as both plea-surable, destructive and inscribed within the dictum that rock is sex. As singer Don McLean observes, 'Take the cock out of rock and it's nothing'.[11]

The emphasis on 'cock' and, indeed, on sex itself is something that differ-entiates the adult from the child, yet in Britain teenage culture is designed to segue seamlessly into adult culture. As Zoe Williams observes, 'British pop is remarkable for its lyric homogeneity with the result that even quintessential pre-teen and teen bands all cleave to acceptable standards of raunchiness as defined by bands that were famous before they were born. This is why songs that are unabashedly aimed at children – 'Wannabee' by the Spice Girls ('I really, really wanna zigazig-aah'), 'C'est La Vie' by B*Witched ('I'll show you mine if you show me yours') – all feature knowing nods to their audience, as if a song that didn't at least show awareness of pop as a sex ritual would be selling itself short' (2001, 37). In contrast, US music appears to reconfigure itself every five years, catering for new teens who seem to show an antipathy for music associated with the previous 'generation' of pop stars. Most recently, this has resulted in the Donnas whose lyrics about dope, unabombers and having sex with lots of different men ('40 Boys in 40 Nights') are stealing the scene from America's virgin pop princesses such as Destiny's Child and Britney Spears. Cast in the mould of 'slapper chick' ('Got an itch underneath my pants/I can smell your sex from here/So I think I'll take a chance'), their attitude has, predictably, provoked criticism from the press. It would seem that 'flamboyantly promiscuous men are merely setting wish-fulfilment to music. Noisily promiscuous women might actually mean it. They might be singing about it because it is so. They might make it worse by turning it into a badge of honour' (Williams, 2001, 37).

Clearly self-identification plays some part in the construction of self-identity and if a person refuses to enact an ascribed identity (as in the case of lang and country music) then there is some sense of contestation regardless of whether this involves identity politics.[12] However, the play on difference and *differance* – the inevitable meaning–creative gap between the object of perception and our perception of it – reminds us that the codes we live by (not least those regarding sex/sexuality/gender) are neither natural nor innocent and that terms such as 'girl' are grounded in the common sense of everyday discourse while emerging as a site of contradiction, conflict and tension. The problematising of the rock chick by Courtney Love, for example, provides one example of the way in which the ironic can be interpreted as gimmick. The angry confessional of her fast and furious grunge rock, her excessive onstage sexuality (the Kinderwhore, 'fucked up Lolita' image of the early 1990s) coupled with her militant 'femmeniste' politics, confrontational lyrics ('Here you come, sucking my energy, Drill it in my good hole so that I can see, you are so much bigger than me', 'Baby Doll') and low-slung guitar were challenging, but her ironic 'teenage whore' image , her parody of the sexualisation of women through the decon- struction of girlhood often misfired. At best it was interpreted as an attention-grabbing gimmick; at its most deprecating, a willingness to cash in on her husband, Kurt Cobain's status within the rock hierarchy.[13] There is, then, the implication of being a 'poseur', an accusation that is often levelled at the emotionally overblown songs of Alannis Morisette, which have been described as 'therapeutic entries from a teen diary set to music' (Freedom, n.d., *Online*)

The problems surrounding the connotations of 'girl' within popular music discourse are, then, both complex and diverse. If the discussion is extended to include 'girly', the emphasis shifts towards performers who are seen as either immature and lacking in musical depth and/or playing on a Barbie-doll image. It is largely the image associated with Anglo-American pop, albeit personified in the petite dimensions of Australian ex-soap star Kylie Minogue who admits that her appeal to gay men is that they love to brush her hair and dress her up. Conversely, the tomboy image, being one of the guys, brings with it a different set of problems. Joplin's fronting of what can be considered an essentially male rock persona – 'one the of the boys', rebellious and hard-living – marked her as both unnatural and deviant, and reverberated uneasily with her underlying vulnerability. As her ex-lover Country Joe pointed out: 'sexism killed her … people kept saying … she was just "one of the guys" … that's a real sexist bull- shit trip, 'cause that was fuckin' her head around … she was one of the women. She was a strong groovy woman' (Gaar, 1992, 107).

Being a girl, then, is not a pre-given fixed human characteristic. Like subjec- tivity, it is continually in the process of formation and is thus capable of reconstitution. Girl power, riot grrrl both endowed 'girl' with the power of the collective voice: the former engaged feminism with a fun identity, the latter with a political voice that challenged media representations of 'girl' as passive while exploring the problems associated with, for example, incest and date-rape.

Different, yet at the same time comparable to the earlier strategies of such artists as Annie Lennox, Madonna and Patti Smith, where an androgynous self-styled image provided a way of combating patriarchal control and power, the term girl/woman was shown to be a construction and, like femininity, inscribed with a set of cultural attributes assigned to the female sex. As Judith Butler argues, part of the pleasure of performance is a recognition of the disciplinary production of gender and the challenges to this that performance makes through, for example, masquerade and/or irony (1990, 66–67).

While my discussion so far has highlighted some of the ways in which 'girl' is inscribed within the discourse of popular music, I want now to explore in more detail the ways in which the childlike femininity associated with Kate Bush, Tori Amos and Björk opens out the debates surrounding the 'little girl', through linking them to mythology, fairytale, childhood and landscape.

As discussed in 'Nursery Crymes' the representation of the little girl within popular culture and popular music plays on the dual concepts of innocence and threat, 'little virgins that might be whores, to be protected yet constantly alluring' (Walkerdine, 1997, 48). The good girl is sugar and spice, she abides by the rules and prefigures the nurturant mother figure. The 'bad girl is corrupted by adult sexuality and is the unsanitised whore to the good girl's virgin. Or is it that simple?

Kate Bush: the red shoes

Throughout her career, Kate Bush (b. July 30, 1958, Bexleyheath, Kent, England) has explored and celebrated female archetypes and iconography, scouring mythology, history, literature, Arthurian legend and Jungian psychology for provisional identities, and using femininity as a cipher of masks and poses. As Joy Press observes, Bush has discovered that she has her own turmoil, her own demons and even her own version of the Dionysian fire that characterises rock rebellion and its relationship to the Romantic. More specifically, she has discovered both a whole set of alternative images and a compositional style which both confronts and extends the premium on passion, confrontation, urgency and extremity of expression associated with the rock rebel (Reynolds and Press, 1995, 235) through an emphasis on the imaginary of art-rock and a musical style that is characterised both by its instinctual 'bright colours and deeply felt emotional hue' (O'Brien, 1995, 189) and, from 1980, her personal expertise as a producer.

Kate Bush's initial impact as 'different' came with the release of her first single, 'Wuthering Heights' (1978), the promo for her debut album *The Kick Inside*. Acclaimed by both critics and public alike, it rapidly reached No. 1 in the UK charts. It was a hauntingly original composition, but its impact was undoubtedly due to the ethereal quality of the vocal, which resonated with the dementia of Cathy, the star-crossed heroine of Emily Brontë's gothic novel.

Although the song can be characterised as a mini-narrative which situates the love of Cathy and Heathcliff within the windy moors of their childhood and the wildness of their adolescent passion, its central axis revolves around the obsessiveness of loss and an erotic longing for her cruel and tempestuous lover which continues beyond death. She is a victim of love, a wild child torn by pain and desire, consumed by the wuthering (literally, wrongful) heights of passion. Written in 1847, Brontë's Gothic novel is dark, angst-ridden and introspective and, like her earlier poem 'The Prison' (1846), the narrator is caught among the harsh, aggressive spear points of the surrounding moors, where 'visions rise and change that kill me with desire'. Its imagery resonates with the sensual longing expressed in the chorus to the song, the vocal line rising and falling like the wind, with subtle shifts in the metre:

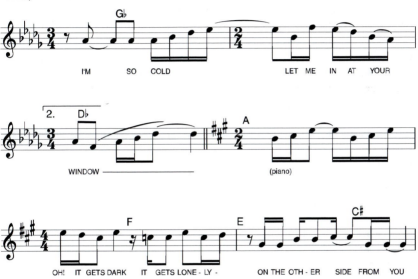

Transcription 4

For Bush, Cathy's need to possess, the sense of being torn between love and hate for her 'one dream', her 'only master', is characterised by a mood of dramatic longing. The eerily-pitched vocal which, like the piano accompaniment, constantly turns in on itself to mirror the obsessive eroticism of desire, is both wispy, wraithlike in its high register, and pleading, childlike in its cry to be recognised:

Transcription 5

It is as if Bush has chosen a never-ending moment in time. She is caught up in the Romantic obsession with the madness of desire, a love-crazed girl who, like Ophelia before her, had no control over her own fate. Cathy can only find resolution through possession of her lover's soul, when they will be united in death.

Transcription 6

But the sense of completion is denied. The ecstatic of the guitar solo, which picks up on the melody of the chorus, and the instrumental build is haunted, once again, by the banshee/siren-like cry and mournful echo, 'You know it's me, Cathy'.

The shock value of the song, the seemingly unnaturally high register of Kate Bush's vocal line, which assumes both childlike qualities in its purity of tone and an underlying eroticism in its sinuous melodic contours and obsessive vocalised femininity, provides the first indication of her ability to create 'a new kind of language, a way of thinking and speaking' that is characterised in Helene Cixous's essay 'The Laugh of the Medusa' (1981, 245–64). Paradoxically, it resulted from a desire to reject 'the representations and representatives of womankind that she saw in pop' and led to a self-definition as musically male, inspired by her heroes (and later mentors) Dave Gilmour of Pink Floyd and Peter Gabriel of Genesis. Not least, Bush wanted to make 'serious' music, 'rather than the kind of girly-girl targeted music that no rock critic would ever take seriously, she had to imagine herself as male in order to create' (Reynolds and Press, 1995, 240–1).

The maleness of progressive rock undoubtedly underpins the guitar solo which, in a manner comparable to Pink Floyd, builds atmospherically. The obsessive 'noodling' around the initial melodic motif, which acts like a structural riff throughout the song, is also comparable to the 'poetic' techniques of progressive rock. Transformed by modulation, compression, extension and transposition, the motif acts as a musical gesture, underpinning the emotion of the lyrics and providing a resonance with the erotic theatricality of the performance.

Transcription 7

However, while 'Wuthering Heights' can be situated within the art-rock genre of Peter Gabriel and Pink Floyd, the subject matter itself is quintessentially woman-centred. In particular, it draws on the traditional concept of the woman who is punished for her sexuality, her wilder side, so drawing not only on the Gothic, but also on the mythological. Heathcliff embodies the beast, the major mythic figure of masculine potency and is both Eros and the source of Cathy's fantasy fixation. In traditional fairytales she would nurture and tame him. In Bush's interpretation, however, Cathy personifies the female erotic: Beauty stands in need of her Beast rather than vice versa and is forever condemned to 'roam in the night'. Her need of him is part of her own carnal nature and, as such, she invokes the darker side of women's fantasy lives.

It is a theme that runs through many of her songs:

> Night after night in the quiet house
> Plaiting her hair by the fire, woman
> With no lover to free her desire
> > ('Room for the Life', *The Kick Inside*, 1978)

> Oh feel it, oh, oh, feel it, feel it my love
> (…)
> I won't pull away, my passion always wins
> (…)
> Synchronize rhythm now
> > ('Feel It', *The Kick Inside*, 1978)

Like the protagonists in Angela Carter's re-telling of the classic fairytales which conjure young girls' sexual hunger and the lure of the wild, and where monsters and princesses lose their place in the old scripts and cross forbidden lines[14], Bush metamorphoses into the lioness for her second album *Lionheart*. The sleeve for the album shows her as a transformed beauty to the lion's beast. Her long red hair mirrors the leonine mane as she drapes herself, catlike in her sinewy body-suit with its fur-like cuffs and tail, beside her sleeping mate. Like the heroines of the Grimms's animal bridegroom tale 'Snow White and Rose Red' she has chosen her beast because his animal nature excites her and gives her desires licence. Like Carter, she has re-imagined familiar tales, borrowing elements from Symbolism and pornography, Gothic romance and mythology, to become transformed into a furry, naked creature like him, so demonstrating the erotic nature of the heroine.

For Bush, the lion, the lionheart, is also England, and the lyrics to track 5 of the album 'Oh England My Lionheart' are handwritten as if to endorse the spontaneous sincerity of the song. 'Lionheart' evokes images of the crusading Richard, but the images are those of post-war London, of London Bridge, the ravens in the tower, the apple-blossom time of music-hall sentimentality and

Peter Pan who 'steals the kids in Kensington Park'. 'Mr. P. Pan whose tricks keep us on our toes'[15] is also included in the album's dedications and is the inspiration for track 2, 'In Search of Peter Pan'. The genderless androgyne of pre-pubescence, who evades adult sexuality and refuses to grow up, seems initially to be a curious antidote to the causality of the lion/lioness. However, for a spirited heroine, his sense of childish wonder and playfulness is attractive. Above all, he is free to fly whereas Wendy is doomed to return to the nursery, eventually marrying and becoming a mother herself. It is a theme that was earlier explored in 'Kite' (*The Kick Inside*, 1978), which juxtaposes the voice of the imagination with the reality of everyday life. Here there is no magic metamorphosis, rather a dream to flee both the fixity of bodily identity and, by implication, the limitations of female biology; to be 'a diamond kite, on a diamond flight'. It is arguably this sense of escape into an alternative identity that informs Bush's identification with Peter Pan. Within the dream of innocence lies the imaginary state of wildness, and the Pan of J.M. Barrie thus becomes linked to the romantic pantheism of rock. In 'Kite', the freedom to fly, 'to get away and go' is compromised, however, by a longing to be 'back on the ground', so establishing a point of friction which is explored further in 'In Search Of Peter Pan'. Here, the groundedness of being a girl, the reality of 'no longer see(ing) a future', where the fun has been taken out of life and where understanding will come with age, is challenged by the recognition that freedom comes with retaining and exploring childlike dreams and refusing domesticity, as embodied in the 'full eyes' but 'empty face' in her mirror image. To free herself of the image of the eroticised girl pop artist that dominated her reviews she has to fly, and the imaginary provides a way of transcending the conflicts of gender and the constrictions of being 'EMI's daughter'.[16] Childhood fantasy, however, has to be tempered with reality. Rock was, and largely remains, a man's world and 'to fly' an artist has to be capable of using her own physicality as a resource and able to redefine herself against the limitations of femininity.

It was a problem that Bush had wrestled with during her early years with EMI. Having been discovered by Dave Gilmour of Pink Floyd, she had been given time to develop her writing, dancing and singing in preparation for what EMI considered to be a long-term career. Her determination to have a say in decisions affecting her work reflected her seriousness as a musician and her own intentions as a composer. Here, she had been encouraged by a family who were themselves involved in the arts: her father played the piano, her mother was a folk dancer and her older brothers were involved in poetry, photography and music. Kate, herself, was an avid reader and had taught herself piano at the age of 11. Her musical precociousness is evidenced by the demo tape of 'The Man With The Child In His Eyes' (which had been professionally produced for EMI by Gilmour), and was one of two included on *The Kick Inside*. As a physically attractive woman, her self-awareness was, however, less well-developed. EMI's promotional poster showed Bush in a tight, sleeveless shirt that emphasised her breasts and it wasn't until the 1980s that she recognised fully the extent to which she was being promoted as 'a female body'. More specifically, the recording of *Lionheart* had been problematic for a young, relatively inexperienced woman (Bush was 20 at the time of recording). 'If you're female, a lot of what you say is not taken very seriously, and so a lot of the points that I would have liked to have pushed, I would have maybe just suggested and would have been told that it wouldn't work, and so I wouldn't push in. But now I would push it all the way. Which is really the way I am' (Gaar, 1992, 268).

The production of *Lionheart* had also caused problems. Unlike *The Kick Inside*, which had been allowed several years of gestation, work on her second album was compressed into two or three months. She was also dealing with preconceptions about her public image: 'People weren't even generally aware that I wrote my own songs or played the piano' (Gaar, 1992, 267) and as a result she stepped up efforts to have more control over her career, forming her own publishing and management companies (Kate Bush Music and Novercia) with herself as managing director and her family on the board of directors. She also planned her 28-day tour (held in the spring of 1979), involving herself in every aspect of the production, choreographing the numbers, designing the sets and costumes and hiring the musicians and crew. Noted for her extravagant mime work (she had earlier trained with maestro Lindsay Kemp) and elaborate sets, the tour was acclaimed a critical and commercial success, and an EP from the show, *Kate Bush On Stage*, gave her another Top 10 hit. It had nevertheless been overly exhausting and it took ten years before she considered touring again.

After guesting on Peter Gabriel's *Games Without Frontiers*, Bush again entered the charts with 'Breathing' and 'Babooshka' from *Never Forever* (1980), her first No. 1 album. As she writes on the credits, thanks to (among others) Roy Harper for holding on to the poet in his music; Peter Gabriel for opening the windows; and all the musicians 'who have worked patiently and understandingly on this album to make it the way I always wanted it to be'. Co-produced by Bush and John Kelly, she wrote and arranged the songs, performing vocals, piano and harmonies, and is pictured on the album sleeve with a multitude of flying creatures and mythological beasts, flying batlike on the back cover which had been conceived and photographed by her brother, John Carder Bush. The songs cover the vocal spectrum characteristic of Bush: the childlike of 'The Infant Kiss' and 'Army Dreamers', the punk-driven dementia (comparable to the Banshee-like screams of Siouxsie Sioux) of 'Violin', and the dramatic poignancy of 'Breathing' with its Floyd-like outro (similar to the final track of *Dark Side of the Moon*) and with Roy Harper on backing vocals. To an extent it provides a retrospective on her compositional output to date in its rich melodicism and sense of drama.

The Dreaming, released two years later in 1982, is altogether different, heavily percussive and fraught with a wild, angry emotion. It was her 'she's gone mad'[17] album but while it was her least successful in the UK, it attracted attention in America where it was hailed as a musical tour de force.

The opening track, 'Sat In Your Lap', released as a promo single in 1981, provided an indication of what was to come. Dominated by the incessant and heavily percussive drumming of Preston Hayman and with all-male backing vocals (including her brother Paddy Bush), the first impression of the song is that of a Broadway show-stopper, the 'big number'. There is a sense of constant build, one mighty climax after the other, with the vocals moving between the sexily intimate of the verse against a heavily syncopated riff and punchy backing vocals (see Transcription 8), a repetitive, multi-tracked section (Transcription 9) and a camp, diva-like delivery (Transcription 10).

Transcription 8

Transcription 9

Transcription 10

While the mood changes dramatically in the second song 'There Goes a Tenner', the sense of pastiche continues, as the song opens with a Berlin cabaret-styled 'Okay remember' which moves slowly into a middle section evocative of Floyd's densely-textured studio compositions, before the final section which evokes, once again, the Berlinesque of Bowie and Siouxsie Sioux.[18]

While there is primarily a feeling of an overwhelming love for the studio in this somewhat overly produced album, not least in 'Leave It Open' and 'Pull Out the Pin' with its helicopter rotors, electronically treated wails and echo and swimmy synth, it nevertheless remains characteristically theatrical in its musical vision. The waltz of 'Suspended in Gaffa' plays ironically with the girl in the 'mirror who don't stand a chance of getting anywhere'; while 'The Dreaming (Dreamtime)' includes animal sounds from impressionist Percy Edwards, a bullroarer against a strongly nasal vocal wail, lamenting the vanishing aborigine, and a narrative set against a didgeridoo rhythm (played by Rolf Harris).

Transcription 11

In contrast, the uillean pipes, penny whistle and fiddle of 'Night Of The Swallow' situate the childlike vocals of Bush in a hauntingly lyrical ballad which reflects back on the need to fly – 'Would you break even my wings?' (an image that is re-explored in 'Waking the Witch') – before the apologia of 'All the Love' which Bush dedicates 'to the friends I make', who 'think I'm up to something weird'.

While the sense of metamorphosis continues in 'Houdini', as Bush embraces the fear of his wife as she watches, 'your spit still on my tongue' as 'we pull you from the water', it is the final song 'Get Out Of My House'[19] that most demonstrates the pent-up anger and sense of frustration that underpins the album. It is, above all, experimental in format, uncomfortable in its aggressive delivery and stance: 'No strangers feet will enter me', and her refusal to let in the wind, the Devil's Dreams.

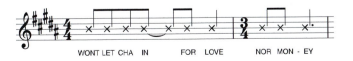

Transcription 12

In contrast, the reflection on the domestic, her recognition that the house is a container 'for m-m-my mess', my 'm-m-mistakes', my 'm-m-madness' effects a retreat into inner space before she metamorphoses finally into the hee-hawing mule. It is a transformation that is, at one and the same time, a reminder that she is something other than an erotic fantasy of girlish femininity while evoking memories of Shakespeare's weaver, Bottom (whose associations with the ruefully absurd icon of male humanity, the Golden Ass, were not lost on his Elizabethan audience). Bush's control of the studio could well be interpreted by her critics as a somewhat absurd intrusion into a male domain.[20] How better to counter the attack than with a well-aimed 'hee-haw'!

After a two-year hiatus, Bush released *Hounds of Love* (1985), a work which was arguably her greatest to date. The gap between her albums was recognised by fans and critics alike as a sign of creative effort and praise of her ability to produce as well as to write her own music is reflected in the reviews.

'Kate Bush produced *Hounds of Love* herself. It is an audacious effort, full of daring and danger.' (Tearson, 1986, online)

'The sound quality on this disc is first rate. Part of this may be attributed to Bush's sensitive approach to producing her own music, competent engineering and digital mixdown.' (Hardy, 1986, online)

'A studio wizard, and a master with synth-sequencing gadgetry' (Bradberry, 1990, online)

'... musical genius and artistic creativity – a reclusive studio obsessive.' (*Washington Post*, 1989, online)[21]

The recognition of Bush's artistry in the studio by such music technology magazines as *Digital Audio* is significant. Across pop history, recordings are characterised by their sound quality and 'artists and producers have enjoyed considerable scope for personal expression and experimentation when composing and recording music in the studio' (Negus, 1992, 91). All genres have their conventions, but with the significance given to the voice – which most explicitly expresses a performer's personality and aurally signals their presence within the music – it is not too surprising that Bush should become obsessive in producing a sound quality that was comparable to the dramatic conception of her own vocal qualities and range. It is also evident that her 'mentors', Dave Gilmour and Peter Gabriel, would also influence her personal sense of direction. *Hounds of Love* is characterised not only by its expansive and dramatic sense of soundscaping, but equally by its sculpting of individual sound moments. Whereas *The Dreaming* suggested an obsessively overproduced album, *Hounds of Love* evidences Bush's ability to transform the emotional content of the songs into well-balanced whole, showcasing her skills as both a competent engineer and as someone who has a mastery of synthesisers and sequencers, so demonstrating an ability to both draw on established techniques while exploring the possibilities offered by new technologies. The result was a beautifully crafted album which revealed her strengths not only as a writer and singer, but most crucially, for a woman, as a producer.

The promo single, 'Running Up That Hill (A Deal With God)', was arguably her greatest work to date, a narrative mini-drama characterised, once again, by an omnipresent rhythmic drum beat (this time with drummer, Stuart Elliot) and a warm atmospheric sound which underpins the driving vocal line to evoke the sense of 'running up that hill'. This time there are no hysterics, no banshee wails, rather a compressed vocal, with neatly tailored backing vocals (again by Bush), which impel the movement, forward and upward through a repetitive motif which underpins the dynamic of movement and where the big-builds characteristic of her earlier songs are contained, providing a sense of thickening texture and occasional cloud-bursts of colour which provide a larger-than-life, cinematic sense of grandeur for her 'deal with God'.

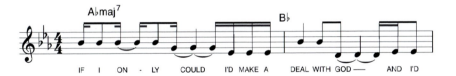

Transcription 13

The mood of running is continued in the title track, 'Hounds of Love', while the conceptual of being one with nature and the universe is expanded in 'The Big Sky' and 'Cloudbusting' (which was accompanied by a video featuring Donald Sutherland) and retained in the second section, 'The Ninth Wave', where 'Hello Earth' and 'The Morning Fog' open out the landscape through songs which again show a delicacy of effect and an indebtedness to Jungian psychology and Arthurian legend in their archetypal dream motifs, 'Dreaming of Sheep' and 'Under Ice': trying to 'get out of the cold water', and the final, spoken 'wake up'. Bush's focus on alienation and the feeling of being estranged from primordial energy is given a specific focus in 'Waking the Witch'. Here, metamorphosis remains a leitmotif and the earlier fear of drowning is resurrected in a chilling track which explores the fate of a young woman condemned as 'guilty, guilty, guilty' through fractured electronic sounds and imagery which evoke the horror of exorcism and torture

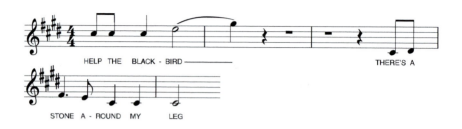

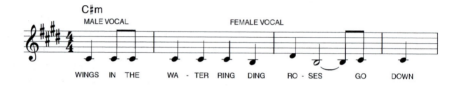

Transcription 14

To an extent, the 'Waking the Witch' is curiously autobiographical. As Joy Press observes, the metaphor of hearing voices, of perceiving creativity not as coming from within, but as coming from outside – another realm to which the artist has access – resonates both with a belief in magic and the traditional rock cliché of 'getting my demons out' as exorcism (Reynolds and Press, 1995, 375–6). In particular, it connects with the visionary, and while this has embraced both the Christian mystic and the occult of Satanism, the association of witchcraft with credulousness, superstition, a belief in magic, and its re-emergence in the Wicca cults of the 1980s (Crowley, 1989) reminds New Age witches that thousands of their fellows perished in the sixteenth and seventeenth centuries largely through the fear of torture that was used to obtain a conviction. As Kate Bush declared in a 1985 *Melody Maker* interview: 'There are always so many voices telling me what to do ... I don't want to disappoint the little voices that have been so good to me' (in Reynolds and Press, 1995, 376).

It is this feeling for 'other-worldly imagery' that most characterises Bush's use of the studio in *Hounds of Love*. Above all, it is sensual in its erotic play on sounds and images that both transform and situate the lyrics and vocal line within an often metaphysical and other-worldly soundscape. At the same time, it is evident that Bush's love for experimentation was not simply confined to the studio and that her musicianship equally involved the exploration of musical form. Her follow-up album, *The Sensual World* (1989), provided further opportunity for evocative and unusual arrangements and choice of instrumentation. It marked a move from EMI to Columbia in the US in an effort to gain greater exposure in the American market but just failed to reach the Top 40. The accompanying single, 'Love and Anger', also failed to register prominently in the charts so resurrecting the debate on whether her voice was right for the heavily commercialised American radio.[22]

The Sensual World is considered Bush's most explicitly female-identified statement and features 'This Woman's Work' and 'Rocket's Tail' with the all-female vocal group Trio Bulgarka. More specifically, the title track traces feminine speech back to Molly Bloom's soliloquy from the close of James Joyce's *Ulysses*. While she was unable to quote directly[23] she takes the non-verbal 'Mmmm' for her chorus, using it as a 'chance for me to express myself as a female in a female way and I found that original piece (Molly Bloom's speech) very female talking'.[24] Contextualised by uillean pipes, fiddle and bouzouki, the non-verbal is explored through exotic and sensuous textures which link the chaos of the inner world to the feminine of Nature. There is an unrepressed emphasis on rhythm, sound and colour and, like the chaos of Kristeva's semiotic chora,[25] the sensual 'Mmmm' is embedded in the psychic, the irrational of sound without syntax.

Sensuality is taken a step further in *The Red Shoes* (1993) (dedicated to the memory of her mother, Hannah, herself a folk dancer). The CD fold-out sleeve is, itself, morbidly decadent in its imagery. The lyrics (printed in white against a black background which evokes the tombstones of Victorian cemeteries) are laid out against a panorama of voluptuous fruits (pomegranates, passion fruits, black grapes, figs) where the seeds spill out in rich and sticky profusion. It is evocative both of Persephone, queen of the underworld and ruler of darkness, and the lyre-playing Orpheus whose search for Eurydice resulted in failure, a relentless hatred for women and a brutal death at the hand of the maenads. There is thus a promise of both the erotic and the thanatic, and this fusion of the love of life and pleasure, and the love of death, is further developed in the black and white of the centrepiece where Bush is shown as a dancer. Her dark hair, dark eyes, dark mouth on a symbolically white body, is thematically linked to the balletic red shoes of Hoffman's sinister fairytale, and to the richly red cornucopia of fruit – strawberries, cherries, grapes, pears, apples, allegories of passion, creativity and desire – with which it is surrounded.

The underlying theme of death is evoked both in 'Lily'

Lily, oh Lily I'm so afraid
I fear I am walking in the veil of darkness

in 'Constellation of the Heart'

> Find me the man with the ladder
> And he might lift me up to the stars.
> (Without the pain there'd be no learning
> Without the hurting we'd never learn)

and in 'Eat the Music' where the Latin-infused melody fuses with the exotic of the fruit (the sticky fingers that play with the papaya, banana, sultana of the chorus) in a rhythmic dance which fuses the erotic pleasure of the fruit with the thanatic of

> Split me open
> With devotion
> You put your hands in
> And rip my heart out
> (…)
> Like a pomegranate

The title song itself evokes both the erotic *jouissance* of shoes that cannot stop dancing and where death is the only release, and the tensions between love, marriage and dance that characterise the 1948 film *The Red Shoes*. Underpinned by the swirling rhythms of an Irish jig and backing vocals which urge her on – 'She's gotta dance … until them shoes come off' – the song juxtaposes dreams of success with faith in the future; yet while the album fulfils Bush's earlier ambition to be on a par with her rock heroes (the album features Eric Clapton on 'And So Is Love' in a nuanced performance where the sweetly melodic of the guitar solo segues into the balladic 'you set me free, I set you free'; Prince [on keyboards, guitar, bass and vocals] in 'Why Should I Love You?', and Nigel Kennedy [violin/viola] on 'Big Stripey Lie' and 'Top of the City') the album evokes overall a sense of nostalgia. 'Moments of Pleasure' draws on memories of 'Wuthering Heights' in its soaring 'Just being alive/It can really hurt', and the early associations with EMI's Abbey Road studios and its hall of fame. 'You're The One' again has a reflexive nod backwards to 'Wuthering Heights' in the melodic line 'She's no good for you baby', a comparable vocal tone 'Take me up to the top of the city', and high vocal register 'And I don't mind if it's dangerous'. Above all, the album sets out what appeared to be a personal agenda, 'The Song of Solomon' juxtaposing the ecstatic of love (I'll be your Rose of Sharon, Lilly of the Valley) against the realism of 'Don't want your bullshit, just want your sexuality'); the 'why should I love you (of all the people in the world)' and the not wanting to leave of 'You're the One'.

The Red Shoes marked the disappearance of Kate Bush who has been curiously hermit-like since 1993. Subsequent speculation has revolved around everything from her mental state, to her smoking habits, to her romantic life. She came 'out of hiding' for the Q awards (2001) in an understated entrance that was met with awe by the audience and a standing ovation from Liam Gallagher, Travis and John Lydon. 'You know what Kate? We are worthy', announced Lydon to the throng. 'Your music is fucking brilliant' (Q, August 2001, 77). The 'fucking brilliant' is no understatement. Bush's 'errant individualism' (O'Brien, 1995, 188) has placed her at the forefront of the singer-songwriter tradition, combining musical skill within the classic rock tradition of originality, rebellion and immediacy. More specifically, she exemplifies one of only a few female performers who have fulfilled the role of composer and producer, so allowing her flights of erotic fantasy full rein. We all look forward to her next album which, at present, is only hinted at (Q, August 2001, 78).

It is arguably at the level of the fantastic that Bush is most remarkable. Her compositions address both the specific subjugation and revitalisation of women's experience, drawing on the tensions between representation and its relationship to history, ideology and culture; marginalisation and its impact on cultural self-expression; and the urge to create and articulate personal perspectives and points of view. Not least, her construction of images and the different ways of culturally defining women reflects both a history of what is meant by femininity, and the ways in which mythology has articulated a cultural sense of what it is to be a women. In doing so, she highlights the significance of dialogics, that meaning is situated both socially and historically, that it works through dialogue – echoes, traces, contrasts, responses – both with previous discursive moments and at the same time with addressees, real or imagined – from Cathy of 'Wuthering Heights', through to Molly of *Ulysses* and beyond. At the same time, she has accessed the revelationary potential of sound through her understanding and use of the recording studio, while emphasising rhythms and timbres that are disruptive and which disturb any sense of ordered time, so creating tension between the rational and irrational, between reason and intuition, rupturing the strictures of thought and syntax to access the chaos of the 'feminine' unconscious. Her music, then, can be characterised as both a strategy of difference and a strategy of defiance, and its otherworldly imagery and neo-gothic sound was, for years, one of the few alternatives to girl pop.[26] Not least, her interaction with mythology, fairytale and literature transcends history by linking her with the experience of other women, what Ian McEwan characterises as the 'unruly unconscious', the 'celebration of sexuality in both its joyous and darkest manifestations'.[27] It is here that the chaos of the unconscious, the passionate and the extraordinary meet and draw into association both desire and dread, the erotic and the thanatic, mythological imagery and the feminine within.

> Freedom consists of voices that have been broken and blood that has been shed. Freedom tastes of pain … There is no objectivity … there is only the vision of possibility.
>
> (Maitland, 1993, 85)

Tori Amos: Lady of the Rings

Tori Amos's debut EP *Me And A Gun* was released in October 1991, and her acclaimed first album, *Little Earthquakes*, followed in January 1992. For the cynic, it prompted immediate comparison with Kate Bush.[28] The front cover picture showed Amos staring out from the confines of a wooden box, long-haired and barefooted, with a child-sized blue grand piano in the bottom right corner. On the back were two phallic toadstools, and song titles which evoked a similar sense of imagery: 'Winter', 'Precious Things', 'Happy Phantom'. More specifically, her vocal style and dramatic delivery was compared with Bush in evoking both the strength and vulnerability of femininity, so implying either an imagined and spiritual union between the two, or an opportunistic leap into the ultra-feminine of the 'unruly unconscious' and its manifestation in both the erotic and thanatic. For other critics, her confessional songs related more strongly to early Joni Mitchell, where there is a similar intimacy and artlessness in the uncultivated quality of the voice and a comparable feel for instrumentation.[29] Time, however, has shown Amos to be an influential and important singer-songwriter in her own right, demonstrating her prowess both as a composer and producer.

Tori Amos (b. Myra Ellen Amos, August 22, 1963, North Carolina, USA) began playing the piano at the age of two and a half years and was acclaimed as a child prodigy when she enrolled in Baltimore's Peabody Conservatory of Music at the age of five. She was the youngest student ever admitted, and her introduction to Mozart, Beethoven and Bartok was matched by an introduction, by the older students, to the Beatles, Led Zeppelin and Jimi Hendrix. Her particular ability was to play by ear, and her love of improvisation and reluctance to read music had initially caused problems: 'If you deviated from a professor's interpretation, you wouldn't win the competition' (Rogers, 1994, 11) – a caution that was related to the practice of yearly auditions, and which finally resulted in Amos losing her full scholarship at the age of 11. She transferred to Silver Spring's Junior High School and in 1977 entered the county Teen Talent Competition, winning first place and $100 in prize money. It renewed her ambition to pursue her career as a performer, not this time as a concert pianist but rather within the popular, and by 13 she was playing everything from Patti Smith to Bootsy Collins and Gershwin at Mr Henry's, a gay bar in Georgetown, Carolina, chaperoned by her father, the Rev. Dr Edison Amos.

Dr Amos holds a special place in the continuing history of Tori Amos[30] and has consistently nurtured her musical career whilst ensuring that she didn't enter into 'a lifestyle that was too destructive' (Rogers, 1994, 23). Early in her career, he had written to Michael Jackson, Charlton Heston and Frank Sinatra inviting sponsorship, and had sent demo tapes to every major record company in the USA. More recently, he has advised on the theological content of such songs as 'God', the promo single for *Under the Pink* (1994).

Religion is one large strand in Amos's family history. Her paternal 'Grandmother Amos' was, like her husband, an ordained minister and has since become infamous through such songs as 'Icicle' (*Under the Pink*, 1994) where Tori Amos rejects her Methodist upbringing through a realisation that 'As a child she was surrounded by women who hadn't been wet between their legs for twenty years' (Malins, 1994, 29). In contrast, her mother's family looks back to a heritage that included Cherokee Indians and a gift for premonitions, dream interpretations and alternative medicine. The philosophical tensions inherent in her background, together with her early sense of being a divided personality, inform her early compositions. 'For all these years, I felt like all these different people at a dinner party. When you've got the virgin and the whore sitting next to each other ... they're likely to judge each other harshly. But it's never about good girl and bad girl ... You can't have your body without your shadow' (Reynolds and Press, 1995, 266).

This sense of shadow is reflected in her first album *Little Earthquakes*, which partly relates to her feeling of desolation when her band, Y *Kant Tori Read* (a word-play that referred to her recent experiences at the Peabody Conservatory), fell apart in 1988. Reviews of their first and only album (produced by Atlantic and released in 1988) had been crushing, not least Amos's relegation to the realm of 'bimbo music' by *Billboard*.[31] More poignantly, she had earlier been raped by a member of the audience whom she had agreed to give a lift home after an LA gig. The associated problems were not fully revealed until 1992 when both the rape and the long-term trauma were broken with 'Me And A Gun' and 'Silent All These Years'.

Although I have provided an analysis in my earlier writing on Tori Amos (Whiteley, 2000, 197–203), the *a capella* account of being raped and the cathartic 'Silent All These Years' are sufficiently important to revisit. Both explore painful memories, working through feelings of victimisation while 'freeing the attacker' inside, 'tearing away all the layers' and so giving vent to the festering negativity that is pent-up inside the body (Reynolds and Press, 1995, 268).

Amos had moved to London in February 1991 at the instigation of Atlantic Records co- chairman, Doug Morris. During the years following the disintegration of her band, she had continued to write, and a demo tape had stimulated both an interest and a belief that her compositional style was more likely to succeed in England than in the US. She was transferred by Atlantic to East West Records (who also managed Tracy Chapman) and started playing small-scale gigs around London. 'Me And A Gun' was released on a debut EP the following October, and was recognised as embodying the feminine voice of courage and power as it communicated, in slow and measured tones, her personal experience of rape. The song is unaccompanied, the melodic line simple and direct, with the emphasis on the words and the immediacy of the moment: 'Five a.m. Friday morning ...'[32]

Initially, the vocal delivery is hesitant, punctuated by irregular pauses as if to underline the trauma of remembering. This is also reflected in the narrowness of the vocal range, the subdued effect of repetition (which confines the singer to a never-ending present) and the Aeolian mode itself and its associations with death.[33] The melodic line is characterised by a rising three note motif, which aurally drags itself up, following the inflection of the words:

Transcription 15

separated by a momentary jerk into self-awareness before it subsides, in step-wise motion, to an uneasy supertonic to create a sense of harmonic tension:

Transcription 16

only to repeat the pattern again in a seemingly never-ending cycle of remembering.

The sense of being at the centre of the trauma is reflected in the constant use of the personal pronoun 'I', 'Me'. At its most dramatic in the octave leap, when the song moves from the remembering of the rape, to the reflective of self-blame ('I know what this means ... Jesus ... said "It's your choice babe"'), it situates the equivocal ('Yes I wore a slinky red thing, does that mean that I should spread ...') within the stark horror of the act itself: 'It was me, and a gun, and a man on my back'. Curiously, the song avoids the leading note (G). It appears twice, but is used contextually as a passing note in the scalic run back to the Tonic:

DO —— YOU KNOW   CAR - O ———   LI —— NA

Transcription 17

so suggesting a certain similarity with plainsong, 'the medium through which the voice of God manifests itself' (Mellers, 1946, 24), in the flexible rhythms, the pentatonic vocal figurations and the avoidance of full closure which suggests a metaphorical gesture for the continuing trauma associated with her rape and the possibility that it was, perhaps, divine retribution.

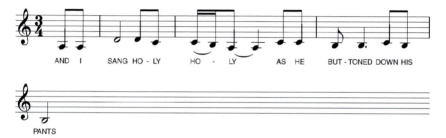

AND I   SANG HO - LY   HO - LY   AS HE   BUT - TONED DOWN HIS

PANTS

Transcription 18

Musically, the expression of the personal is characterised by the interval of a fourth which draws into association the desire to live, the horror of rape and the talismanic of prayer:

AND   I   WAN-NA   LIVE

IT WAS   ME AND A   GUN

Transcription 19

AND I   SANG HO - LY   HO - LY

and momentary shifts in colour as when, for example, Amos muses on her beloved Carolina and the childhood memories of soft, sweet biscuits. It is both a magical touchstone and one of two words that appear in capitals in the lyric printout of an otherwise stream-of-consciousness song. Personal survival depends both on clinging on to previous happy moments (CAROLINA) and a will to go on. The second word BARBADOS ('but I haven't seen BARBADOS yet, so I must get out of this) is thus symbolic of the future. Musically the thoughts of escape, Carolina and Barbados are linked by a descending motif which sinks to the Tonic (home note) A:

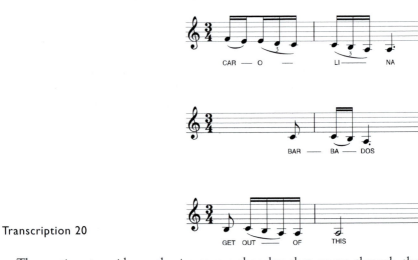

Transcription 20

The sentiments evidence the innocuous thoughts that course through the mind in moments of crisis, so providing a sense of personal insight and a sense of the ironic: 'these things go through your head when there's a man on your back'.

The performance of 'Me And A Gun' can be interpreted both as personal catharsis and as a way of identifying Amos as part of the continuing history of women who campaign against violence and oppression, who recognise that rape is centrally involved in personal identity and that it is the kind of crime that makes 'her less of a person by depriving her of bodily autonomy' (Tong, 1992, 111). There is, then, both a sense of speaking to and speaking for others, so energising the activism which characterises such grassroots organisations as the Rape Crisis Centre Movement. More specifically, her experience of rape encouraged Amos to voice her support for the Rape, Abuse and Incest National Network (RAINN). The re-release of the single 'Silent All These Years' (from the *Little Earthquakes* CD) and the 'Unlock the Silence' show at Madison Square Gardens, New York evidence her personal commitment to giving and receiving support for those who have gone through similar experiences.[34]

First, however, she had to work through her feelings of victimisation and it is not too surprising that *Little Earthquakes* is largely about self-examination, reflecting on the tensions between her religious upbringing, her rebelliousness, her relationships and the struggle to find her own voice – 'Silent All These Years'. As Amos recalls, 'the bumble bee piano tinkle came first. This one evolved slowly but stayed an obsession until it was finished. I entered boxer occupation – part of me not wanting to hear what "I" was saying, the other part fighting off "The Brain Drain"'.[35]

The song is chillingly perceptive in its reflections, the feeling of being somehow dirtied by her experience

> stripped of my beauty and the orange clouds raining in my head
> will it choke on my tears till finally there is nothing left
> one more casualty

recalling the 'scream' that 'got lost in a paper cup', the prayer that 'I bleed real soon' and the momentary reversal of guilt 'it's now your turn to stand where I stand everybody lookin' at you'.

As Amos noted, the 'bumble bee tinkle' with which the song opens is significant in providing a musical metaphor for the obsessive self-exploration that characterises mental torment, and the post-traumatic inability to communicate with the outside world

Transcription 21

The simple and unadorned vocal line of the verse is again evocative of introspection in its repetitive phrases and narrow range, and the childlike tone of the opening lines is quietly subdued, asking simply for a new body, to be someone else

Transcription 22

The advice that 'my DOG won't bite if you sit real still' suggests a metaphor for her gnawing anxieties as she talks of the Anti-Christ in the kitchen 'yellin' at me again', of the redemption promised by 'the garbage truck' and the reality of having 'something to say but NOTHING comes'. Moments of escape, the 'what if I'm a mermaid' of the chorus, are warmed by accompanying climbing strings before the reflective of 'sometimes I hear my voice …' The constrictive phrases which characterise the verse are opened out as the vocal tone warms then subsides as the iterative of the 'bumble bee' motif returns and the verse(s) once again return to a stream-of-consciousness rambling.

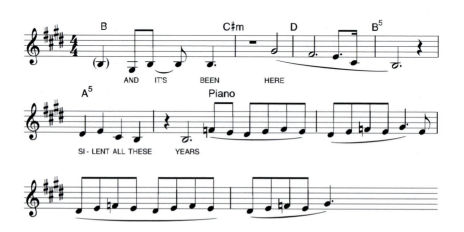

Transcription 23

'Silent All These Years' was later accompanied by a video by Cindy Palmano who had also designed the cover for the *Little Earthquakes* CD. Citing her as one of the most important influences in her life, Amos believed that 'Cindy helped to put my vision out to the world, and without her it would never have been interpreted in the way it was. She has such a pure eye that she was able to go in there and capture my soul on film'.[36] The full video of the CD (again featuring Cindy Palmano's realisation of 'Crucify', 'China' and 'Silent All These Years', along with live performances shot at New York City's Bottom Line, at a concert in Rotterdam, Holland, and 'Me And A Gun' as sung for MTV Asia) was released in October 1992. The video also includes Amos's personal commentary on her songs, adolescence, faeries and personal monsters, so providing an insight into the ways in which her chameleon-like character resonates within the individual songs. 'China' explores the paradox that being with someone can be more lonely than being apart, 'I can feel the distance getting close', and that attempts to build bridges cause withdrawal, 'you just look away'. 'Crucify' reveals a sense of self-tormented recognition, a realisation that the relationship between God and the victim is one of reciprocity – 'God needs one more victim ... I gotta have my suffering so that I can have my cross', and an awareness that the search 'for a saviour beneath these dirty sheets' reflects more a need for sexual release than a resolute cry for absolution.[37] The sense of self-torment is opened out in 'Precious Things' which evokes painful memories, crawling into the wound and discovering hidden fears that can be dissipated through the metaphor of bloodletting and haemorrhage – 'let them bleed'. The metaphor of bloodletting[38] is characterised across the CD which, in its intense and often vitriolic explosions, expresses the tussle with her own sexuality and the conflict inherent in her desire to please others (her father, her lover, her mother) while coming to terms with her own problematic persona and the associated trauma of her rape.

As Amos notes, 'A hole opens sometimes that I fall through, a bit like the mad hatter I guess, where memories coughing in loose molecules come and chase me around for a while. I felt like I had lived 20 different lifetimes from birth through death'.[39] Her tussle with her strongly-felt sexuality is evidenced in 'Leather':

Transcription 24

and the plaintive 'Thoughts':

Transcription 25

providing particular insights into the pressures and problems of her 'Upside Down' 'little blue world'.

Little Earthquakes debuted at No. 15 in the UK charts and was released in America in February 1992. The MTV broadcast 'New Artist Spotlight' (March 1992) celebrated the video of 'Silent All These Years' as a 'buzz clip', while the April edition of *Rolling Stone* gave her songs the accolade of 'smart, melodic and dramatic'. On September 9 she was nominated for Breakthrough Video, Best Cinematography, and Best Female Video (with 'Silent All These Years'), and Best New Artist at the Los Angeles MTV awards. Extensive touring stimulated further interest and journalists, generally, homed in on her 'weird chick' persona.[40]

The human voice is often interpreted as a metaphor for the internal, subjective world of the individual, and *Little Earthquakes* can, and has been, interpreted as 'a talking cure', 'turning suffering into a story' (Reynolds and Press,1995, 267). While this has a certain sense of perception in reflecting on the way in which suffering can have a commercial outcome,[41] it is more a case of the artist rediscovering her personal voice by reflecting back on conflicting and painful experiences. Amos's vocal style, in particular, is sometimes innocent, sometimes edgy, enticing and mischievous as it moves through and re-enacts her memories of childhood, teenage angst and trauma. Her performance is, above all, characterised by gendered emotions and truthfulness to experience yet, as Amos often notes, her inspiration for her music is due largely to her 'faerie muses'. Her songs already exist in a certain form, and she is the conduit, taking them 'up to the third dimension – maybe the fourth' (*Tori Amos*, 1994, 71)

Amos also alludes to the way in which her music is an expression of who she is and who she has been, and her second album, *Under The Pink* (1994), was recorded in her newly acquired studio in Taos, New Mexico – a land characterised by its *pueblos*, horses and desert plains. The album marks a shift from the piano accompaniments and orchestration of *Little Earthquakes*, this time incorporating industrial loops in songs which evoke the impressionistic rather than the intimate of the confessional. Even so, there are comparisons. The tussle with the metaphysical remains, but this time the emphasis shifts to God (*Tori Amos*, 1994, 71) rather than his son, and the 'Under the Pink' of the title explores what lurks beneath the concept of 'girl'. As Amos observed, it 'is actually about emotional violence between women, rather than between the sexes. There's a definite pecking order, which men don't usually see'.[42] The UK promo single 'Cornflake Girl' had two different EP releases, one featuring three cover versions (tributes to Jimi Hendrix 'If 6 was 9', Billie Holiday 'Strange Fruit', and Joni Mitchell 'A Case of You'). The other included her version of 'Home on the Range' (subtitled the Cherokee edition) together with a piano suite.

The first track of the album, 'Pretty Good Year', opens with a flowing piano line and a vocal which is sweetly intimate in its reminiscence about 'a man (who) don't wanna be a boy'. Although there is a characteristic build which impels the rhythm, and where the high-pitched vocal wail dramatises the commonplace 'Hey what you gonna take till my baby's alright', the multi-tracked harmonised vocals ('Let me tell you something about America') and occasional warming strings evoke an overall impression of personal reflec-tion.[43] In contrast, track two, 'God' (which was released as the American promo), moves into a laid-back soft-rock feel, with bass, percussion and guitar filling out the piano accompaniment. The song is, above all, a reproach to God who 'makes the pretty daisies grow' but who 'always goes when the wind blows'. Characterised as self-centred, with a '9 iron in the back seat', the multi-tracked vocals (which act as a chorused rebuke to the God who sometimes 'doesn't come through') imply a feminised statement of reproach. This is heightened by a rhythmic change on 'here a few witches burning' (from an alternating 3/4, 4/4 to a sinuous 5/4 and back again), the scratchy, dissonant tweaking on the guitar which provides an underlying edginess, and the totemic rhythm on the toms. Not least the occasional shrill ululating evokes both a mocking gesture and a sense of admonishment for a God who is more at home in his 'new 4 wheel', who is, perhaps, a little crazy, and who might 'need a woman to look after' him.

The video (directed by Melody McDaniel) extends the sense of a Christian 'Westernised' God to one who is worshipped and appeased in the exotic of Indian religious ceremonies (where live rats crawl over Amos's body), and the extremes of fundamentalism where large snakes symbolically evoke the perverse communion between Eve and the devil which led to the 'fall' of Adam as told in Genesis. The significance of dialogics and its relationship to previous discursive moments is important. Medusa, Eve, Cleopatra, Lilith, Lamia and Salammbo have all been brought into association through a perverse communion with snakes. As a personification of sin, there is the possibility for a range of depic-tions and descriptions, from the subtly symbolic to the overtly pornographic. Arguably, all relegate woman's personal identity to her sexuality.

> The Medusa, with her bouffant of snakes, paralyzing eyes, and bestial proclivities, was the very personification of all that was evil in the gynander ... Fernand Khnopff ('Istar', lithograph, 1888) ... showed a bestial Venus, arrogantly self-possessed even while chained in punish-ment to the walls of subterranean lust, while the polyplike tentacles of a giant medusa head, screaming in frustration, covered the feminine loins whose barren symbol, whose aggressive 'vagina dentata', the Medusa's head was widely thought to be, with its nearly masculine, phallic, yet hypnotically ingestive powers.
>
> (Dijksra, 1986, 309–10)

Tori Amos is thus drawn into association with addressees, real and imagined, and in doing so she provides a personalised insight into the ways in which women's sexuality is perceived as dangerous to the paternalistic of religious worship.

In contrast, the childlike piano introduction and accompaniment to 'Bells for Her' provides an omnipresent and minimalist requiem for a lost friendship, while 'Past the Mission' features Trent Reznor, of Nine Inch Nails, on backing vocals in a haunting song with an equally evocative video which was shot on location in Spain. Imagined as a female pied piper, Amos draws a following of women, skipping through the streets, watched by men and boys, before a vitriolic confrontation with a young priest. The exploration of conflicting emotions and their realisation in the changing moods of the songs continues with the childlike wistfulness of 'Baker Baker' which reflects on her emotional withdrawal after her rape, 'make me whole again'. The sense of 'wholeness' is drawn into association with the imagery of cake-making in an introspective song which examines self-doubt and the problems of communication earlier explored in 'Silent All These Years': 'he says that behind my eyes I'm hiding and he tells me I pushed him away that my hearts been hard to find'. The retrospective is again hinted at in the waltz-like accompaniment to 'The Wrong Band', and her own sense of violence in 'The Waitress'. Introduced by dissonant electronic effects and reverse samples on the cymbal, the quietly declamatory vocal, which expounds in measured tones 'I want to kill', is suddenly broken by a heavy rock backing, so effecting a dramatic underpinning for the outburst 'But I believe in peace. Bitch'. The contrasts between anger, hurt and numbness are explained by Amos in an interview in the February 1994 issue of Ireland's *Hot Press* magazine: 'People out there must be told about the self-loathing that follows rape and how it's the greatest breakage in divine law to mutilate themselves, as I have done'.

The themes of self-victimsation and retribution are developed further in 'Cornflake Girl'. The predominately black and white video (shot by the BBC) draws on the tornado scene in the *Wizard of Oz* and shows Amos spinning through space, along with a burning house, shells and feathers. Weighed down by a piano tied to her foot, and dressed in a tattered white dress and Inuit boots, she falls and is caught by an enormous spider's web. The surrealistic video relates strongly to the sense of 'hurtling' engendered by the song itself. Driven by a heavily syncopated piano accompaniment, the high vocal register on 'this is not really happening' is opened out by the multi-tracked vocal harmonies 'you bet your life it is', and a background whistling evocative of Spaghetti westerns. The sense of being out of control, which is induced by the high feminine voice, is maintained on the final section of the song 'Rabbit, where you put the keys girl'. The unvoiced 'uh, uh, uh, uh!' moves the song into a thicker textured multi-tracked vocal section which heightens in emotional intensity with the final reprise of 'Rabbit', before a sudden, almost unexpected silence. This sense of momentary tension effects a transition to a dramatic piano interlude, which builds into an underlying mood of anger through a theatrical use of dynamics and dissonance, before seguing into the tinkling introduction to 'Icicle'. Beginning with a changeable motif in the upper register of the piano, reminiscent of a child's musical box, hinting at innocence through a timid, almost anxious dynamic, the musical accompaniment underpins the imagery as Amos sings, in frayed tones, about the hypocrisy surrounding female masturbation and the moral imperatives of the established church. More specifically, the song rejects her Methodist upbringing: 'Father says bow your head like the good book says ...' (Malins, 1994, 29).

As the volume increases, the chords become harsh and dissonant, a persuasive metaphor for inner conflict 'getting off, getting off, while they're downstairs singing prayers'. The repetitive drive of masturbation is reflected in the accompanying ostinato figure, played by the right hand, which gradually builds throughout the verse, finally resolving into full chords as if to effect a sense of orgasmic climax. The vocal line also imitates the gathering momentum, the pitch rising, the dynamic level increasing so that each individual phrase becomes an ecstatic rush until the moment of release when the voice soars climactically to the octave. Amos's attitude towards the pleasures of female autoeroticism,

Transcription 26

her challenging stance against Holy Communion ('and when they say "take of his body" I think I'll take from mine itself') and her controversial:

> Believe in love and peace, my child and it'll all be over
> Well, fuck you
> – that isn't the answer

provide a specific voice for her anger. As Germaine Greer observes, 'A Woman's body is the battlefield where she fights for liberation. It is through her body that oppression works, reifying her, sexualising her, victimizing her, disabling her' (1999, 94). Amos's specific response to the issues of victimisation were reflected in her storyboard for the US video of 'Cornflake Girl' which she co-directed with Nancy Bennet. Inspired by Alice Walker's novel,

Possessing the Secret of Jo – which recounts the story of a tribe where mothers allow their daughters' genitalia to be removed as part of a traditional ritual – Amos deals with betrayal and is seen driving a pick-up truck across the desert accompanied by what she calls 'the girls of tomorrow' in the back. Her 'point of view' is focused by watching through the rear-view mirror as one girl's neck is lassoed, the end of the rope attached to another girl's finger. Ending with a lone cowboy who is cannibalised by the girls, the video explores the equivocal relationship between the bully and the bullied, so drawing together many of the issues explored on the album itself.

Cannibalism, as Marina Warner, observes, is 'a key metaphor of outrageous transgression and lives on in modern mythology as the underlying connection with rampant and uncontrolled conduct (rape, incest) ... When the perpetrator isn't a God, eating human flesh becomes a distinguishing radical sign of the Beast – all devils are ravenous, and in Christian images of hell, covered in multiple orifices, busy gorging on themselves and one another' (1994b, 70–1). The imaginary of swallowing and being swallowed also evokes fears of a loss of identity, a cannibalised past (Warner, 1994b, 70–1) and while *Under the Pink* moves from the confessional, the songs, intentionally or otherwise, evoke memories of *Little Earthquakes*. 'The Wrong Band' is not dissimilar to 'Leather' in its cabaret tone, while 'Bells for Her' evokes 'Winter' in its use of a deconstructed piano. Track 10, 'Cloud on my Tongue' also draws on images of cannibalism, 'it won't be fair if I hate her, if I ate her', situating the image of the woman within the hundreds 'who are freezing cold'. The sense of being personally trapped in the traumas of the past is reflected in the vocal outro 'Circles and circles (got to stop spinning) circles and circles again I thought I was over the bridge now'.

The final songs on the album, 'Space Dog' and 'Yes, Anastasia', move from the small portraits characteristic of the earlier songs. These had centred primarily around two musical ideas, which are developed by fluctuating metres so heightening the dynamic inflections of the lyrics. While the full dramatic potential of Amos's vocals and pianistic skills continues, 'Space Dog', and the nine and a half minutes of 'Anastasia' are more ambitious in their orchestration and scale, evoking the epic drama of the Romantic tone poem. Coloured by wide leaps, sweeping arpeggios, powerful chords and dynamics which open out the lyric inflections as in, for example, the coloratura of 'we'll see how brave you are Anastasia', and the childlike evocation of 'and all your dollies have friends', they are, as Mike St Michael comments, 'either ambitious or indulgent according to your point of view' (1996, 91). What they evidence is Amos's ability to orchestrate, to develop ideas and a confidence to stretch her abilities as a composer. What they lack is the sense of intimacy and spontaneity that characterise her more poignant songs. Her virtuoso piano playing, for example, becomes part of the overall orchestration, albeit that it dominates the texture in a manner often comparable to a solo concerto.

Figure 2 Tori Amos

It is, however, the sense of spontaneity that is so valued by her fans; her live performances, not least in the pre-band days, were characterised both by personal anecdotes about her childhood and friends and the dramatic virtuosity of her pianistic style. The relationship was reciprocal. As Amos observes, 'You're not even thinking any more (when performing). You just free your mind and express. There's nothing calculated. I don't play the piano, the piano plays me … I'm just a conduit for some kind of power … You just put your hands on the voltage and it surges through you and if the crowd are giving that out too, it can completely energise you back' (St Michael, 1996, 97). In contrast, her recent performances with the band are more like a visual and musical onslaught, with the songs rushing in, blow by blow, never slowing down to take a breath. As one fan wrote after seeing the promotional tour for *from the choirgirl hotel*, 'One was assaulted by the visual imagery of Ms. Amos clutching her belly – which once held the child she miscarried, as she sang mournfully "Why has it got to be a sacrifice?" and then knocked back again at the sight of her arching back in erotic ecstasy with one hand playing the piano and one the electronic keyboard as the "Raspberry Swirl" beat pulsed through the auditorium. It's a tough experience to be drowned and electrocuted and thrashed about …'[44] The comments about the before and after are interesting in raising the question of 'just how long does a little girl remain a little girl?'

Kate Bush was 31 when she released *The Sensual World*, her most explicitly female centred album, and 35 when she disappeared after the release of *The Red Shoes*. Tori Amos was 28 when *Little Earthquakes* was released, and 33 when *Under The Pink* topped the UK charts. Her next album, *Boys For Pele* (1996), provides a partial answer to the aforementioned question in the sexually-charged songs which suggest a powerful combination of artistic and erotic liberation. The CD cover shows Amos with a pig suckling on her breast, and generally the broader approach to instrumentation that characterised some of the songs on *Under The Pink* is continued. Not least, the girlish and winsome personality of the early Amos is transformed into a feminisation that draws heavily on the Gothic novel and horror film genres. Described as overly dramatic, tracks such as 'Hey Jupiter' nevertheless continue to reflect a love of words and play on nuance. The result is a confusion of pronouns

Transcription 27

and a play on gendered identity and sexuality

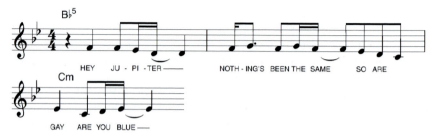

SOME — TIMES I — BREATHE YOU IN AND I KNOW YOU KNOW YOU

Transcription 28

which climaxes on the final enigma of the extended coda with its orgasmic 'ooh
… yes'.

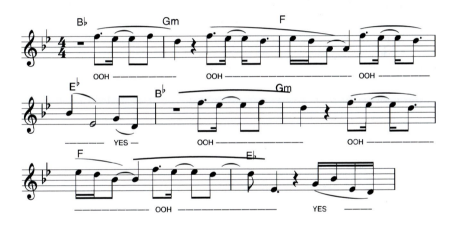

OOH ——————— OOH ——————————— OOH ————
————— YES — OOH ——————————— OOH ——————
—————————— OOH ——————————— YES ———

Transcription 29

For her numerous fans, both gay and straight, the esoteric quality of the lyrics
was an added bonus. There is no single correct interpretation, and Amos herself
seldom reveals the meaning behind the words. As evidenced on the numerous
Web pages and discussion groups dedicated to Tori Amos, 'Hey Jupiter' is seen by
some as a personal revelation. It is about the discovery of a female friend's
romantic attachment for her. Others situate it within the reality of Amos's life, as
a biographical song about the break-up of her long-time relationship with Eric
Rosse. The 'who it is', however, is the not the real significance of the track.
Rather it is about the emotions surrounding relationships and the thoughtful
sparseness of the arrangement and the powerful vocal lines remain a defining
characteristic of Amos's musical style. At the same time, there is a sense that the

early traumas that characterised her first two albums had been replaced by a more mature but equally tempestuous self-characterisation. Public performances of 'Me And A Gun' became increasingly rare, but as Amos commented at the end of the *Under The Pink* tour, 'things are changing so fast', although 'there's such a lot of guilt to work through. I'm not totally free yet' (St Michael, 1996, 115).

The sense of a personal journey into adulthood is reflected in *from the choirgirl hotel* (1998). The inside of the CD booklet is full of photos of Amos – alone, supported by two long-haired girls, curled up in foetal position, sleeping bare-footed by a map which draws heavily on the mythical lands of Tolkien's *Lord of the Rings*. However, rather than the Hobbit lands of the Shire and the blue mountains of Eriador, there is a sense of the anecdotal in the 'I'm wrecked' of the standing stone, the 'Oh Jeez Tower', the 'Still defending Richard III Troll Bridge'[45] and the 'Wannabe Rockies'. The listener also has to enter into the sense of exploration. The lyric printout is architectural, building patterns with the words, and drawing songs together in a different order from that on the CD itself: 'She's Your Cocaine' and 'Raspberry Swirl', for example, appear together on the same page and resemble a towered building with 'She's your Cocaine' on the summit.

The roof is created by a line from 'She's Your Cocaine' and the final line of 'Raspberry Swirl', so suggesting a curious elision between the two songs

If...you...want...me...to   boy you better make her raspberry swirl

Individual words are blocked to form the outer walls, inviting a list like scrutiny

you				you
and				you
something				frame
and				you
So				came
She's				Cocaine
She's				legs
She				back
got	me	takin	it	in
getting		mine		back
lasting		mine		evil
I'm				easel
and				checks
you				Darkness
try				dimness
please	don't	help	me	with	this

while inviting attention to the enigmatic of individual words and the 'founda-tion' of the bottom line.

Amos's use of language here focuses attention on the way in which 'meaning' and language are active transitive forces which are always capable of infinite adaptation. Her dissection of the sentences undermines any sense of the rational, albeit that their architectural structure and juxtaposition suggests both a confinement within a drug-induced state ('She's My Cocaine') and the *jouissance* of orgasmic release in 'Raspberry Swirl'. There is, then, a plurality of meaning, a *dérèglement de tous les sens*, which is heightened by their contextualisation on the CD. 'Raspberry Swirl' is sandwiched between two ballads, 'Black Dove (January)' and 'Jackie's Strength'. The first is characterised by the evocative of Amos's childlike vocal and lyrics

> she never let on how insane it was
> in that tiny kinda scary house
> by the woods

and the assertive 'but I have to get to TEXAS ...', which provides a sense of the talismanic earlier found on 'Me And A Gun' and the highlighting capitals of CAROLINA and BARBADOS. 'Jackie's Strength' is more consistently lyrical in providing both a personal retrospective on the 'where were you when Kennedy was shot?', but this time reflecting on the need for strength, 'I pray I pray I say I pray for Jackie's strength'. 'She's Your Cocaine' is preceded by the sombre mood of 'Liquid Diamonds' and followed by 'Northern Lad'. Comparable to 'China' in evoking the sense of a relationship 'falling apart', it harks back to the imagery of 'Baker Baker' in the feeling that 'this cake just isn't done'. The sense of intimacy, remembering the lad who 'moved like the sunset', is underpinned by a gentle and hesitant piano accompaniment, with minimal drums, bass and guitar which supports an almost world-weary vocal which is broken only by the anguished rise on

> girls you gotta know
> when it's time to turn the page
> when you're only wet
> because of the rain

The contextualisation is thus intriguing. In one sense, it provides a sense of contrast, 'She's Your Cocaine' is jagged and has (as the CD notes) 'weird sounds', an often menacing vocal nuance and extremes of contrast. 'Raspberry Swirl' creates a heightened sense of drama in its electronic dance-feel (comparable to Armand Van Helden's remix of 'Professional Widow' from *Boys for Pele*). The layered production techniques and instrumentation provide, once again, a pulsating sonic soundscape for her own swirling vocals and assertiveness; 'If you want inside her well, boy you better make her raspberry swirl', a line which evokes a comparable sexual innuendo to the 'Honey, bring it close to my lips' and 'It's gotta be big' of 'Professional Widow'.

At the same time, the sense of a personal journey (as hinted at in the 'Lord of the Rings' map) is one which partly explores the traumas surrounding her recent miscarriage. 'Spark' juxtaposes strength and weakness, 'she's convinced she could hold back a glacier, but she couldn't keep Baby alive'. Her 'fear of the dark' is explored further in the ballad to Jackie Bouvier, and 'Playboy

Mommy', 'then my baby came before I found the magic how to keep baby happy'. While there is a sense of an autobiographical past in 'January Girl' and the 'I'm still alive' of 'Hotel' and 'She's Your Cocaine' (which also extends the sense of addiction in 'Spark' ('she's addicted to nicotine patches'), but which, this time, contrasts the sense in avoiding unnecessary health problems with the 'carelessness' in losing her child. There is also a referencing to mythology in 'Pandora's Aquarium' with which the album ends, and which is, significantly, the first on the lyric printout, so suggesting a mental cycle. Here Amos uses her full vocal range, in a nuanced performance where the 'ripples come and ripples go and ripple back to me' are echoed by the piano accompaniment. The vocal phrasing, and her use of the full colour spectrum of tonality, from the breathy 'little girl' voice of 'Pandora', to the warmth of her middle range, and sexy intimacy of 'she dives from shells', is evidence of the amazing sense of control that characterises her singing. This is encapsulated in the final word of the song, 'sound', which gradually expands upwards both in dynamics and register.

There is little doubt that Amos possesses a quite extraordinary talent, not least in her ability to sculpt the music around the lyrics, so giving them a sense of rhythmic fluidity. This is also reflected in the way in which the band are never intrusive, but rather provide a backing which allows her voice a new freedom, working within the varied textures, while retaining its characteristic nuance of expression and vocal range. While this does not mean that Amos has abandoned her piano-centric performances, it does mean that she is no longer a loner. The *a capella* isolation of 'Me And A Gun' is, it seems, over. The 'little girl' voice remains, but it is part of a musical contextualisation, one which relates to the more vulnerable aspects of emotion. There is thus a comparability with her pianistic skills which give a sense of occasion to her performances by using the full resonance of the keyboard. Both evidence her musicality and the ability to open out the lyric content through challenging and personalised emotional nuance. There is, then, a heightened sense of maturity. Amos has moved from being a little girl to a woman, one who is confident of her success and her ability to cope with the traumas of her personal world by relating her life journey to her art as a singer-songwriter.

This sense of self-confidence and personal integrity was also reflected in her refusal to contribute three songs to the film *Natural Born Killers*. Written by Quentin Tarantino and produced and directed by Oliver Stone, it was to grow to cult status on the back of the high incidence of alleged copycat killings and the reluctance of many censors worldwide to grant it a certificate. Amos, it seemed, had fitted in perfectly with the plot which saw the heroine (Juliette Lewis) kill no fewer than 47 men. An added attraction was the possibility that Patti Smith might appear. Even so, she turned the opportunity down. Her reason revolved around the problem that her song 'Me And A Gun' was meant to represent peace in the movie. As she explained: 'Well, if I represent peace, I'm not doing a very good job, am I? See it's always been difficult for me to sing "Me And A Gun". And when I sing, "I must get out of this", I don't mean go kill 47 people' (St Michael, 1996, 112).

Amos's personal growth has continued. *Venus* includes both her classic singles (Venus. Live still orbiting) and new releases (Venus orbiting), while her album, *Strange Little Girls* (WEA/Atlantic, September 2001) covers such male-written/dominated songs as Eminem's '97 Bonnie and Clyde' and Neil Young's 'Heart of Gold'. The latter, in particular, provides an intriguing twist on the original's need for a nurturing woman. The delivery is ironic and ascerbic and contrasts with the vocal and string arrangements of '97'. This is Amos at her scary best, as her ex-husband makes their baby daughter an accomplice to her murder. Although the album is interesting, it doesn't really compare with her earlier covers, such as 'Smells Like Teen Spirit' and 'Angie' on her *Crucify* EP, and, as such, it was great to see her return to form in *Scarlett's Walk*, her first release for Epic and her sixth album since *Little Earthquakes* (1992). Amos calls the album, a 'sonic novel'. Following the title character (Amos's shiftless anima) across all 50 U.S. States, it moves from frustration – 'even a glamorous bitch can be in need' – to separation, 'your cloud'. Her excursions into one-song stands (none of the men last more than a single track) are melodious, well-arranged and adventurous and it is, without doubt, her best album since *Under the Pink*.

While *Scarlett's Walk* still invokes an emotional striptease which informs the narrow line between seduction and confrontation (Reynolds and Press, 1995, 267), her ability to harness the 'little girl' inside through an exploration of female sexuality is powerful. Her musical language reflects both intimacy and desire, violence and self-negation, within an imaginative compositional framework, and while her vocal style and register have resulted in media images that focus on her ultra-feminine delivery, there is nevertheless an underlying strength of purpose. 'I'm like "OK sister, you get raped and ready to get cut up, and then write about it and sing it" – that's why I wrote "Cornflake Girl" and "The Waitress". That to me is a lizard running around with pussy. It's not a woman like me. She ruined her rights as a woman. So what if I sing like the Little Mermaid?' (Mundy, 1995, 12–13). Not least, Amos has had a profound effect on preconceptions regarding the nature of women. Her songs are about experiencing her world as art, and she remains a constant reminder that 'Human beings invented Original Sin because the alternative hypothesis was worse. Better to be at the centre of a universe whose terrors are all a direct result of our own failings, than to be helpless victims of random and largely malevolent forms' (Byatt, 1997, 80).

Björk: the Icelandic elf

> Björk is not weird. She is not a white witch, an elfin eccentric, or a preten-
> tious pixie. She is certainly not, as some sections of the media would have it,
> barking mad. What she is, though, is a bright, driven, hugely talented musi-
> cian and singer.
>
> (Connolly, 2001, 4)

Born in Reykjavik, Iceland on November 21, 1965, Björk Gudmundsdóttir has,
it seems, always attracted attention for her eccentricity and elfin image. She
made her debut 'proper' in 1977, with an album that included cover versions of
pop standards and folk songs. It was produced by her stepfather, Saevar
Arnason, with a sleeve design by her mother Hildur. It went platinum in
Iceland and Björk was quickly labelled as an 11-year old child prodigy. Even
then, she was somewhat of an oddity, 'wearing my mum's orange sheets. I cut a
hole in them, put a funny hat on, had green hair' (Raphael, 1995, 65). At 13
she performed with a short-lived punk band, Exodus, and by the age of 14 she
had left home – 'Nobody thought it strange – I was ready' (Connolly, 2001, 5).
– recording two albums (between 1981 and 1983) with Tappi Tikarrass (which
translates as 'Cork that bitch's arse'). At 18 she joined the Kukl collective, an
experimental punk rock/jazz band which provided an opportunity to experiment
both with vocal sounds and lyrics. Two albums were produced for the British
anarchist label Crass, but were considered too experimental for commercial
success. In 1986 she joined a new band, The Sugarcubes. Half of the six
members had been with Kukl, and included Thor (who she married at 18 and
who is the father of her son Sindri), Einar Orn and Siggi Baldursson. They had
come together as a like-minded party band and thought of themselves as part of
Reykjavik's alternative scene, sharing an enthusiasm for music, art, poetry and
literature. Characterised as surreal pop, they released a total of five albums
before they split in 1992. The Sugarcubes had not anticipated the success of
their singles, 'Hit' and 'Birthday' (*Life's Too Good*, 1987, which introduced the
general public to Björk's swooping vocals and her secretive elf-sprite whisper),
but despite their growing popularity Björk was becoming increasingly interested
in British dance music. In 1992 she moved to London, teaming up with Nellee
Hooper (who had also produced Soul II Soul, Massive Attack and Sinead
O'Connor) at the One Little Indian studios to start work on her first international solo album *Debut* (1993).

Björk's personal background has had a profound effect upon her musical
legacy. An only child, she was brought up in a large house, with her brother and
sister, parents, and eight of their bohemian friends. Music was a vital ingredient
in her life, both at home and at Barnamusikskoli Reykjavikur where she studied
piano and flute from the age of 5 to 15. Her stepfather (Saevar Arnason) was a
guitarist and had introduced her to Johnny Winter, Eric Clapton and Frank

Zappa, a useful antidote to her 'just shut up and listen for an hour' classical training, while engendering a broadminded approach to music. 'I could be either the jazz freak … or bring Jimi Hendrix or right-out pop tunes … then go to my grandparents and play them Sparks, Ravel or something. I really liked being the outsider coming with something' (Raphael, 1995, 63). She was also passionate about Thorbjorn Egber, whose music and plays for children exhibit a comparable sense of narrative to her own future songs and where there is a similar sense of mood, 'the happy song, the sad song, the aggressive song, the sweet song for the sweet person' (Raphael, 1995, 62–3). More specifically, her unconventional looks (at school 'I remember people coming up and calling me "Chinese", 'cause I look different, not really Icelandic, and I just went: "Really? Great! I'm one of them? Cool!"' (Raphael, 1995, 65), her ethnicity, her eccentric little girl image and her enthusiasm for role play – which extends into both videos and films – has led to a characterisation as both other-worldly and spontaneously natural.

Björk's decision to leave Iceland was seen as partly a sacrifice: 'Leave the country with my child, live where I don't know anyone – just go on a mission. I had that urge. Not to take anything for granted, not to play it safe, not do an easy record' (Raphael, 1995, 69). But, paradoxically, *Debut* was easy to make. She had spent two years collecting material and ideas, writing everything down, including sentences and lyrics. All the songs had been mapped out, with an intro, bass line, chords, music, melody, lyrics, with the result that the process of recording took, on average, two days for each song. Timing is everything in pop music, knowing how to tap into the zeitgeist, and here Nellee Hooper provided the necessary flexibility, smoothness and know-how. He also provided an introduction to studio technology, with Marius De Vries as programmer, so giving the original songs a contemporary feel. Vries's imaginative use of synths and keyboards in particular give the album its dance chart potential, and this was enhanced by the inclusion of well-known names on the sample mix. These had chiefly come to prominence in the early 1990s dance charts and included Underworld[46] and Bassheads ('Human Behaviour'), Black Dog ('Venus As A Boy'), Tim Simenon of Bomb the Bass[47] ('Play Dead', which was also used on the soundtrack to the film *Young Americans*, featuring a distinctive Jah Wobble bass hook) and David Morales,[48] Justin Robertson[49] and Fluke ('Big Time Sensuality').

Debut is both accessible and authoritative in its 'state of the art' feel. Not only is Björk's vocal delivery clear and confident – each word accessible despite the often quirky delivery – but there is an interesting mix of styles which range from the upbeat narrative of 'There's More To Life Than This', with its four-on-the-floor (i.e., a kick on every crotchet beat) house groove, to an avant-garde jazz pastiche ('The Anchor Song') and an upbeat love ballad ('Violently Happy'). The first song on the album, 'Human Behaviour', is finely tuned to the period with its bass-heavy sound. By the 1990s, samplers (which had earlier underpinned hip hop) had become a key ingredient in the house sound, and by

November 1991 half the records in the British Top 10 were house instrumentals. In 1993 computer-aided music makers such as the Orb and Biosphere were producing chilled-out soundscapes of great expressiveness, and Björk's melancholic and troubled vocal provides a sense of her making her own version of the house sound. The seamless rhythm of the track is held together by a steady four-on-the-floor beat on the bass hook, with 16ths on the cymbals, and a brushed snare drum effect with a finger snap on the second beat. The repetitive grooves allow Björk a certain indulgence in her vocal delivery which is often jagged and rhythmically erratic, and characterised by a concentration on the syllabic quality of words. These are sometimes extended through repetition with an emphasis on the individual consonants and vowels ('terribly, terribly, terribly smooth', 'Ever so, ever so sat ... isfying', 'yet so, yet so, yet so irr-e-sis-ta-ble'), or coloured by an upward yodel which provides an atmospheric swoop to her top register ('there's no-o map'). The shape of the words are also underpinned by a very clean and precise sound which effects a sonic contrast with the double-time feel of the vocal outro. Presaged by a violin sample (which is deep in the mix), the repeat of the multi-tracked chorus ('behaviour') effects an almost aggressive reflection on confusion:

> there's no map
> to human behaviour

The four-on-the-floor feel continues into track 2, 'Crying'. This time, the funk rhythm on synth provides a bitter, melancholic edge (evoking memories of 'All Night Party' by A Certain Ratio) which is enhanced by the locomotive rhythm and sampled train whistle with which the song opens, and the dissonant synth riff which separates the verses. Metallic samples provide an edgy feel and suggest a certain underlying resonance with Björk's earlier love of hardcore industrial,[50] which enhance the defencelessness inherent in her 'little girl' voice as she sings, in a close-miked breathy vocal:

> No-one here
> and people everywhere
> everyone
> is so vulnerable
> and I'm as well

The 'broken English' of the lyrics open out her sense of 'aloneness' when abroad. 'At Reykjavik, I'm just *Bjerrk*', she says with full Icelandic resonance, 'but when I'm abroad, I'm the alien Icelander. When I go to Manhattan, I don't sleep. I feel most the time when I travel I might as well be on the moon' (Baker, 1997, 18). As the song moves into its final verses, Björk moves to a more jazz-driven feel, cruising around the lyrics:

> only if a ship would sail in

swooping up to her top register for the outburst on 'I care'. Again, the song waits until the end for the multi-tracked vocals. This time, there are no words, rather a rising and unaccompanied 'duh duh duhrrr' which provides a sense of linguistic frustration before a gradual fade into a stuttering drum sample.

While the intro to 'Venus As A Boy' is also characterised by electronic samples, the song itself is both melodic and poetically eloquent. The vocal is sinuous and breathy, and its simple melodic shape is echoed by parallel octaves on the strings so providing a minimalist feel which underpins the personal reflection of the lyrics. Here, each word is separated, providing an almost tactile and voluptuous quality to 'his fingers (which) focus on her touches'. Individual syllables are eroticised through the exotic quality of the strings:

Transcription 30

and Björk's vocal as she moves into the evocative of the chorus,

Transcription 31

while the laid-back mood of the verse provides a space to vocally caress the memories of arousal, taking time, with the implication that every memory of his body is precious:

> he's exploring
> the taste of her
> arousal
> so accurate
> he sets off
> the beauty in her

It is no wonder that 'Venus As A Boy' became a Top 10 single. Its melodic hook is immediately memorable, inviting participation, and generally there is a lack of complication, so aligning the feel of the music (the parallel octaves of vocals and strings over the reggae groove, the accompanying slurred violins which suggest an unsophisticated folk feel) with the evocative beauty of sexual awakening. At the same time, the song is highly personalised and individual-istic. Björk's heavily punctuated vocals evoke the sense of an eroticised space, aligning Venus, the goddess and principle of erotic love, with her lover, a boy whose 'wicked sense of humour suggests exciting sex'.

Track 4, 'There's More To Life Than This', returns the listener to a classic House feel and evokes a party mood, reminiscent of the warehouse raves of the early 1990s. The sampled conversations (which are deep in the mix) are opened out by electronic swoops and multi-tracked vocals before the four-on-the-floor bass hook establishes the omnipresent beat 'come on girl, let's sneak out of this party, it's getting boring'. The semi-rapped:

> We could sneak off to an island
> There's more to life than this

provides the first taster of Björk's mischievous persona. The tone is impudently persuasive, concealing a hidden chuckle ('we could nick a boat …'), with the flattened vowels and occasional growling 'rrr's' (ghettoblasterrr') situating her as exotically different. In contrast, 'Like Someone In Love' (accompanied by Corky Hale on harp) fronts the wavering 'little girl' voice in a somewhat unconfident cover, while 'Big Time Sensuality' returns to the early 1990s house style reminiscent of the Hacienda.[51] While there is no direct mention of ecstasy, the 'coming up' and the reference to 'the hard core and the gentle bit time sensuality' evoke memories of the throbbing rhythms of house, with the emphasis firmly on the repetitive rhythms and the Hammond organ stabs.

Transcription 32

Björk's strange and often eerie vocal colouring and melodic contouring has frequently been linked to her empathy with the Icelandic landscape, and track 7, 'One Day', provides a particular example of her idiosyncratic shaping of words as a musical metaphor for the 'unnatural' beauty of a country shaped by ice and volcanic eruptions. 'One Day' opens with curious 'helium'-inflected speech samples, a sustained string sound and electronic samples which suggest 'other world' associations, before moving into a sinuous vocal, accompanied by a repetitive bass riff. The emphasis throughout is on the vocal line and Björk's melodic gestures with their characteristic swoop and fall shape.

I   CAN FEEL   IT ————————

Transcription 33

Individual words are again caressed, tonally lightened ('the atmosphere'), inflected with momentary dynamics ('the volcano with the eruption that never lets you down') to effect a sense of storytelling, the 'one day it will happen' of the opening lines. The narrative of the verse is coloured throughout by the vocal mix and the contouring of the melodic line, rising ethereally on phrases which reflect on the Land of the Midnight Sun ('two suns ready to shine just for you'), separating and enjoying the voluptuous quality of words which soar upwards, following the trajectory of 'the beauty-full-est fireworks', or curving gracefully with the aeroplane as it moves across the volcanic landscape. Ending with an evocative multi-tracked vocal with echo on the 'one day' the song provides a particular insight into Björk's sense of communion with the Icelandic landscape and its contextualisation by a somewhat curious techno beat. 'When you live in a place like this', she says, 'it doesn't matter how techno you get … It's not just the volcanoes and earthquakes that are stronger than us; it's the sun and this galaxy and all the other galaxies. Basically, I would say I believe in nature' (Baker, 1997, 16).

In contrast, 'Come To Me' is a love ballad, sung in a sweetly intimate tone against a string accompaniment with a bottom-heavy bass sample which shifts from 3/4–4/4 and back again. The emphasis is, once again, on the vocal line, with a characteristic overemphasis and spacing on key words ('I understand'), and upward soaring on the 'I adore you', 'I love you'. Björk succeeds, here, in fronting a sense of vulnerability which is curiously at odds with the 'Come to me, I'll take care of you' of the opening lines. The slurred melismas:

YOU ——— KNOW ——

Transcription 34

are inflected with an echo, and seem to slide across the surface of the words to create a sense of enchantment: 'don't make me say it (I love you) it would burst the bubble'. This time there is no multi-tracking. Rather the monosyllabic effect of the words imply a sense of aloneness. The accompaniment is simply there as a platform for her vocal and there are no dynamic changes. It is an example of vocal tone painting at its best, a flickering flame that, on paper, is reduced simply to a flickering of black ink.

'Violently Happy' returns to the four-on-the-floor house feel, enlivened by maracas, Hammond organ stabs and occasional cymbal-like splashes. Here there is an interesting use of alternating minor/major harmonies which effect the shifts of emotion inherent in the 'violently happy, but you're not there'. In direct contrast, 'The Anchor Song' is almost surrealistic in its minor feel saxophone accompaniment and widely spaced tonal register. The final song on the album 'Play Dead' is, arguably, the 'big number' and evokes memories of Kate Bush's 'Running Up That Hill' in its lush instrumentation and orchestration. It is also a showcase for the versatility of Björk's vocal range, with massive swoops up to her top register ('the city of fear'), the flattened dynamic of her breathy 'little girl' voice ('darling stop confusing me'), the long sustained 'ache' which is suddenly inflected by a low growl before soaring up again. Above all, it embodies not simply a raw naturalism but also a unique individualism and originality. As her producer, Nellee Hooper writes: 'I must have listened to each of these tracks more than 500 times since we started. Everything's long since finished but I'm still listening to these songs everyday ... We are so lucky to have Björk's voice'.[52] The critics and general public agreed and *Debut* sold more than four million copies worldwide.

Her next album *Post* (1995) did even better. Again, it was an eclectic album, including the hard techno beats of 'Army of Me', the shimmering 'Hyperballad' and the hit single 'It's Oh So Quiet'. Produced, once again, by Nellee Hooper, the album overall shows little real shift in direction, rather a consolidation of the vocal style which characterised *Debut*. The success of *Debut* and *Post* resulted not only in Björk's acclaim as an international artist, but equally in the problems associated with stardom. At their least threatening, she had been lampooned both by comedienne Dawn French and by Spitting Image which showed her screeching along to fax machines. On a darker note, the media's running commentary on her private life, including her traumatic break-up with drum 'n' bass artist, Goldie, had turned her into 'an *adrrrenaleen* junkie' – touring, hotel rooms, endless flights and back-to-back interviews. She was, however, in west London, where she had been living for four years, when a potentially lethal letter bomb was posted to her home address by an obsessed American fan. After sending the device, Ricardo Lopez filmed himself as he blew his brains out with a shotgun while listening to one of her songs, 'I Remember You'. Although the bomb had been intercepted on its arrival in England, it changed her life. 'I was very upset that somebody had died. I couldn't sleep for a week. And I'd be lying if I said it didn't scare the fuck out of me. That I could get hurt and, most of all, that my son could get hurt' (Baker, 1997, 12). Two days after the incident she went to southern Spain and remained there for six months, recording her new album *Homogenic*, this time without the glossy production style of Nellee Hooper. Instead, it is co-produced by Mark Bell and the songs are 'all one flavour. I'd used up my back catalogue. It's just tunes from now, from a similar place. It's kind of like a 31-year old female – me' (Baker, 1997, 14).

For me, this is a very Scandinavian-sounding album, comparable to Norway's Bel Canto in its dark melancholy, and its sombre mood provides an evocative backdrop for the often limpid purity of Björk's vocals. The arrangements (by Eumir Deodata) are complex, with tracks 1 'Hunter', 2 'Joga', 6 '5 Years' and 9 'Pluto' characterised by the lush, sweeping sounds of the Icelandic String Octet. Overall, the album evokes memories of *Debut*'s 'The Anchor Song', exorcising the past and documenting her 'crash' after the bomb incident and the break-up with Goldie. The first track 'Hunter' creates an emotional bleakness which is enhanced both by the solo cellos, tattoo-like snare drums and the electronic sound samples which spark against the flatness of the vocal line 'so you left me on my own'. Although Björk rarely explains the meaning behind her lyrics, she does provide some insight into 'Joga' (the first single from the album, and the name of her best friend). 'It's about having a conversation with a friend where you load off your emotional luggage and you're just back at point zero, with the past behind you and the unknown in front, and it's exciting. Anything could happen' (Baker, 1997, 14). The slow tempo and dark cello line initially maintain the sombre mood of 'Hunter', providing a bleak background for the flattened dynamic of the vocal line 'all these accidents that happen …' The sense of trekking through large emotional landscapes is then intensified by the introduction of sweeping strings and dynamically sparking electronic sounds which swoop upwards, cutting through the surface of the strings which momentarily open out in a repeated lyrical arpeggio against an ecstatic 'state of emergency, how beautiful to be, state of emergency is where I want to be'.

The momentary highs associated with volatile emotional states are, however, transitory and the underlying darkness of being suddenly alone is re-explored in track 3 'Unravel' where timid vocals are almost hidden under the orchestral accompaniment. Initially, Björk's wavering melodic line evokes momentary memories of Norwegian saxophonist Jan Garbarek (*Officium*) in the juxtaposition of a plaintive solo against dark-voiced strings, 'while you are away my heart comes undone'. It is, however, the beautifully constructed vocal counterpoint that most poignantly constructs a musical metaphor for the slow unravelling of a ball of yarn – 'our love … he'll never return it'. Ending with a dark organ ostinato it seems, for the listener, that the feeling of encroaching isolation will never be lifted, and while 'Bachelorette' is more up tempo, with an underlying tango beat, the mood continues as Björk laments a lost love in a song which situates her within the tradition of the torch singer: 'You are the one who grows distant (my love) when I beckon you near'. Heavily punctuated by electronic incisions and a heavy bass ostinato on piano, her voice is fronted, projecting a mood of subjective emotion, 'drink me, make me real (my love)'. This time, Björk uses her full vocal range, climbing up to her top register and often making use of a quavering effect to reinforce the underlying passion of the lyrics: 'the game we are playing is life (my love) love is a two way thing'. While the 'little girl' voice is used to express vulnerability – 'leave me now' – the vocal is characterised overall by a powerful delivery which soars, diva-like, above the densely orchestrated minor accompaniment, weaving through the dark texture with poetic images that draw heavily on nature:

> I'm a whisper in water …
> I'm a path of cinders …

and mythology:

> I'm a tree that grows hearts … You're the ground that I feed on.

It is an image that evokes legends of trees that are transfigured into men and women and where, instead of sap, the severed ends gouge blood.[53]

> I'm a fountain of blood (my love) in the shape of a girl.

Björk's evocative use of imagery and tone-painting continues in track 5 'All Neon Like', where an impressionistic use of instrumentation and change of tempo effects, initially, a well-crafted sense of contrast. Her opening vocals 'not til you halo all over me' seem to shimmer, effecting a musical metaphor for the imagery of the lyrics, before they are grounded by a heavy bass tattoo which continues throughout the song. Again there are references to mythology as Björk aligns herself with Arachne who, sentenced to become a spider by Minerva, entices the unwary into her web:

> I weave for you
> the marvellous web glows in the dark, neon like
> the cocoon surrounds you
> embraces all so you can sleep, foetus like

While Björk's vocal tone here is alluring, there are nevertheless characteristic vocal swoops that momentarily cut through the surface dynamic, and the mood remains dark, 'with a razor blade I'll cut a slit open and the luminous beam feeds your honey. I'll heal you'. Given the contextualisation, the 'heal you' seems, at best, equivocal. Female spiders are known to eat their unwary mates, and a military-like tattoo on snares and simple melodic ostinato on pipe organ create an underlying mood of aggression which supports the 'in yer face' vocal delivery of '5 Years'. While the harmonies remain resolutely minor, so suggesting a possible uncertainty, the final 'I dare you to take me on' is inflected with growls and snarls, confronting the sense of futility inherent in the 'you can't handle love' by an implicit 'you can't handle me'.

In contrast, the dynamic of track 7, 'Immature', is restrained, although still minor in feel, effecting an underlying reflective mood for the 'how could I be so immature to think he could replace the missing elements in me'. The spacing of the words is crucial to the overall effect. Each syllable is weighted, shaping the sense of deliberation and growing frustration: 'how could I be so lazy'. The five line stanza (which constitutes the total lyric content) is repeated three times, confining the vocal within a never-ending present which is broken only by the tortured vowels and growling inflection on 'elements' and a scream-like howl on 'immature'. The need to break out of the imprisoning past is opened out in the stream-of-consciousness 'alarm call'. Opening with fractured bells and a syncopated bass, the multi-tracked vocals support the sense of breaking free – 'I want to go to a mountain top … play a joyous tune'. However, as anyone who has been through personal trauma knows only too well, rejuvenation often involves a nightmare journey and the jagged electronic samples and frenetic 140 bpm of 'Pluto' creates an uneasy feel. Characterised once again by unvoiced sounds and screams of anguish against the stuttering staccato bass, the 'I just want to explode' is finally resolved in the final track 'All Is Full Of Love'. After the frenetic and exhausting rhythms that characterise Björk's personal sense of rebirth ('a little tired, but brand new'), she re-finds her 'little girl' voice. Against a background of shimmering strings there is a sense of fragile reawakening 'you'll be given love'. Harps, strings and a gradually warming texture support the feeling of being in tune with oneself. Self-knowledge, 'your doors are all shut', 'your phone is off the hook', is tempered by the recognition that 'you have to twist your head around', that 'love is all around you'. This is effected musically by Björk's vocal line. She sings in counterpoint with herself, capturing the 'all is full of love' in a song which promises a happy ending to an otherwise dark and introspective album.

After *Homogenic*, Björk could never again be regarded as a quaintly elfish pop artist. There is a new sense of maturity in the mesmeric quality of the songs that provides a personal insight into 'what it is to be a woman'. This is captured both by the lyrics – which engage with echoes, traces, responses and reactions to her past – and through her musical expression. In essence, the album is about Björk's own nature, which embodies both desire (as opposed to reason) and defiance as she searches for freedom from the contours of the past through sensual and erotically shaped vocal gestures and tonal inflections. This is also reflected in the morphing of Björk into Geisha on the cover of the CD booklet. The self-styled kookie image with bleached hair that marked her presence at the 1996 Brit Awards is replaced here by an impenetrably whitened face with tight rosebud lips and an elongated neck encased in glittering gold rings. The electronic manipulation of her features, and the hyper-real Ming Dynasty clothing (by fashion designer Alexander McQueen) create a bizarre image.

While recognisably Björk, it is, at the same time, the face of a bonded Japanese girl, trained to provide entertainment (as conversation, performance of dance, traditional songs) for the pleasure of men, so drawing into association Björk's own sense of personal frustration and the need to break free.[54]

While *Homogenic* suggests a personal exorcism, it also marks a shift from her earlier naivety. Her earlier upbringing among people she could trust had left her ill-prepared for the 'real' world and it took her a long time to realise that not everyone meant well. Her role as Selma in *Dancer in the Dark* (directed by Lars von Trier) won the Palme d'Or at Cannes and Björk was given the award for best actress. However, as she recounted, Lars was dictatorial and she was the naïf abroad in the unfamiliar world of cinema. Characteristically she walked out

Figure 3 Björk

at one point and also defended her music from 'the butchers of Denmark who had begun chopping and meddling with her songs'.[55]

Björk's reaction to interference, together with her growing maturity, may well account for the singularity of her album *Vespertine* (2001). The American electronic act Matmos are in a supporting role, and Marius de Vries contributes to the programming, but the album is quintessentially Björk, albeit in a quietly understated romantic mood. In essence, this is a delicate collection of love songs with evocative colours that sparkle and light up the melodic lines. The sound effects and orchestration are often impressionistic, occasionally abstract (as in watery sounds of 'An Echo. A Stain'), sometimes referential (as in Björk's music box arrangement), and lit by female choirs. It seems, then, that the growls and shrieks and hard techno beats of the past are gone. Rather, there is an increasing sense of control which allows the 'little girl' vocal to float around the gentle textures of the album, to soar effortlessly in a newly found freedom of expression. While it would be somewhat ungracious to suggest that the 'ugly duckling' has become a swan (for Björk has always been fascinatingly different in her elfish beauty), there is nevertheless a certain feeling that she has moved on from the angular and dysfunctional mood of rejection that characterised *Homogenic*. 'All Is Full Of Love' had promised a new beginning and the image of the swan on the CD booklet, sketched in lightly over the sleeping Björk, finally emerged at the 2001 Oscars where she appeared dressed in a white swansdown dress.

Little Girls revisited

Images have a fundamental influence on the development of our preconceptions regarding the nature of women, as anyone familiar with the popular arts can attest, and the persistence of the 'little girl' within popular music iconography has shaped the reception of Kate Bush, Tori Amos and Björk, suggesting both a shared vulnerability and a certain eccentricity. To an extent, it is an initial response to their personal vocal style, but it is equally a result of their media characterisation as childlike, winsome and other-worldly.

The characterisation of femininity as 'childlike' has its roots in the late eighteenth century. Mary Wollstonecraft viewed it as a form of romantic illusionism which prevented women from exercising their reason. Her main contention was rooted in the observation that society functions under the false belief that women are, by nature, less intellectually and/or physically capable then men, thus excluding them from the academy, the forum and the marketplace. If they were given the same educational opportunities and access to civil liberties they could then achieve their true potential. While Wollstonecraft's discussion focused primarily on eighteenth-century married, bourgeois and, hence, privileged, women, the strength of her analysis was her recognition that women should be treated as, and act as, autonomous decision-makers. 'Woman is not', she asserted, 'the toy of man, his rattle' which must 'jingle in his ears whenever, dismissing reason, he chooses to be amused'. Rather, she should be a rational agent whose dignity consists in having the capacity for self-determination (Tong, 1992, 16). While Wollstonecraft's celebration of rationality is evident, one hundred years later, in the writings of John Stuart Mill and Harriet Taylor Mill and, in the 1960s among such feminists as Betty Friedan (*The Feminine Mystique*), the equation of the intellectual capacities of women as one of arrested development, and hence childlike, can be traced to the writings of Darwin (*The Origin of Species*). Here, the notion that education could provide women with a responsibility for their own development and growth was effectively countered by the contention that women's intellectual evolution had not progressed beyond the condition of childhood.

Although the notion that women's brains are smaller and softer than men's has been largely consigned to a repertoire of sexist jokes, the legacy has continued in the construction of innocence (and its relationship to immaturity) as part of the ensemble of representations that constitute women's gendered subjectivity. While the term innocent evokes an underlying childlikeness in its association with simplicity and guilelessness, it can equally suggest a certain eccentricity. Childishness in an adult is often construed as emotionally immature and freakish, prone to petulant outbursts. Tori Amos, for example, has been described as flakey, 'a cornflake girl', 'a Grade A, Class One, Turbo-driven Fruitcake' (*NME*, January 11, 1992), a 'weird chick';[56] Björk is strangely exotic with little hands, little fingernails, a diminutive pixie who 'talks in such an ethereal, emotional vocabulary that ... she does not always seem to make sense' (Smith, 2000, 34). This sense of an overflow of emotions can also be seen in the critiques of Kate Bush, not least in her early associations with Peter Pan (*Lionheart*, 1978) and the primordial energies that characterised her girl-child evocation of freedom and imagination.

It is also apparent that the representation of femininity as childlike resonates with both an underlying mysticism and a contextualisation of childhood within the fairytale world of legend and mythology. Kate Bush has referred to 'the little voices' that have been 'so good to me ... telling me what to do' (Reynolds and Press, 1995, 376); Amos has credited her inspiration to her 'faerie muses'. While less direct, Björk also feels that the mythical legacy of her cultural heritage has played a significant part in her compositions: 'In America, people talk about the supernatural. It's so obvious that people are talking about something they don't know. They have *The X Files* and *Ghostbusters*, and talk about these things that *maybe* exist; *maybe* there is something more. In Iceland, it's like, *of course* there is. We live it every day – there's no question about it ... All spiritual things are part of life ... Here, it's not like you're a freak if you believe in it. Everybody *knows* it, and that includes elves, Odin and Nordic mythology' (Baker, 1997, 16). Their beliefs in the metaphysical, however, do not constitute passivity. Rather, as Joy Press observes, their self-effacement 'connects with the post-structuralist idea of 'the death of the author'. Here, the artist as godlike, omnipotent is replaced by a conceptualisation that suggests that 'language speaks us'; 'that poetry occurs at the point of friction between the impersonal system of language and the individual's unconscious desires'. Genius, then, 'is just an ability to go with the flow, to be flooded with visions' (Reynolds and Press, 1995, 376).

While external voices provide one way of conceptualising the creative process by invoking spectral or other-worldly images, the unconscious has long been central to feminist accounts of femininity, not least because it represents a resistance to identity. For Helene Cixous, female writing is a way of unleashing an unruly babble of desire and disgust, and her notion of *écriture feminine* is one way of approaching the more fantastic elements in Bush, Amos and Björk's compositions. All three, for example, resort occasionally to wordless singing, Björk in 'monstrous starburst gushes of ecstasy/agony, a mix of orgasm, birth-pang, hiccup and mystic wonder that seems to explode in the listener's head' (Reynolds and Press, 1995, 379); Bush in the 'feminine speech' which revels in the 'sensuousness of sound without syntax, affirming her sense of connection with Nature' (Reynolds and Press, 1995, 380) and *The Sensual World*; Amos in 'Little Earthquakes' where an incantatory 'Give me life, give me pain, give me myself again' is followed by a wavering yet intense passage of wordless singing. All three provide a particular insight into 'language as a bodily product, a product of our earliest intimacies and desires, from the babble of the infant at the breast to the impassioned discourse of the visionary who tries to speak what is yet unformulated and unshaped' (Byatt, 1997, 64).

Despite the evidence that all three women employ their full vocal registers, it is their 'little girl' voices that are most commonly drawn into association and interpreted as demonstrating their girlish femininity. To an extent, this can be attributed to the fact that all three employ their top registers to situate the vulnerable within the context of their lyrics. For Bush it involved her eerily high voice in, for example, 'Wuthering Heights'; for Amos the edgy insecurity implied by the childlike tone in, for example, 'Silent All These Years'; while for Björk it most recently suggests rebirth, finding herself in her vocal duetting, 'All Is Full Of Love'. It would, however, be misleading to suggest that these examples constitute the totality of their femininity as childlike. All employ the full spectrum of tonality. The yelps, howls, screams of anguish, that have been described as constituting childish outbursts are balanced by an ability to tap into the more sensitive and sensual middle ranges, eroticising the childlike by a close-miked breathy intimacy. As such, generalisations have to be countered by reference to the explicit context of the song, both in terms of lyrics and melodic gesture. Not least, it is important to situate the innovative vocal timbres within the dramatic realisation of the narratives. All three artists are, primarily, story-tellers, looking before and after, referring to past events and wisdom, and envisaging the future in the light of these interpretations.

It is here that the simple contextualisation of childlike and its association with mythology and fairytales is often misconceived as naive and whimsical. As Marina Warner tellingly writes: 'Wonder has no opposite; it springs up already doubled in itself, compounded of dread and desire at once, attraction and recoil, producing a thrill, the sudden of pleasure and of fear. It names the marvel, the prodigy, the surprise as well as the responses they excite of fascination and inquiry; it conveys the active motion towards experience and the passive stance of enrapturement' (Warner, 1996b, 3). It is useful here to briefly examine both the notion of prodigy and the historical development of the fairytale or *wunder-marchen* (which frees this kind of story from the moralising tendencies of the nineteenth century and the happy-ever-after of Walt Disney's adaptations).

Kate Bush, Tori Amos and Björk were all hailed as musical prodigies. All had a musical precociousness which set them apart from other children and which resulted in their initial stereotyping as different, as child wonders. Kate Bush had been discovered by Pink Floyd's Dave Gilmour while still at school; Tori Amos had begun playing the piano at two and a half and had enrolled at the Peabody Conservatoire at five; Björk had also exhibited a gift for music and had enrolled at the Barnamusikskoli at five. All three equally exhibited a sense of errant individualism, and came from families who were, themselves, well-versed in music, literature and the arts and, in the case of Tori Amos, a heritage that included Cherokee Indians and a gift for premonitions and dream interpretations. The sense of being 'different' is also evident in their music, not least in the lyrics which focus in on feminine subjectivity, whether through legend, mythology and fairytale, the exotic of landscape, or in the problems surrounding girlhood and, for example, Amos's personal sense of alienation from her Methodist upbringing. Femininity is thus shown not as a fixed set of characteristics (as implied by the media fixation on childlike) but rather as fluid, troubling and emotional.

It is here that Bush, Amos and Björk relate most strongly to the original conception of the wondertale. Written initially by urbane, aristocratic women, who knew one another's work and exchanged ideas in the various Parisian *hotels particuliers* where they entertained, they consciously invented the modern fairytale at a quintessential moment in a city (Paris) under the Sun King, Louis XXIV. They were produced for adults by adults, to deal with actual, urgent dilemmas such as tenderness in friendship between men and women, the reform of language, and for equal rights to intelligent talk. They also focused on matters of more immediate material urgency: asking for control of their own money, for their right to choose not to marry; or, if they were married off, the same social permission, as men, to take a lover. Above all, they wanted to decide for themselves, to have similar opportunities to learn and to travel. These demands are buried in the tales; they were driven into the coded language of enchantment by the most penetrative state censorship on the one hand, and fervent religious revivalism on the other. By pleading native, Gallic tradition, the storytellers could include anything and everything they pleased. Hence the pleasure in the grotesque, the unlikely and the incongruous, the mixture of tragedy and comedy, the frank eroticism, and the casual cruelty (Warner, 1996b, 3–17). Their legacy is encountered in the writings of Angela Carter, Sara Maitland and Marina Warner whose retelling of myths, fairytales and medieval legends are anchored in both the imaginative and consciousness of women. It is this sense of a shared past that draws into association the mythological imagery, the erotic imagination and the feminine within of Bush, Amos and Björk.

As Sheila Rowbotham observes: 'The writing of our history is not just an individual venture but a continuing social communication. Our history strengthens us in the present by connecting us with the lives of countless women. Threads and strands of long-lost experience weave into the present. In rediscovering the dimensions of female existence lost in the tangled half-memories of myth and dream, we are uncovering and articulating what it is to be a woman in a world defined by man' (1993, 86). The subjugation and revitalisation of women's experience described by Rowbotham is undoubtedly central to Bush, Amos and Björk. The inspiration for much of Kate Bush's work has been mythology, the supernatural and fantasy, history and literature; Tori Amos has countered the problems inherent in established religion, not least in relation to her own sexuality; Björk has inflected her songs with Nordic mythology and a love of the Icelandic landscape – its vast expanse of freezing glaciers, volcanoes, geysers and the Aurora Borealis. At the same time, imagery is used to open out the painfulness of rejection and loss, and the ecstatic of love, so providing individualistic insights into what it is to be a woman, 'tracing the boundaries of oppression and the practical assertion of the self against their confines, the erosion and encirclement, the shifts and tremors of new forms of resistance. We are heaving ourselves into history, clumsy with the newness of creation, stubborn and persistent in pursuit of our lost selves' (Rowbotham, 1993, 86).

The 'little girl', 'girl child', 'child woman' associations are thus problematic and suggest that reviewers and the media alike all too often fall into the trap of stereotyping in their attempt to present snapshot reviews of arguably different women. To an extent, this is understandable. Popular music has a tendency towards a generic categorisation (blues, R & B, rock, metal, rap, disco, dance), and while this blurs hybridisation and fusion, it does help in situating an artist. For women such as Bush, Amos and Björk this has meant that they have often been relegated to the singer-songwriter tradition, albeit that their music far extends the original contextualisation as folk. It is also obvious that despite the extremes of femininity that have been thrust upon them by well-meaning reviewers, they are far from passive in their interactions with the music industry. Indeed, it could be argued that their early experience of a wide range of music (including classical, jazz, popular and folk) has both influenced their own writing while exerting a pressure for excellence (in production, orchestration and arranging). What is evident here is that all three were sufficiently mature to accept the guidance of their early mentors (Kate Bush with Dave Gilmour and Peter Gabriel, Tori Amos with Cindy Palmano – who made many of her videos – and Eric Rosse, whose passion for unusual sound effects created a sympathetic atmosphere for her songs on *Under the Pink*; Björk with Nellee Hooper and Marius de Vries).

While there is no doubt that all three artists exhibit an amazing musicality, it is also apparent that the session musicians and programmers who contributed to their albums are also important to their realisation. It is to their credit that Bush, Amos and Björk are never reluctant to attribute credit and while they are all now competent producers it is evident that they learnt a great deal from friends, musicians and producers along the way.

Finally, it is interesting to note their historical contextualisation. Kate Bush, despite the success of 'Wuthering Heights', was all too often 'underrated because of the prettiness of her music and image' (Reynolds and Press, 1995, 268). Her rise to fame coincided with the more confrontational style of punk and singers such as Siouxsie Sioux and Poly Styrene. As Lucy Toothpaste, editor of the feminist fanzine *Jolt* observed: 'Boy bands were getting up on stage who couldn't play a note, so it was easy for girls who couldn't play a note to get up on stage as well. By the time that they developed, women were singing about their experiences in a way which I don't think they'd done before' (Savage, 1991, 418). Siouxsie Sioux, for example, brought a new sense of individuality in her confrontational style and image and her songs were aggressive, full of brutalities and characterised by what John Savage calls 'controlled hysteria'. In contrast, Bush appeared overly contrived in her eerily pitched vocals, virtuoso piano accompaniments and extraordinarily contorted mimes. Moreover, the excellence of production on her albums, her identification with the heroes of rock (Peter Gabriel, Dave Gilmour), and her romantic and sensual style of writing and experimental song structures seemed curiously out of step with the more anarchic ambitions of punk. The result was an initial perception of Bush as an artist who was unlikely to stay the course.

Tori Amos also suffered by comparison with the tougher image and confrontational rock style of Courtney Love, L7 and Babes in Toyland. As Joy Press observes, 'she does come over as the cute girl performing for Daddy's attention, too inculcated in "feminine wiles" to be considered a real she-rebel' (Reynolds and Press, 1995, 268). Clearly her songs did not have the defiant noise and direct sexual confrontation associated with, for example, L7, whose song 'Fast and Furious' pays tribute to someone with 'so much clit she don't need balls' and who had pulled down their pants and thrown a used tampon into the audience while performing live on *The Word*. Nor did she have the aggressive stance of Courtney Love whose motor-mouthing about heroin and extreme on-the-edge image was couched in fast, furious and frustrated grunge rock. Rather, Tori Amos's virtuoso piano playing and stream-of-consciousness lyrics initially suggested a devotion to music that was curiously at odds with both early 1990s grunge and all-female speed metalheads. As Jon Wilde wrote in 1992, 'It would seem that Tori Amos has nothing to declare but her own, erm, (c'mon man, cough it up) ... genius' (1992, 8).

In contrast, Björk's first solo album *Debut* was underpinned by the imaginative synths, keyboards and programming of Marius de Vries, Nellee Hooper's studio production and an ingenious arrangement of harp, Hammond organ, brass, tabla and strings. To an extent, her vocals suggested an opposition with the 'real' talent of her producers, implying that they provided the musical innovation. As Björk later observed, 'If a boy does a record with beats, say someone like Tricky or Goldie, and they have several singers on it, that's cool, but if a singer does a record and gets several people to do the beats, they're stealing' (Elliot, 1997, 5–7). As I wrote, in my earlier work on Björk (Whiteley, 2000, 212), it might be suggested that *Debut* attempted to corner the lucrative corner of club culture while attracting jazz and indie fans, but there is little doubt that her imaginative lyrics, unique vocal style and gift for melody (as well as her earlier experience with The Sugarcubes) marked her as a competent and innovative musician who was, simply, 'different'.

Over the years, Björk, the 'quirky torch singer/dance diva with the Voice' (Raphael, 1995, xxvi), Tori Amos, 'the daffy, kooky character with Kate Bush vocals' (Raphael, 1995, xxvi) and Kate Bush, the 'ethereal, almost demented' (Larkin, 1999, 207) vocalist, have proved that they are a force to be reckoned with. They are artists in their own right, bringing particular insights into the debates surrounding femininity and subjectivity, fully at home with the studio, technology and production, using videos as tools to express and extend the connotations of their music and lyrics, and credited authors of their own work. Not least, they have expressed their authenticity as individuals, opening out both the strength and vulnerability of femininity as performance.

Part III

Little Boys

Introduction: the rules of the game

While 'little girls' have had to both confront and challenge the gendered stereotypes imposed by the media and the more generalised critiques surrounding popular music, 'little boys' have had to take on the generic conventions imposed by a 50-year heritage. For each genre, there is an established lineage that has imposed a sense of collective identity, a family tree, which charts the development of bands back to the founding fathers of style and image. While this is most obvious in the dynastic framework of rock, where tradition (blues, country and folk roots), authenticity, originality and self-expression have traditionally provided a larger-than-life arena for its heroes and geniuses, a comparable list of criteria can found for soul, reggae, hip hop and rap. Here *process* (an emphasis on the open-ended, improvisatory inflections of 'groove', an aesthetic of 'engendered feeling' [Keil, 1966, 227–49]), *intensional development* (where the *simple* entity is that constituted by the parameters of melody, harmony and beat, while the *complex* is built up by modulation of the basic notes, and by inflection of the basic beat), *nuanced vocal and instrumental style* (off-pitch notes and inflections, 'swoops, 'bends' and 'smears', call and response, cross rhythms and syncopation) and *cultural politics* provide defining parameters for what is often defined as 'black music' (Chester, 1990, 315–19). The effect has been to impose both cultural and musical criteria, which effectively control what is/what is not acceptable within the stylistic conventions of the respective musical genres.

Although such over-arching definitions provide some indication of generic categories (and clearly one could add dance, to include disco, rave, house and so forth to the list of family trees), it is equally obvious that such categorisation obscures as much as it reveals. Many of the stylistic characteristics not only inform, for example, the repertory of pop music, but equally many of the lineages themselves interact, so creating inter-textual relationships and, by the late 1990s, an increasing hybridity. As Michael Bakhtin has successfully argued, genres not only define and influence each other through constant interplay (as, for example, in the adoption of rock/soul/rap techniques in pop music), but individual genres are themselves the product of an ever-mutating dialogue between historically contingent features. As such, individual interpretations often exceed generic criteria even as they refer to them, so creating a sense of 'centre' and periphery.[1]

Even so, it is evident that chart pop music (as distinct from popular music as a whole) is perceived as less weighty, less significant, more knowingly formulaic, clichéd and transient than its more elite musical betters. Not least, there is an aesthetic distinction, which juxtaposes knowledge of genealogy and history with knowledge of the star and his/her personal lifestyle (as reflected in the contrast in editorial between, for example, Q, Mojo and MixMag, and Smash Hits, Top of the Pops, TV Hits and Bliss). This distinction is at its most extreme in the more generic magazines such as Blues and Soul, Kerrang, Metal Hammer and Rap Sheet where there is a particular commitment to the genre culture and its associated music. It is equally apparent that such magazines also assume a masculine readership – not least in their advertisements and overall mode of address – which contrasts both with the more egalitarian New Musical Express and magazines which are aimed primarily at a young female readership such as Smash Hits, where key rings, bars of soap and other novelty items featuring favourite pop stars are often attached as a free gift. What is evident is the investment made by musicians, marketing departments and producers in creating the effect of authenticity and in attracting a particular readership.

While authenticity can be traced back to its Romantic roots and the attempts by both folklorists and anthropologists to defend traditional and communal cultures from commercialisation, the concept itself is both discursive and contextual. At different historical periods authenticity has focused on sound (acoustic, 'real' vs synthesised), on economic autonomy, on creativity (ideally self-composed) or on performance style (honest, natural, expressive). Yet, as Richard Middleton observes, 'the degree to which authenticity can be acquired (the straining voice, the contorted pose, the wild "spontaneous" guitar break) and conversely the impossibility of calling up "sincerity" to order, performance after performance, casts doubts on this theory ... Techniques aren't settled (the electric guitar, first often heard in relation to the acoustic instrument in terms of pop falsity, later became a symbol of authenticity to place against the "unreal" sounds of synthesisers) ... Moreover, the knowing insincerity of pop can itself take on a kind of authenticity, if it comes to seem more true to the real situation than the pretensions of honesty' (Middleton, 1997, 34).

Honesty is equally a slippery concept, not least in its relationship to authenticity. While it implies both integrity and sincerity, it is also associated with a lack of commercialism, so returning it to the earlier association with Romanticism. However, it is apparent that for the young audience of pop music, the suggestion that their idols are insincere, that they are only there for the money, is implausible. Honesty, here, is associated with truthfulness – about their lives, their likes and dislikes, their often overt consumerism (what they buy, what they wear, what they eat) – and the fact that they don't compose their own songs (an important criteria within rock and the singer-song writer tradition) is less relevant than the seeming sincerity and/or enthusiasm with which they deliver their lines and engage with their fans. It is also apparent that within the cult of the boy group/girl group, individuality (in terms of personality) is important; fitness is something to be aspired to (in relation to dance routines) and a contemporary image (slim, appropriate hairstyle, clothing, make-up and so forth) is paramount to success. Most specifically, there is an emphasis on youthfulness, and while older stars such as Madonna, Cher, Prince, Michael Jackson, Elton John and so forth, continue to achieve chart successes, their significance lies more in their iconic status and their ability to engage with audience expectations.

The emphasis on youth (and its relationship to popular culture) is long-standing[2] and while it is accepted that musical processes take place within a particular 'space' – a space configured physically, sociologically and imaginatively – it is also argued that the contours of this space are inflected by the specificities of the musical context (Middleton, 1997, 28). As suggested earlier, generic conventions play a significant part here in determining what is/what is not acceptable. If new bands/groups simply conform to current style indicators they are considered at best unoriginal, at worst mere pastiche. If they exceed the conventions imposed by style and image they are considered as either transgressive or as problematically challenging the dictates imposed by the dominant genres. Either way, authenticity is at risk, and with the established canons of greats (as conferred by the accolade of 'the best' singer/instrumentalist/ band/ album/CD of the last 50 years) they can, at best, be 'one hit wonders'.

Although it is problematic to simply identify the 'alps' of popular music – inasmuch as they tend to obscure significant co-existent and emergent styles of the same era which can, themselves, become dominant – it is nevertheless constructive (in terms of canon) to briefly focus on what are generally identified as some 'defining' moments within the evolution of popular music and how these relate to age and identity. More specifically, I am concerned with how and why the association of 'boyishness' (and its conflation with boyish man/mannish boy, lad/laddishness) continues to exert a powerful presence in contemporary pop(ular) music. It is recognised that my discussion is selective and that a different genealogy would inform the development of, for example, soul, funk, reggae and rap and their relationship to masculinities.

Age, identity and the slippery divide of the rock/pop binary

While the release of 'Rock Around The Clock (Bill Haley and the Comets, 1954) represented the pivotal moment for the popularisation of 1950s rock 'n' roll,[3] eventually selling 15 million records worldwide, Bill Haley can also be cited as its first big failure insofar as image is concerned. Already in his mid-forties, and with an established R & B band (featuring saxophone), his kiss-curl quiff and somewhat paunchy appearance was clearly at odds with the underlying sexuality of his songs. In effect, he marked one moment in the complex development of rock 'n' roll. Little Richard's frantic, anarchic and uncompromisingly 'black' 'Tutti Frutti' was another,[4] but the release of Elvis Presley's 'Heartbreak Hotel' was by far the most significant. As John Collis observes, 'Those early-fifties American teenagers who picked up on black music were an elite; to the rest of us Elvis was a revelation' (Collis, 1980, 13). Not least, his simple espousal of black music with hillbilly and his dangerous sexuality marked the arrival of the 'generation gap' of adolescent rebellion. Whereas the stars of the early 1950s, including Johnny Ray, did not appeal specifically to the teenage market, the injection of black influences into country music, together with the new emphasis on image and, hence, teen appeal, gave popular music its missing ingredient.

It is significant to note, here, that 'pop music' emerged in the 1950s almost as a synonym for rock 'n' roll and that it was not until the end of the 1960s (when the tensions between values of pop chart music and those of counter cultural or progressive rock became clear) that the pop/rock distinction became embedded (Middleton, 1997, 33). As such, the image of Elvis Presley was not only significant to the emerging discourse of rock, but equally to pop music itself. As David Sanjek notes, 'one can observe in the features and voice of any number of musicians – the well known, the unknown, and the obscure – the shadow cast by a young Southern man to whom fortune and talent ascribed the figure of royalty' (Sanjek, 1997, 138). Not least, his image, described by Nick Tosche as constituting 'the face of Dionysus, full of febrile sexuality and sense-lessness' (1980, 230) and who Greil Marcus considered the embodiment of rockabilly, 'the sexy, half-crazed fool standing on stage singing his guts out' (1982, 169), constituted the future image both of rock and rock-influenced pop. A sexy, guitar-playing, heterosexual,[5] caucasian whose rebellious energy and mean, surly image constituted a sense of wild boys at play. It marks, equally, the moment when 'boys were men and men were boys', so establishing one of the defining parameters of 'boyishness' within popular music discourse, and which may well account for the unprecedented level of fandom for 'the king'. The 25th anniversary of his death (August 16, 2002) at the age of 42, by an over-dose of prescribed drugs, was celebrated by thousands at Gracelands. Lookalikes, singalikes, an all-night vigil and a virtual reality concert provided a rare insight into the extremes of fandom and why the history of modern pop and its predictable tales of male heroes traditionally begins with Elvis.

By the 1960s, the initial popularity of rock 'n' roll had faded as record producers, convinced that it was only a temporary fad, looked for the 'next big sound' – including calypso – failing to recognise that the music had grown from strong folk roots that were embedded in American culture. The most noticeable effect was the creation of the 'teen idol', parodied to perfection by satirist Stan Freberg in 'Old Payola Blues' where 'a kid is pulled off the street and turned into an instant star' (Collis, 1980, 14). Unlike the first generation of rockers who were already performing musicians, the new 'pop idols' were chosen primarily for their looks and their ability to copy the rock 'n' roll gestures – pouting lips, gyrating hips, surly gaze – that had characterised Presley's performances. They were also given appropriately evocative names – Adam Faith, Tommy Steele, Marty Wilde, Tab Hunter – so drawing on Presley's two most notable contributions to the language of rock 'n' roll: the assimilation of romantic lyricism and 'boogification', where the basic vocal rhythms are triplets and where the off-beat quaver is often given an unexpected accent, producing cross-rhythm and syncopation. The effect is physical, demanding movement, jerking the body into activity. In addition, extra off-beat notes (not demanded by the words or vocal lines), the splitting up of syllables and consonants and the slurring together of words, disguise the verbal sense to create a sexy, jittery effect (Middleton, 1993, 18–19). The techniques were not difficult to copy, and while Presley was the most significant influence, other mannerisms were also adopted from the first generation rock 'n' rollers, most notably Buddy Holly's boyish hiccup (so modifying the ostensible meaning of the words) which became a defining gimmick in Adam Faith's 24 UK chart hits. Most notably, however, the guitars gave way to huge violin sections which sawed away at songs that were intended to represent rock music, with titles that arguably misrepresented the actual power of the music: 'I'm a Man', 'Tiger', 'Hound Dog Man' by Fabian (1959). The effect was to commercialise what was originally a largely improvised and undemandingly simple musical format, and to bring to the fore the manufactured pop idol – single, boyish, white, good-looking and replaceable, so allowing for swings in fashion both in terms of music and image.

By the mid-1960s the rock/pop binary – and the associated images of rebellious, dangerous/conforming, boy-next-door – was encapsulated in the tensions between the Rolling Stones and the Beatles. The early success of the Stones is well documented. In part it was attributable to the 1960s British R & B scene, with Mick Jagger and Charlie Watts gaining experience in Alexis Korner's legendary band, Blues Incorporated. In June 1962 the embryonic Stones gave their first performance: 'Brian Jones and Mick Jagger and the Rollin' Stones'. In January 1963, having replaced drummer Tony Chapman with Charlie Watts and securing Bill Wyman on bass, the band went on the club circuit with a repertoire based largely on Chuck Berry/Bo Diddley material. After an eight-month residency at The Crawdaddy, in Richmond, London, the band attracted the attention of Andrew Loog-Oldham. Formerly in public relations, he recognised the potential of the band's nihilistic image and, as their manager, promoted them as sensual, insolent and undesirable. In terms of market potential, it was a shrewd move. The Beatles (Paul McCartney, John Lennon, George Harrison, Ringo Starr) were fast becoming established as a clean-living, clean-cut Beat band and the Stones provided an ideal counterpart. Jagger's stage performance exploited the sexual connotations of the lyrics and while their first release (a cover version of Chuck Berry's 'Come On') only edged into the lower end of the UK Top 30, an appearance on ITV's *Thank Your Lucky Stars* served to publicise their image. Their next single, Lennon/McCartney's 'I Wanna Be Your Man', made the Top 20. Compared with the Beatles's version (best remembered, perhaps, for its coda of improvised blues riffs over a mixture of whoops, shouts and harmonised repetitions of the refrain line), the Stones displayed a rawness in delivery with Jagger, in particular, subverting the connotations of 'want' to one of possession through an overtly arrogant delivery. 'Not Fade Away' (Buddy Holly, February 1964) took the Stones to No. 3 in the UK charts and heralded their first inroad into the American market.

The early descriptions of Mick Jagger are remarkably consistent: sexist, an enemy of decency and society, uncompromising, rough, sensual, rebellious. The image was consolidated with the band's cover version of Willie Dixon's 'Little Red Rooster' (1964). Riots had broken out in Chicago when the Stones had attempted to give interviews after recording the 'Five by Five' EP with Chess Studios. With 'Little Red Rooster' banned in the US for its overtly sexual lyrics, it is not too surprising that the attendant publicity propelled the Stones into the limelight. Jagger's menacing swagger and his portrayal of aggressive masculinity and male sexual autonomy established a particular legacy for the young, male rock star which is recognisable today in the Manchester band, Oasis. Not least, they attracted a largely male audience. 'Guys started sticking posters of Mick and Brian up on their walls and what happened was the audience became more integrated. Then, it was the boys fighting their way to the front as much as the chicks ... The Stones ignited that and Jagger in particular' (Hotchner, 1990, 114–15). Inspiring an analysis as 'cock rock' by Simon Frith and Angela McRobbie, their phallocentric style established a male-dominated agenda, 'an ideal world of sex without physical or emotional difficulties, in which all men are attractive and potent and have endless opportunities to prove it' (1990, 382).

In contrast, the Beatles confirmed the ideal of the boy-next-door. In particular, they attracted a frenzied adoration by young female fans, both in Britain and America during the peak of Beatlemania. Described by some feminists as the most dramatic uprising of the *women's* sexual revolution, it signalled an abandonment of control and a protest against the sexual repressiveness of female teen culture (Ehrenriech *et al*, 1992, 85). Essentially a mainstream band, their ability to popularise even the most esoteric trends in British and American rock, and the extent to which their music achieved worldwide dissemination, has meant that they have remained one of the most significant forces in the history of popular music. Unlike the Stones, whose members were all characterised by a surly indifference, the Beatles, despite their earlier promotion as the four mop tops (an allusion to their hair style designed by Stu Sutcliffe's girl friend, Astrid Kirchherr) had four unique personalities, so allowing for identification by a diverse fan base. Paul, the boyish figure with the big spaniel eyes; John, the sexy one; George, the quiet one; and Ringo, the loveable (if undistinguished) drummer. Their legacy has curiously informed not only the so-called Britpop bands of the early 1990s (which included groups as diverse as Pulp, Blur, the Lightning Seeds and, in particular, Oasis) but also equally the personality-driven boy groups where, once again, there is an emphasis on individual charisma, so allowing both for group allegiance and personal favourites.

While the Stones and the early Beatles provided two contrasting role models for would-be bands, overall the 1960s was characterised by a growing tension between rock and pop. As Richard Middleton observes, by 'the 1970s, splits within rock itself into "roots" and "art" branches were part of a wider fragmentation of the whole pop/rock audience, and this, along with the apparent co-option of the music's rebelliousness by corporate strategists, put rock's claims to both centrality and moral superiority in question' (1997, 32–3). David Bowie's manipulation of pose and cliché established a new credibility for pop in his adoption of multiple personalities and sense of theatricality. In contrast, the return to basics of punk provided a vigorous assault on the pretensions of rock (evidenced in the performance of bands such as Yes and Genesis) and its constant internal referencing. Again, image was crucial to effect. The principal mode of address was one of confrontation, 'dramatising the last days as daily life and ramming all emotions into the narrow gap between a blank stare and a sardonic grin' (Marcus, 1992, 595). Shouted or snarled vocals emphasised sound rather than lyrical meaning and groups generally featured a strict 'buzz saw drone' guitar, monadic bass and an often breakneck eight-to-the-bar rhythm. Plastic garbage bags, safety pins, old school uniforms and hairstyles that were either close-shaven or dyed in bright colours (or later, spiked Mohicans) added to its DIY ethics and sense of confrontation. The emotion love, in particular, was singled out as both outmoded and weakening. Described by punk idol Johnny Rotten (John Lydon) as 'two minutes of squelching', the self-explanatory 'This Is Not A Love Song' assaulted sentimentality as a distraction from the vital business of hate and rage and disgust. Small wonder then that the unbridled negativity of punk had little attraction for the more conforming teen market who continued to buy the more romantic ballads of David Soul, David Essex and Donny Osmond or the more dance-oriented Bay City Rollers and Abba. Even so, Lydon's legacy of anti-love has continued with the Smiths ('William, It Was Really Nothing', 1984), Guns 'n' Roses (*Appetite for Destruction*, 1987) and Nirvana (*Nevermind*, 1991).

By the 1980s, the growing knowledge (on the part of fans, music critics and academics) of rock/pop's histories 'led to a situation in which, if anything, pop's knowing, even ironic use of cliché and convention could be seen as *more* "credible" so leading to discussions surrounding "the death of rock"' (Middleton, 1997, 34). Largely attributable to such groups as Soft Cell ('Tainted Love', 1981), Frankie Goes to Hollywood ('Relax', 1984), the Pet Shop Boys ('West End Girls' 1986, 'Domino Dancing' 1988) and the continuing influence of David Bowie, 'masculinity became moodier, referencing inner-city streetscapes, albeit in sanitised and glamorised form' (Mort, 1988, 199). Not least, gay culture was brought into the centre of mainstream pop via the euphoric sound of gay disco[6] and such artists as Boy George. Even so, the dichotomy (between rock and pop) remained active. In the 1990s the rock 'anthems' of Oasis were pitted against the pop 'craftsmanship' of Blur, the 'creative honesty' of rocking singer-songwriter Alanis Morisette against the sophisticated pop ballads of Celine Dion'

(Middleton, 1997, 38). Today, it would seem that the commercially produced and marketed musical genres most commonly equated with 'popular music' have become increasingly driven by the 'anyone can do it' attitude of early rock 'n' roll and punk. Fame-hungry wannabes and a succession of anodyne bands playing middle-of-the-road guitar pop evoke a feeling that we've heard it all before, only better. Inventiveness seems sadly missing and 'hot sounds' continue to be those that draw on garage rock, psychedelia and electro, as evidenced by Primal Scream's *Evil Heat*. Hailed by the *Observer* (August 4, 2002) as 'Pop CD of the week', it seems to indicate how musical magpies, provided they demonstrate the appropriate swagger and passion, have increasingly displaced the sense of inventive rebelliousness that earlier characterised the rock canon. As John Peel tellingly observed in his interview at the 2002 Glastonbury Festival, 'British bands know little about the rich history of the rock genre and, for them, everything started with the Manchester sound associated with Stone Roses and Happy Mondays.' Small wonder, then, that rock is constantly chasing its own tail and that innovation is seen increasingly in terms of fusion and hybridity – Nu Metal's blend of rap and rock being one such example.

Even so, those rock stars who have survived a lifestyle dominated by excess continue to attract critical acclaim, albeit tinged with a certain nostalgia. Eric Clapton ('god'), Bruce Springsteen ('the Boss') and Bono (the 'messiah'), among others, continue to embody the essence of rock – an inventive musical mind and the techniques to express it. Cover bands provide a further arena for the veneration of rock heroes (including Pink Floyd, Sting, Beatles). Meanwhile, the dead (Jim Morrison, Jimi Hendrix, Kurt Cobain) continue to be likened to the gods within rock pantheism. In contrast, and with few notable exceptions (e.g. David Bowie, Elton John), pop idols are quickly relegated to the dustbin of chart histories and pub quizzes. The essential quality, it seems, is not musicality but rather a sense of novelty and youthfulness. What this constitutes, in terms of definition, however, is as complex and contradictory as the problems surrounding use of the term 'girl'.

Who's that boy?

Despite the complex relationship of sexuality or sexual orientation to identity or gender category and, more specifically, homosexuality and masculinity, there is still a problematic, underlying assumption that there is some existing identity that can be understood through the category of 'man'. Films, TV programmes, the press, advertising and popular music constantly bombard the public with images and representations that invite the public to recognise masculinity as *naturally* heterosexual. Clearly, men do not passively accept this dominant myth, but despite the occasional flirtations with same sex desire in soaps, series such as *Six Foot Under*, *Will and Grace*, Graham Norton's chat show, and the high profile afforded to such films as *Philadelphia* (BBC, 1993) – where closeted lawyer Tom Hanks finds himself ousted from his job after his homophobic law firm discover he has AIDS – the cultural domination of the masculine myth, and its presentation in popular culture, is, it seems, inescapable. Homosexuality continues to resonate with camp, with being different, with being 'other' or, at worst, with being threatening and deviant.

While feminist and gay studies have made masculinity more visible, popular music, as an ideological and cultural form, continues to operate both as a form of sexual expression and sexual control. As suggested in *Sexing the Groove* (1997), the imaginary sense of wholeness, the pleasure that popular music affords to its fans lies in its affirmation of sexuality – in heterosexual equals norm, in gayness equals norm, in androgyny equals norm. Yet despite the ambivalent sexuality of many of its most notable performers, it is still apparent that rock continues to provide a cultural expression of normative heterosexual masculinity. The aesthetic judgement of Beavis and Butthead on whether music is 'cool' or 'sucks', for example, remains largely relevant to metal and its many offshoots where the quality of the video is dependent on the 'quantity of smoke, fire, explosions, guns, death images, violence, leather, and 'chicks', and the extent to which the soundtrack conforms to the rapid hard-driving beat of heavy metal. Groups such as AC/DC, Metallica, Black Sabbath, Motorhead, Slayer, Danzig, Judas Priest, Iron Maiden, Pantera, White Zombie, Soundgarden, The Beastie Boys, The Red Hot Chili Peppers *rule*, while Glam Rock, Billy Joel, Depeche Mode, Huey Lewis and the News, Michael Bolton and others *suck*, as does all 'college' music (Best and Kellner, 1998, 74).

While the extremes of metal provide a particular insight into normative heterosexuality, pop music's emphasis on adolescent love initially suggests a powerful reversal of the dominant image of the masculine ego. Men, here, are allowed to ache, to cry, to suffer – so forging a curious alliance with rock ballads, which resonate with messages of self-doubt and self-pity. There is also a strand of gay sensibility that runs throughout pop history, from Little Richard's 'Tutti Frutti' through to Bowie, Morrissey, Boy George, the Pet Shop Boys and Frankie Goes to Hollywood. Michael Jackson, Prince and Madonna also draw attention to what has been termed the 'production of confusion', while k.d. lang's early recordings provided fans with the opportunity to read *against* dominant discourses. While the complexity of sexual identity within popular music warns against overly simple generalisations, it is nevertheless apparent that the dominant stereotypes underpinning the pop field continue to affirm heterosexual desire and, hence, a normative masculinity. Thus while it is recognised that performers are adept at putting their own identity in quotation marks, the 'surprise' announcement by the popular press, that Will Young (winner of the 2002 reality TV programme, *Pop Idol*) had 'come out' as gay, highlighted the problems associated with the masculine myth. For teenagers, despite the current debates surrounding sex education and the inclusion of same-sex desire, heterosexuality is resolutely maintained as the norm. Young's No. 1 position on the charts was ousted the following week by rival Gareth Gates. Clearly, there is no empirical research to justify a claim that this was due to his sexuality, but it nevertheless suggests that pop's imaginary sexual world continues to privilege dominant conventions of masculinity. A pop idol must be seen as desirable by his legion of girl fans, and this clearly does not mean fag hags.

While sexual honesty remains a thorny problem for pop stars and their promoters, the consequences of being 'outed' continue to plague George Michael. 'George is now trying to make social comment. This is the guy who hid who he actually was from the public for 20 years' (*Sunday Times*, July 28, 2002). Although Noel Gallagher's comments on 'Shoot the Dog' can be construed as a somewhat vitriolic reflection on George Michael's inability to be straight, it is also evident that it effects a less-than-subtle endorsement of his own honesty as a heterosexual performer in an arena that continues to extol the extremes of machismo. At the same time it is a reminder that popular success continues to reflect the traditional gendering of public space and the expectations generated by pop music's social context. For that reason, the everyday, commonsense definitions of being a man, being a boy, remain potent. They constitute, in effect, the continuing masculine myth of normative heterosexuality.

At its simplest, a man is most commonly defined as a 'grown-up male', and that 'male is the sex that begets (not bears) young' (Kirkpatrick, 1985, 148). This, in turn, implies both sex roles and gender traits, and terms such as masculine continue to be defined in terms of prevailing cultural stereotypes. As such, biological males who manifest feminine gender traits are classified as 'exceptional', 'deviant' or simply 'different' in societies that privilege 'culturally constructed cages of masculinity' (Tong, 1992, 30). Socialisation also continues to encourage and/or coerce the adoption of sex-appropriate personalities as well as interests, professions and, in the case of popular music, genre-specific gendered identities. The plurality of meanings and interpretations available to the term 'man', then, is all too often relegated to the characteristics regarded as 'masculine' by a prevailing group or society. Boys are still instructed to be 'masculine', and in white, middle-class, protestant societies this entails, among other attributes, being ambitious and independent.

Most commonly, however, the state of being a boy includes such synonyms as a male child, a lad, a son, a young man, with underlying connotations of boyhood, boyish, boyishness. There is also the implication that boy's play is somehow trifling, and that the dubious accolade 'boys will be boys' involves an expectation that one must expect and put up with foolish or childish behaviour (Kirkpatrick, 1985, 148), as instanced by the associations of lad culture and such Britpop groups as Oasis. In common with the female child, sexual experience (in this instance, ejaculation and sexual intercourse) is also associated with growing biological maturity. However, unlike the underlying patriarchal assumption that a girl is an unmarried woman, the state of boyhood is unmarred by implications of being left on the shelf. An unmarried man is a bachelor, but the term equally carries with it definitions of 'a young knight following the banner of another, as too young to display his own', and as one who has taken his or her first degree at a university (Kirkpatrick, 1985, 89). Both, however, suggest a certain rite of passage into adulthood and in some tribal communities this can involve both the confrontation of the wild, the killing of an enemy or some form of mutilation (including circumcision and/or tribal scarring).

> Among the Sambia, in New Guinea, a tribe where men are warriors and hunters and women are feared and despised, boys are removed into exclusive male control around the age of six, and begin a series of violent initiations which will turn them into men like their fathers.
>
> (Warner, 1994b, 28)

As Marina Warner observes, 'proper cultural masculinity doesn't come naturally, it seems, to a New Guinea Highlander. Why should it to a child living in Kentish Town or Aberdeen?' (1994b, 28). Her question is answered in part by the poet Robert Bly and his personal growth bestseller, *Iron John* (1991). His recognition that rites of passage are significant to the development of 'manliness' inspired a Men's Movement in America, co-founded by 'guru' Bly. Based on his observation that feminism has taught women self-knowledge and a will to challenge outmoded ideologies, he believes that men must follow their example and challenge the constraining dictates of patriarchy. More specifically, he urges men to reawaken the 'Wild Man' or 'Warrior Spirit' within, to commune with the spirits of their fathers and so regain their lost virility. It is significant that Bly thought of his father 'not as someone who had deprived me of love and attention or companionship, but as someone who had himself been deprived, by his mother or by the culture' (Reynolds and Press, 1995, 43). The contemporary 'soft male' was thus associated with too close an identification with women, and in particular, with their mothers. Drawing on mythology, and the ideas of Carl Jung, Bly urged men to change their allegiance, and to identify with the phallic Serpent. Drawing on the example of the Kikuyu tribe, whose practice of shared bloodletting and other symbolic woundings provided an appropriate sense of bonding, he advocated the appointment of surrogate fathers – men who will take younger men under their protection – and rites of passage. Socialising weekends, including homoerotic physical contact were also considered empowering, although, as Warner observes, 'so far none of the men's groups have started practising fellatio of men by boys, as do the Sambia in order to transmit the necessary semen for manhood from generation to generation' (Warner, 1994b, 29).

Bly's attempts to generate a proactive approach by men, whereby they 'regain' their lost masculinity and connect this with the feelings that have been denied them, relates to the eighteenth-century legacy of the Enlightenment, where reason was placed above emotion. Not least, the Descartian notion of mind/body dualism meant that the mind, as the reasoning decision-maker, was seen as the principal organ of progress. In contrast, the body, with its inherent biological processes, was seen as governed by nature and therefore inhibiting. This resulted in men supposedly *knowing* what they wanted and needed. Not only were they the rulers of their own lives but they had the power to rule the lives of women and children. It also led to the hiding of anxieties, uncertainties and emotions that threatened society's definitions of male identities

While men's emotional powerlessness cannot be compared directly with the subjugation of women (in terms of lack of political and economic power) there are, nevertheless, certain parallels in that both aim to break free from the tyranny of patriarchal oppression. For example, the universalising argument about male nature informed a prominent American rights lawyer, Catherine McKinnon, to argue with reference to war and rape 'that men do in war what they do in peace, only more so', and that 'similar acts are common everywhere in peacetime and are widely understood as sex' (in Warner, 1994b, 28). As Warner observes, 'these sweeping assertions work against mobilising change; they present as sovereign truth beyond history, beyond society, the idea that the swagger and the cudgel come naturally to men, due to their testosterone, a hormone that according to this view, is always in excess. The Serbian rapist[7] thus becomes the summation of male nature' (1994b, 29).

To return to my earlier discussion, masculinity and its cultural manifestations remain central to popular music discourse. As discussed earlier, rock is centred upon a testosterone-loaded culture that dates back to the 1950s. In the 1990s the ironic glorification of masculinity was asserted through the humorous use of stereotypical images such as football, lager and the female body as sex object, as in the 'New Laddism' which informed such TV programmes as *Men Behaving Badly*, the magazine *Loaded* and the Manchester band, Oasis. What is obvious, however, is that monsters are made, not given, and that while boys are not deprived of strong masculine role models, they are still suffering from a compulsion to conform. My case studies are based on two contrasting rites of passage: rock pantheism and its relationship to the 'wild boys' tradition of rock culture, and 'nice boys', a representation that includes boy bands and teenage pop idols, and the acceptable 'gay' image of such stars as Boy George. While it is recognised that my discussion is rooted in the well-established distinction between the rock rebel and the more conforming image of the pop idol, it is considered that these codes continue to exert a powerful and controlling influence on contemporary performers. As such, my aim here is to discuss how and why they emerged and the extent to which citation, reference and stereotype[8] effectively control what is/what is not acceptable within the stylistic conventions of the respective musical genres.

Death and my cock

As Roland Barthes observed, 'the mythical is present everywhere sentences are turned, stories told' (1977, 169). My earlier discussion of Jim Morrison and his enactment of the Oedipal myth in 'The End' provides one particular insight into mythology and its relationship to rock culture. For his many fans, however, it marked not only his severance with his own past, but also his emergence as the 'Lizard King' of rock[9] and the embodiment of a particular definition of masculinity that was to situate death as the ultimate form of excess.

While it is recognised that 'myths don't necessarily command faith (in the same way as religious observance) ... they can represent ways of making sense of universal matters, like sexual identity and family relations', and frequently 'intense emotional upheavals pass through a mesh of common images and utterances which are grounded in ideas about nature and the supernatural, about destiny and origin' (Warner, 1994b, xii). Morrison's birth as the 'Lizard King' is unequivocal in his celebration of the phallus as an object of desire

> Ride the snake, ride the snake
> To the lake, the ancient lake ...
> Ride the snake, he's old
> And his skin is cold.

Sandwiched between a softly intoned stanza, which situates 'the end' within the ritualistic of death and the climactic 'murder' of the father, Morrison's identification of 'the snake', and the final outro provokes a direct comparison with Blake's illustration of Lucifer for Milton's *Paradise Lost*, 'rousing his legions' and railing against the repressive Jehovah.[10] As Ray Manzarek (co-founder and keyboards, The Doors) recalls, after the explosive scream 'Mother, I want to ... fuck you!' the band exploded.

> Drums, organ, guitar in a frenzy of volume ... the sounds of chaos, of hell, of an orgy or madness ... And then John (Densmore, drums) upped the ante and took the rhythm into a twice-as-fast meter ... The whirling became dervish frenzied ... Jim was gone ... the faun was now onstage, leaping about on his little split hooves, priapic and intoxicated. Robbie (Krieger, guitar) and I were racing to keep up with John, driving and pushing each other faster and faster until we had no place left to go and exploded in an ejaculatory climax! An aural orgasm. A smashing explosion of come. We shot our sonic wad out onto the heads of the collective and anointed the faithful with holy chrism. Jim, or the satyr, shrieked into the microphone, 'Kill, fuck, kill, fuck!'
>
> (Manzarek, 1999, 199–200)

Manzarek's identification of Morrison as the new Dionysus and his relationship to the satyr is discussed earlier in his book. As he notes,

> Satyrs are the familiars, the attendees of Dionysus. Also of Bacchus, the Roman god of wine and revelry. They mill about Dionysus, waiting for the fun to begin. They wait for the maenads, those frenzied women who take part in the wild, orgiastic rites that accompany his worship. They wait for the bacchantes. They wait with Dionysus for the rock concert to begin. For

the *groupies* to appear. And this particular faun came out of the ether because he saw a *new* Dionysus walking down the street in Venice Beach, California, and he knew the fun was going to start again. Jim Morrison was going to assume the mantle of Dionysus, as had Rimbaud and Nijinsky, Modigliani and Mayakovsky and Picasso, Brendan Behan and Jackson Pollock, Neil Cassidy and Michael McClure and Allen Ginsberg and Jack Kerouac. Dionysus. The shaken-loose god of the green powers, the resurrection, the rebirth, the fecundity of the planet. And the wildness. *That* was Jim's calling. The wildness. ... A man who knew no bounds, acknowledged no restraints, no rules, no laws

(1999, 129, original emphasis)

I make no apology for quoting, at some length, from Manzarek. For those not immersed in rock mythology the language may seem somewhat over-the-top, yet Morrison's following in the late 1960s and early 1970s, and his continuing position as a 'god' (evidenced by the countless pilgrimages to his Paris grave in the Père Lachaise Cemetery) provide an indication of his status within rock mythology. 'Crawl out now, King Snake!', 'Jim Morrison is God' are examples of graffiti now perpetuated by a third generation of rockers. He is also the 'Electric Shaman', the 'Acid King', the 'Lizard King', the 'Poet Priest' who many believe was overtaken by his own mythology of wild excess. As The Doors's drummer John Densmore observed, 'as long as there's young people, they can look to Jim to help them cut the umbilical cord' (1991, 208), so providing yet another comparison with Bly[11], this time with his identification of surrogate fathers who will both protect and initiate a reborn sexuality:

Awake
Shake dreams from your hair
My pretty child, my sweet one
Choose the day and choose the sign of your day

Morrison's self-proclaimed identity as the mythological 'Lizard King' is revealed most clearly in his psychedelic song-cycle 'The Celebration of the Lizard' (*Absolutely Live* 1970).[12] Starting with the death of his mother (so linking it with 'The End'), the song explores the paranoia often associated with an acid trip ('once I had a little game, I like to crawl back into my brain') and his awakening in a motel room with a sweat-drenched reptile in his bed: Bly's serpent, symbol of the lost phallus. By the end of the song-cycle, Morrison assumes the mantle of the 'Lizard King'. Presaged by what he terms 'sounds of fire' (whistles, rattlesnakes, castanets) Morrison addresses his audience as his nomadic tribe.

Now I have come again
To the land of the fair, and the strong, and the wise
Brothers and sisters of the pale forest
Who among you will run w/the hunt?

The significance of the song lays both in its insistence on hallucinogenic experience, as enabling creativity and a temporary trip into psychotic disorientation, and his personal credo – accept no limits to desire. 'I am interested in anything about revolt, disorder, chaos, especially activity that seems to have no meaning' (in Manzarek, 1999, 349). 'Let the carnival bells ring, Let the serpent sing … I am the lizard king, I can do anything'.

The association between Morrison's Oedipal fantasy, his rebirth as the 'Lizard King' and his association with Dionysus is pivotal to rock mythology. Influenced by Nietzsche's *Birth of a Tragedy*, Kerouac's *On the Road* and Norman O. Brown's *Life Against Death*, and 'ancient fertility religions that ensured their follower's survival and prosperity by choosing a monarch (young, male and virile) who would be sacrificed (usually by young, nubile females)' (Reynolds and Press, 1995, 124), Morrison was the first rock icon to see himself, from the onset, in messianic terms, as a wild boy, sexually omnivorous[13] and obsessed by the dictum of love as sex and sex as death. It is interesting to note that Morrison had been thinking about and writing portions of 'Celebration' as early as the summer of 1965 and that it was written and rewritten before its printed version appeared on the cover of The Doors third album *Waiting for the Sun* (1968). As such, its recorded version on *Absolutely Live* (1970) represents more a testament to his status as 'Lizard King' than an annunciation.[14] It is also suggested that he recognised a musical lineage in his testament, relating his birth as the Lizard King to his blues forefathers. 'Crawling King Snake' (John Lee Hooker) is covered on the 1971 album *LA Woman*. Unlike Blind Lemmon Jefferson's 'Black Snake Moan' which exhibits an underlying ironic humour, 'Crawling King Snake' is identified from the onset as the embodiment of the singer

> I'm the crawling black snake in the room of the damned
> Call me the Crawling King Snake in the room of the damned

Sung with both ferocity and a slippery lasciviousness, Morrison's vocal encapsulates his ability to both taunt and provoke. Comparable to his mythologised exposure in Miami, where 'the audience saw snakes where there were no snakes' (Manzarek, 1999, 315), the vocal entices a fixation on Morrison as the phallic embodiment of sexual excess.[15] There is, then, a continuum of thought, a self-perception that runs throughout his life with The Doors which is encapsulated not simply in his songs but equally in his extensive poetry: 'Forget your past, create your future, travel to the "end of night" and "break on through to the other side"'.

Morrison's 'Lizard King' persona was enhanced by his image, wearing calf or reptile skin trousers which accentuated his sexuality, so relating the metaphor of the snake to the theatricality of his stage presence and to his personal life. Renowned for his drinking[16] and sexual excesses (his numerous relationships included Nico, the Valkyrian angel of death, singer with the Velvet Underground

Figure 4 Jim Morrison

and Andy Warhol's show, the Exploding Plastic Inevitable), his machismo stance links him to such writers as William Burroughs and de Sade, while situating the penis at the continuing hub of rock culture. As Robert Pattison observes, 'the ideal rock star is young, male and horny' and while the legacy is most apparent in such iconographic record sleeves as Andy Warhol's design for the Velvet Underground's *The Velvet Underground and Nico* (where a yellow banana is peeled back to reveal pink flesh), and the Rolling Stones *Sticky Fingers* (which features a crotch shot of a bulging pair of jean complete with zipper), the rockumentary satire *Spinal Tap*, and plaster casts made by groupie Cynthia (Cynthia Plaster Caster) in the late 1960s early 1970s, the emphasis on the penis persists as an image of ritual worship' (1987, 114). Identified by Morrison in his personal anagram 'Mr Mojo Risin' ('LA Woman') which is associated both with erection and ritualistic power, the concept of phallic power linked to apocalyptic sex – love is sex and sex is death – moved rock in a pivotal direction.

It is considered relevant, at this point, to provide some further insights into the distinction between the erotic and the thanatic and how these relate to Morrison. Although both erotica (from the Greek *eros*, love or the creative principle) and *thantica* (from the Greek *thanatos*, death or a destructive principle) relate to sexually explicit descriptions and depictions, it is apparent that the one can have an uneasy and perverse relationship to the other. Within human nature, the worship of Death and the worship of Beauty and Pleasure are not necessarily distinct. Both evoke and celebrate sensuality – the erotic its joyous, the thanatic its darkest manifestations. Both work in the imagination, in the not said, and it is arguably the case that the liberation of passions can lead to 'refinements of pleasure, of ecstasies of perception of courtesies and reciprocities undreamed' (Byatt, 1997, 204). As Simon Reynolds observes, 'sexual congress, for Jim Morrison, was not about anything so prosaic and limited as a union with a specific, flesh-and-blood woman … Rather he took the phallic model of rebellion (transgression, penetration of the unknown) to the limit'. 'Women constituted his "soul kitchen", a nourishing hearth that provided a brief resting place before he hit the road again' (Reynolds and Press, 1995, 118).

> Lying on stained, wretched sheets
> With a bleeding virgin
> We could plan a murder
> Or start a revolution.

The association between sex, murder and revolution relates strongly to Morrison's personal identification as shaman/lizard king, situating the penis and the worship of the penis within a love of death. It was a creed that revolved around the Romantic mythology of self-destruction and is present in his earliest songs. 'Light My Fire' (1967) is trance-like and sinuous, evoking an underlying hallucinogenic feel in its obsessive keyboard motif. Underpinned by a cool Latino beat on drums, the principal keyboard motif (a left-hand Bolero-like figure against a right-hand Chicano comping) unfolds through small variations and a consistent dynamic to create a feeling of a never-ending present. This sense of absorption is heightened by Morrison's vocal which gently oscillates between Am7 and F#m7, creating once again a hypnotic feel, inviting, rather than commanding, participation in a love/death ritual which draws together heightened awareness, sex and death through a rhyming structure which links the first two verses: untrue/through; liar/mire; you/lose; higher/pyre.

The F#m7 (on higher/pyre) is pivotal in moving the invitation to the assertive rock mood of the chorus where major harmonies support the

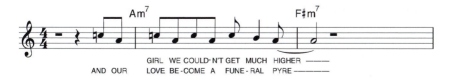

Transcription 35

commanding 'Come on baby light my fire, try to set the night on fire'. While the connotations here are strongly sexual, the rhyming structure again draws into association the final words of the verses – that passivity results in death, and that active participation will 'set the night on fire'. It is clear, however, that this will be no normal sexual congress. The lengthy solo implies hallucinogenic flight in its obsessive noodling around the principal motif. Based on a circle of fifths (G to D, F, Bb, Eb to Ab [two beats to each chord]) and a semitone step to A over two bars, 'with Bach-like filigrees over the top in a kind of turning-in-on-yourself Fibonacci spiral' (Manzarek, 1999, 151), the mesmeric effect is enhanced by the guitar which provides an additional timbral colour whilst remaining within the trippy contours of the keyboard improvisation. This, in turn, is intensified by the reprise of the second verse and the chorus, which is repeated three times before it finally rises to the assertive:

Transcription 36

It is interesting to note that while the song was initially conceived by Robbie Krieger (who wrote the first verse), all four members of The Doors were involved in the musical realisation. As such, it is intriguing to probe further into the sinuous nature of the arrangement and its analogies both with tripping and with Morrison's emerging persona as the Lizard King. As Ray Manzarek relates, the challenge for The Doors was to move blues-based rock in a psychedelic direction (1999, 102) and the early days of the Band were marked by LSD ingestion. There is thus a sense of a shared experience; 'You are everything, all there is, and you are rested, relaxed, charged with energy and ready to create a world to occupy. You are eternity. You are infinity ...' (Manzarek, 1999, 123), and while the specifics of tripping relate to the individual's own state of mind, there is nevertheless a sense of bonding. As Joel Fort writes:

strong emotional bonds or positive feelings for each other; changes in time (and other sensory) perception; unusual genital sensations; diminished inhibitions and symbolic overtones can be part of an LSD experience and will in some circumstances produce a mystical or ecstatic sexual union which may seem endless.

(1969, 130)

Thus, while Manzarek and Morrison never discussed the details of their LSD trips (Manzarek, 1999, 123), the shared knowledge of hallucinogenic experience is evident in the trance-like feel of the music. While this is reflected most specifically in the extended solo, it is also suggested that Manzarek's obsessive noodling around the circle of fifths equally provides a musical metaphor for Morrison's persona as the 'Lizard King'. The sinuous mantra-like accompaniment to the vocals provides a symbolic metaphor for the hypnotic powers of a reptile, enticing the listener to embrace the wild child within. In conjunction with Morrison's vocal there is thus an analogy with both the snake and the snake charmer who transforms the initial sentiment of the song into the transcendent thanaticism of a love/death ritual.

Hallucinogenic experience, then, was a crucial ingredient in The Doors's creative mind, providing access to the metaphysical – ' ... and we were off! Flying on the wings of love ... to Nirvana, to the pure land ... It was divine. It was expansive and harmonious and beatific in one' (Manzarek, 1999, 120) – combining the psychedelic with the thanatic of Morrison's personal cosmology 'death and my cock'. Although his subsequent addiction to drink[17] accounts more for his increasing paranoia and his alienation from many of his friends, it also underpins the move from the transcendent mood of such songs as 'Light My Fire' and 'People Are Strange' to the malevolence of 'LA Woman'. 'His voice, ravaged by drink and three packets of Marlboro a day, rode roughshod over the chromatic soundtrack, a brooding, menacing voice that was resigned, desperate and tired. He was a man exposed, a man saying goodbye in the only way he knew' (Jones, 1990, 169). 'Riders on the Storm', the final track of the album, can thus be seen as somewhat of a swan song which reverts back to the earlier hallucinogenic tracks. It is dark, sinister, mystical and morbid with the iterative shape of the vocal motif drawing into association love ('you gotta love your man') and death ('there's a killer on the road') through an identification of alienation:

Transcription 37

Morrison's commitment to death as the ultimate form of sexual excess is reflected in the rock creed of live fast and die young.[18] Although his death at the age of 27 was a self-inflicted martyrdom (caused by an excessive addiction to drugs, alcohol and a wild lifestyle) it has meant that he has symbolically joined the ranks of the Romantics, Byron and Shelley, while foreshadowing the deaths of such rock icons as Michael Hutchence (INXS) and Kurt Cobain (Nirvana). In doing so, he has fulfilled the myth that self-annihilation is perfect self-realisation. The fact that the cause of death has never been formally established, that he was buried without an autopsy or proper identification, has fed the legend that he is still alive and that he will, like King Arthur before him, return.[19] As one fan has scratched on his tombstone: 'When are you coming back, you bastard?' The answer, it seems, lies in those who have followed in his footsteps, whose credo of sex, drugs and rock 'n' roll is also marked by a fascination with both the metaphysical and the reality of death. It also links him to the other iconic figure of 1960s rock, Jimi Hendrix.

'Scuse me while I kiss the sky

Hendrix, like Morrison, was arguably destroyed by the pressures of stardom and the demands of countless public performances. Both had performed at the Isle of Wight Festival (August 1970), an event that was effectively destroyed by running battles between the organisers and a loose grouping of bikers and anarchists who wanted to turn it into a free festival. Both suffered the consequences. Morrison sang without passion, without any commitment to the words and, at the end of the set, picked up the heavy mike stand and smashed it over and over again into the old plank flooring of the stage. Exhausted, he finally just stood, looking at the audience while the band finished the chorus of 'The End'. He died the following year (July 3, 1971). Hendrix was equally exhausted, tormented and trapped by an audience who would not accept that he was no longer interested in power-trio hard rock. On stage he already appeared three parts dead, and his death, 'less than three weeks later, seemed hideously appropriate' (Shaar Murray, 1989, 8). They were both aged 27, thus establishing the totemic of rock mythology, that 'the gods die young'.

Morrison and Hendrix are also connected through their shared idealism which is reflected both in their concern for the environment (e.g. Morrison, 'Not To Touch the Earth', Hendrix 'Up From The Skies') and the problems concerning state ideology (e.g. Morrison, 'The Unknown Soldier', Hendrix, 'Star Spangled Banner'). In terms of rock mythology, however, it is their 'supernatural' powers, their addiction to drugs and their omnipotent sexuality that is most significant. More specifically, while Morrison provided the iconic model for the lead singer-songwriter, Hendrix was the messianic embodiment of the guitar hero – as attested by his consistent topping of the Lead Guitar polls some 30 years after his death.

Jimi Hendrix (b. Johnny Allen Hendrix – his father subsequently changed his name to James Marshall Hendrix – November 27, 1942, Seattle, WA, USA, d. September 18,1970, London, England) is unquestionably one of rock's most influential figures, with an unparalleled vision of electric guitar technique. Left-handed and self-taught, his strongest influences came from the serious blues guitarists of the American South – Robert Johnson, Willie Dixon, Little Walter and B.B. King. Prior to his move to London, his musical career had included package tours with Solomon Burke and Wilson Pickett and other temporary engagements included backing Little Richard, Jackie Wilson and Curtis Knight. He also played with the Isley Brothers, the first band to give him the chance to play lead guitar. While this broad-based experience made him equally conversant with jazz, saxophone swing, rhythm and blues, gospel and soul, the question nevertheless arises as to 'what the hell happened to Jimi in the summer of 1966?' (Ellis, in Potash, 1966, p. 201).

There is little in Hendrix's early career that even hints at the electrifying music that emerged, fully formed, in 'Purple Haze'. 'As a sideman on Curtis Knight recordings cut at that time ... you hear a merely competent R&B player ... then came Jimmy James and the Blue Flames, the short-lived petri dish in which Jimi cultured his newfangled ideas.' (Ellis, in Potash, 1966, p.201) This was the band Chas Chandler (former bass player of the Animals and subsequently a rock manager) heard at the Café Wha in Greenwich Village in 1966. Recognising the power of Hendrix's explosive guitar-led rock, he brought him to London, where he was joined by Noel Redding (bass) and Mitch Mitchell (drums). The Jimi Hendrix Experience played their first public performance at Paris Olympia and spent four months playing the London underground scene, the Marquee, the Upper Cut, the Bag-O-Nails and the short lived 7 ½ Club. While the press initially focussed on his image, 'The Crazy Black Man', 'The Wild Man From Borneo', it was obvious from the onset that this was a totally new music, one that explored the full potential of his Stratocaster guitar, and where the sounds were inseparable from the song. As Nick Jones wrote, in his 1967 article in *Melody Maker*, 'The Hendrix sound is what England hasn't yet evolved – but desperately needs. It's a weaving, kaleidoscope of tremor and vibration, discords and progressions'. (p.8) In retrospect, it is evident that the strange textures and timbres, the kaleidoscopic sounds, were part of his personal vision, something that he had nurtured when alone and unknown, but which had emerged with its full dynamic force in the single, 'Purple Haze' and the debut album *Are You Experienced?* (September, 1967) Even so, as Hendrix informed Chris Welch, in an interview for *Melody Maker* (15 April, 1967), 'the style was formed here in England. When I first came over I was having little plays with Mitch and Noel. Noel can play really fast bass, and Mitch – well he is one of the best drummers. He can do anything' (cited in Potash, 1996, p.10), an ideal duo for the free-form performances associated with the early Hendrix.

Hendrix's showmanship, the unusual racial combination of his group – a black American guitarist leading a white rhythm section – his innovative guitar techniques[20] (most notably the unusual sound effects, devised with his recording engineer Eddie Kramer), his use of the recording studio as a compositional environment and his idiosyncratic vocal style provide a particular insight into what constitutes the Hendrix sound. Typically it was full-textured, loud, sustained and usually avoided a rigid rock beat. What gave it its particular feel was his expressive use of timbral nuance, unusual sound effects and his distinctive guitar sound. He was also a poet, comparisons including Charlie Mingus (Miller in Potash, 1996, 55), addicted to narcotics[21] and psychedelics, and like Morrison, a superstud sex symbol – this time, one whose celebration of phallic potency ('Voodoo Child') was tempered by a craving for female salvation ('May This Be Love', 'Gypsy Eyes', 'You Got Me Floating').

By 1967 Hendrix had been voted the world's top pop musician by the annual *Melody Maker* Readers' Poll, *Are You Experienced* was in the Top 10 in both Britain and the USA, and 'Love or Confusion', 'Are You Experienced' and 'Purple Haze' had situated Hendrix as the inventor of psychedelic guitar music. In the contemporary world of synthesised music, it is almost impossible to realise just how radical his music sounded in 1967 as he 'stretched the concept of sound, soungwriting and social behaviour.' (Ellis, in Potash, 1995, 202) As Michael Nesmith (of The Monkees) told him a week before his death, 'nobody ever played this before you came along' (Duff in Potash, 1996, 91). His observation is supported by Andy Ellis: 'Anyone who has listened to Hendrix while tripping knows that Jimi *played* the sound of LSD ... Jimi gave us "Purple Haze" and blew our minds ... He was a pathfinder (and) to devotees of the psychedelic state, he was a cosmic cartographer, exploring uncharted territory and recounting his journeys in song' (Ellis, in Potash, 1996, 201–2).

Named after a particular brand of acid, 'Purple Haze' is overtly concerned with LSD experience and its effect. Beginning with a bass pedal E under A# on bass and lead guitar, the first two bars create a jarring underlying pulse which continues into the bars three and four. Here the A# disappears as Hendrix moves into the opening riff with its characteristic bends and dipping vibratos. The riff has the typical feeling of muscle and crunch common to much of his repertoire, not least in the tonal quality created by the electronic distortion, the fuzz and the resultant discordant partials. The feeling of disorientation is enhanced by the vocal. The word 'haze' in particular vibrates, dips and swerves upwards, creating a feeling of floating around the beat, an effect also present on 'funny' and 'sky'.

The guitar solo, in particular, moves towards an overt theatricality with hammered and pulled-off notes, and jittered bursts of broken words, before moving into an almost frenzied noodling around the principal motif. This is supported by the bass which moves into a fast but even pulse in quavers, so maintaining a steady groove. Throughout the entire solo there is an effect of doubling at the octave, and for the listener, the sheer volume of sound obliterates consciousness, as background becomes foreground in an intense barrage of noise. The pulsating rhythm (Hendrix often described himself as a rhythm guitarist and habitually played lead and rhythm simultaneously, thus keeping his solos in perfect counterpoint with the rhythm), the sinuous tripping around the basic motif, the distortion and overload create a disorienting effect which feeds the connotations of spinning, out-of-control, spaced-out by 'Purple Haze'.

The sensation of being absorbed into the trip is further enhanced by the obsessive repetition of the vocal motif. While there are minor variations based on inflection, these only enhance the feeling of obsession. The final vocal phrase, in particular, is characterised by its swerving inflection and is supported by a pulsating beat which stops abruptly as Hendrix , once again, utters a cry for help which resolves into a resigned acceptance of the inevitable. The effect is that of a loss of time, the underlying pulse has gone and all that remains is the mixed-down voice and a feeling of dislocation, of being in a different space.

The psychedelically-charged mood is also present in 'Love or Confusion' (track 5 of The Jimi Hendrix Experience). The association of colours with the feeling of disorientation that accompanies tripping is intensified by the rise and fall contouring of the vocal line and the intensity of the guitar, which pushes through the texture, dominating the sound. Based on a simple harmonic structure (G-G6-F-F6), so facilitating improvisation, the initial impression is one of theatricality and noise. Generated in the main by Hendrix's use of fuzz tone which sounds at times almost like snare drum accents articulating the beginning and end of phrases, and the low grinding sound of the bass guitar against rests and a drum roll, there is the implication of a new language of sound and colour which equates with the hallucinogenic. In particular, the use of distortion and fuzz, the excessive string-bends, the use of wah-wah pedal to create a unique psychedelic drone, and the extremes of feedback often obscure the actual notes played. Layers of sound appear to grow out of one another in a continuous flow to create a kaleidoscopic effect, while the energy, volume, and guitar effects – as Hendrix slides effortlessly from one note to another – communicate the experience of hallucinogenic disorientation to his audience.

The correlation between psychedelic experience and Hendrix's guitar style is evident not simply in the mode of address in the lyric line but also in the mystical feel of his performances. While the lyrics provide the initial clues, the colouring of the guitar line and the fixation on specific sounds and effects relate strongly to acid experience. As Joel Fort observes:

> the main dimensions ... are perceptual ... With the eyes closed, kaleidoscopic colors and a wide array of geometric shapes and specific objects ... are often seen ... Illusions can occur ...
>
> (1969, 182)

This is often born out by his fans who considered that his 'art rock songs had a more specific purpose than ordinary rock: they served to help induce in the listener a state similar to that which inspired the composition of the songs'. Their length was also a contributory factor – often lasting from 7 to 20 minutes, they 'were less momentary stimuli and more comprehensive "experience"' (Goertzel, in Potash, 1996, 111). It is this sense of comprehensive experience that is crucial to an understanding of Hendrix's live performances, for while the press focussed in on his pyrotechnics – his flambuoyant performance style which had included the destruction of his guitar – it is apparent that each song was carefully composed, the effects thought through to enhance the connotations of the lyrics. Not least, he was an interpreter of history, sensitive to the empty rhetoric of politicians, as evidenced in his performance of 'The Star Spangled Banner' at Woodstock (August 1969), a festival dedicated to celebrating 'Three Days of Peace with Music'.

As a musical allegory of the cultural crisis surrounding the Vietnam War, 'Star Spangled Banner' is apocalyptic in its vision and considered by many to be Hendrix's most complex and powerful composition. For Americans, their anthem is probably the most familiar of all songs, and its sentiments ('the land of the free', 'the home of the brave') are intended to inspire both patriotism and fervour. Its performance at Woodstock (not the first, so suggesting a carefully rehearsed composition) is thus far more than a showy display of power-driven rock. Rather, it is a compelling statement that forces the listener to hear the horrors of war and to question the rhetoric of 'my country, right or wrong'.

Opening with crackling feedback, the familiar refrain is played slightly out of pitch, the feedback and sustain providing a chilling commentary on the flag ('broad stripes and bright stars') as the sounds plunge, then hover. The gathering sense of desolation is heightened by the waivering strains of the guitar, summoning courage before the tension is shattered by the simulated sound of a fighter plane coming out of a deep dive against the lines 'the rocket's red glare'. When the straight melody is finally heard ('gave proof through the night'), there is little sense of the heroic. There is no victory, no glory. Rather, the soundscape evokes images of death – cluster-bombs, the rotating blades of helicopters, the crackle of flames – before the final ear-shattering grind of the guitar strings are treated to a crude bottle neck slide against the microphone, which gradually resolves on the opening chords of 'Purple Haze'.

The juxtaposition of the 'Star Spangled Banner' with the psychedelically-charged 'Purple Haze' is, surely, far more than a gesture to the audience's desire for 'golden oldies.' Rather, they provide a challenging contextualisation for the anti-war movement of the 1960s, questioning the ideology of patriotism through the vocabulary of acid-rock. Hendrix's performance was thus both culturally and politically perceptive, tuned into the collective consciousness of an audience who were only too aware of the demands of the parent State.

He was not the first to highlight the overt militarism of 'The Star Spangled Banner'. The Music Supervisor's Conference of America (1931) had also felt that its patriotic fervour reflected more the ideals of a nation at war, rather than one committed to peace and good will. As a commemorative poem on the attack on Baltimore (Francis Scott Key, September 13–14, 1814), it establishes a heroic narrative that links flag and nation to victory over its enemies, and its melody (originally published as The Anacreontic Song, London, 1770–1780) had already been used as the setting for about fifty printed American patriotic songs. It is also apparent that the onomatopoeic evocation of the sounds of jungle warfare resonate with Hendrix's earlier dedication of 'Machine Gun'

(New Year's Eve, 1969) to the 'soldiers' fighting in Chicago, Milwaukee, New York (a reference to the Civil Rights battles at the time) and Vietnam, where Black GIs represented 2 per cent of the officers, yet were assigned 28 per cent of the combat missions. (Shaar Murray, 1989, 22-23) The ironies surrounding the performance at Woodstock were, as Charles Shaar Murray writes, 'murderous: a black man with a white guitar; a massive, almost white audience wallowing in a paddy field of its own making ... One man with one guitar said more in three and a half minutes about that particularly disgusting war and its reverberations than all the novels, memoirs and movies put together'. (1989, 24)

While Hendrix's sense of vision and musicianship are more than sufficient to earn him his place as the top lead guitarist of all time (most recently, a 2003 Opinion Poll placed him 1st out of 100 other contenders) the status of 'god' can be attributed equally to his sexual prowess that informed not only his relationship to women, but also his relationship to his music. Hendrix reportedly 'slept with his guitar at night and called it his Electric Lady (hence the title of his third album, *Electric Ladyland*)'. He also admitted that 'Manic Depression' was 'a song about a cat wishing he could make love to his music, instead of the same old everyday woman' (Goertzel in Potash, 1996, 110). This was reflected in his live performances where he often played guitar with his teeth[22] or writhed on the ground, simulating sexual intercourse. At the 1966 Monterey Pop Festival he had pelvic-thrusted his guitar against the wall whilst making it wail above a wall of feedback. At a gentler level, he would caress and twist the strings, bending the neck of his guitar, spinning round, not even looking at his audience while he spun out his electric, sexual dreams. In the early part of his career, he smashed and burned many of his guitars, as well as harpooning his speaker cabinets – sometimes out of frustration, sometimes for acoustical effect. His use of the 'whang' bar on his Stratocaster was also highly visual, manipulating the bar with his picking hand, but also using less orthodox and almost masturbatory techniques – vibrating it rapidly with his chording hand while tightening and loosening the machine heads, or pounding on the guitar's neck.

Hendrix's erotic relationship to his guitar was extended in live performance by his knowing attitude towards women. As Charles Shaar Murray writes: 'He would lean over to women in the audience, rapidly lapping his tongue in an explicit mime of cunnilingus (at a time when it was still considered an exotic sexual activity that only wicked, depraved men would perform, and even wickeder and more depraved women would want); the guitar would become either a sexual partner or his own sexual organ' (1989, 71). The sensationalism surrounding his sexuality was compounded by Cynthia Plaster Caster's life-size model of his erection which was deemed the most impressive of all current rock stars, and his public humiliation of Mick Jagger with his ostentatious pass at Marianne Faithfull.[23] She was but one of numerous women in Hendrix's life and his general aversion to saying 'no' is reflected both in his legendary on-tour encounters and the gallery of female archetypes who emerge from his writings. There are strutting bimbos like 'Foxy Lady' or 'Little Miss Lover', the insipid clingers of 'Stone Free' and 'Crosstown Traffic' or the castrators such as 'Dolly Dagger'. However, as Shaar-Murray observes, 'pop mythology generally being a loose conflation of lies, rumours, old newspaper cuttings and snap judgements, it is less than surprising that unrestrained sexuality and all-purpose King dick-ism remains one of the cornerstones of Jimi Hendrix's legend.' For many critics, his music in its entirety was simply dismissed as 'cock-happy guitar heroics.' (1989, 68)

As such, the harem-groupies, the 'Dolly Daggers' and 'Foxy Ladies' are simply part of his 'Cross Town Traffic', separated from his feminine muse, the elementals 'Little Wing', 'Waterfall', 'Gypsy Eyes', 'Angel'. But why, I wonder, this separation, this emphasis on essentialism? What these legend-makers fail to appreciate is that Hendrix was both 'knowing' and 'experienced'. Thus, while he was disparaged for his staged acts of cunnilingus, the critics seem blissfully unaware of his skills. This was no grudging going-down on his woman, nor an invitation to the macho imagination – a probable interpretation of their reaction. Rather, it is playful, giving. His tongue is dexterity, and his erotic exploration is both pleasure and performance, the vibrations on the guitar strings relating to the vibrations on the clitoris. He knows how to 'touch the live wire', 'using a lingual, instead of a phallic, function to mobilize the (dis)play of eroticism.' (Grosz and Probyn, 1995, 38) He is, then, no macho stud, 'leering at a woman in the audience'. (Shaar Murray, 1989, 69) Rather, his knowledge of the petite venus, shows him to be a 'cunning linguist', a knowledge-able lover, rather than a disparager of women. With cunnilingus still a punishable offence in some American States, it is small wonder that his gestures provoked such attention at the time.

The relationship between Hendrix and his 'electric lady' is, then, the anima, the activating spirit, of Hendrix's sexuality, which allows him access to his elemental muses who, in turn, arouse his own sex. It also relates to the power of the music itself, so raising the (unanswerable) question: what came first, the lyrics or the sounds. It was, perhaps, neither. Rather it was the feel of playing a guitar. As his father, Al Hendrix reminisced, 'He just taught himself. He just picked it up. It was just in him, and the guitar became another part of his anatomy … And his guitar began to love him and he began to love it like no other love he had known … It understood his frustrations', (Henderson, 1990, 19) his desires and his vision. In effect, he spoke through his guitar and his guitar spoke through him. As such, the mood of his music could only effect a reciprocal response. The making love to his 'electric lady' would thus involve passion and tenderness, hard-grinds and playful eroticism. As his singular love, she embodied every aspect of woman – consciousness, freedom, subjectivity, and feminine sexuality in all its manifestations. It is both an acceptance and integration of male and female, suggesting that both gender and sexuality are transferable. By engaging with risk and defiance, he/she/he embodies a desire for desire itself. His musical language thus combines male desire and feminine pleasure, female desire and masculine pleasure. It is both an exploration and confirmation of erotic sensuality in all its complex subtlety.

Hendrix was also a perfectionist. As Eddie Kramer, the chief engineer at Hendrix's Electric Lady Studios explained, shortly after his death: 'He had to have everything just perfect by his standards. He'd lay down tracks, and every time he put his guitar over it, and played it different. Sometimes he'd take tapes home and listen to them all night, and the next day he'd come in and do it entirely different. You should have seen him – he'd be down there grimacing and straining, trying to get it to come out of the guitar the way he heard it in his head. If you could ever transcribe the sound in a man's head directly onto the tape ...' (Morthland, in Potash, 1998, p.45) Kramer also forecast the greed that would follow from Hendrix's death: 'I'm certain there's all kinds of unscrupulous people in the business, who shall remain nameless, that will release tapes of Jimi now ... The thing is, these people will put them out on the basis that any Jimi Hendrix music is good music. And that's not true! I knew it and Jimi knew it.' (Morthland, in Potash, 1998, p.45)

Hendrix recorded only three studio albums with the Experience and one live album with his Band of Gypsies. *Smash Hits* was the only other Experience title sanctioned during his lifetime, yet the number of reworked/reissued/repackaged/rereleased albums are testament to the greed forecast by Kramer. As Chris Potash (1998) writes, 'Don't buy them; you'll risk bad karma.' (p.211) Having recently watched the Channel 4 programme on the problems surrounding the Hendrix Estate (September 25, 2003) I have to say I agree.

Valued at around $150m, the Hendrix legacy has become the most litigated rock estate in history and as the programme argued, it is a case of brother against sister on who gets what. Hendrix had only $20K in the bank when he died, and reputedly had as many debts as he had assets. Significantly, he had not left a will and his father, Al, was left to handle his affairs. Matters were complicated by the fact that he had remarried, and his step-daughter Janie, recognising that the legal issues were complex, advised him to take on the entertainment lawyer, Leo Brandon Junior to handle the estate. It was clearly a good move, and as the years rolled on, millions of records were released and the estate grew to an estimated value of between $5–7m. Brandon then advised Janie to sell the Hendrix business to the MCA Record Company, obtaining a $2m settlement for Jimi's brother, Leon, and step-sister, Janie. While Leon accepted his $1m share, Janie went to an attorney and decided to retain her rights to the Estate. Supported by Micro-Soft co-founder Paul Allen (the 4th richest man in the world and himself a Hendrix fan), Leo Brandon filed a law suit. This was to have taken place in 1995, but was settled out of court and Al and Janie Hendrix won the business back. By then, it was worth some $80m.

From 1996, the estate was handled exclusively by Janie and her cousin Bob under the company name, the Hendrix Experience. Since then, they have remastered Hendrix classics and issued previously unreleased material, with concert DVDs, films and memorabilia. Golfballs, rocking chairs printed with Hendrix's head, and bottled red wine are included in the merchandise. The company is now worth between $150-$160m, so establishing Hendrix on the top tier of dead musicians. While the company attracted adverse comments about their crass merchandising, matters were further complicated by Al Hendrix's 1999 statement that he was not Leon's father. Twelve years earlier, in 1987 his will had claimed Leon as his only living child and suspecting the machinations of his sister, another lengthy law suit ensued. Claiming both legal and moral rights as Al's son, Leon agreed to take DNA tests, the results of which have not yet been revealed. In the meantime, supported by his lawyer, Craig Diffenbach, Leon went to Court to obtain a copy of his father's will and discovered that his only inheritance was a Hendrix souvenir gold record. Clearly wills can be changed and Janie attributes the disinheritance to Leon's behaviour, for making bad choices in life – smoking weed, taking crack. In turn, Leon blames Janie for manipulating her step-father and is stepping up the fight, taking on the Experience and trying to get the will overturned.

It is not insignificant that Janie and Bob Hendrix moved Jimi's body to a newly erected memorial mausaleum. Claiming it was her father's vision, no-one in the family was informed; the body was taken there in the middle of the night, and on the memorial itself is a sculpted right-handed guitar. As Leon observed, 'they didn't even know the man or his music.' Nor is it insignificant that the family trusts established by Al in 1997 remain in the hands of the Hendrix Experience. Thirty-three years on, the litigation continues. As Charles R. Cross, biographer of Hendrix observed, 'it's a sad reminder that no-one can be trusted when large amounts of money are at stake.' From personal experience, I wonder just what image of Hendrix is being perpetuated. My request for copyright permission to quote four lines of 'Purple Haze' and two transcriptions ('Purple Haze', 'Love or Confusion') were refused by Experience Hendrix, LLC, Seattle who describe themselves as a 'Jimi Hendrix family company'. Apparently they didn't like my interpretation. It seems, then, that for the countless fans, writers and critics who valued his psychedelically-charged power rock, and his strong, sensitive, sensual performances, such discussions are taboo.

The fact that Hendrix has been made a god by his countless fans, is 'not because he asked to be one. It was because those people needed a god ... to make their decisions for them; and because modern mass communications provided the means of god-making.' (Potash, 1996, 208-9) It is a requiem that could equally stand for Kurt Cobain who, like Morrison and Hendrix before him, could not cope with the extremes of stardom and who, like them died at the age of twenty-seven.

Myth and reality

The association of death with the heroic, which was triggered by the god-like status conferred on Morrison and Hendrix, remains a powerful signifier within rock culture. It confirms the creed that 'sex and drugs and rock 'n' roll is all my brain and body need' (Ian Dury) and situates death as the ultimate form of excess: 'live fast, die young'. By 1972, the deaths of Brian Jones, Janis Joplin,

Jim Morrison and Jimi Hendrix had provided a chilling testimony to the morbid extremes of rock culture. The year also marked another rock 'n' roll suicide, when David Bowie unveiled Ziggy Stardust, his pop alter ego.

Ziggy is introduced by a slow drum beat, bringing the sound, the concept and the guitar into play before the piano and twelve-string guitar situate the lyric context of 'walking the market place'. Set in the supposedly drug-crazed world of a future on the brink of catastrophe, it is nevertheless evident that the album is set firmly within the context of the 1970s. Rock lifestyles had proved to have terrifying analogies with the mythical Faustian bargain as iconic figures died from the excesses of superstardom after a magical five-year life span. If 1967 is taken as the year when stars such as Hendrix and Morrison first achieved international success, then the fact of their deaths in 1972 suggests that the conceptualisation of Ziggy, the Nazz of Bowie's parable, is both an ironic and knowing commentary on the entire rock process. Like his real-life counterparts, Ziggy dies from the excesses of stardom when he is killed off in the last track of the album, a rock 'n' roll suicide, five years on.

Bowie is spell-binding as a storyteller and his voice is kaleidoscopic, ranging from the overt, viper-like tones that accompany the verbal caresses of the 'Lady Stardust', the soulful, preacherman recitative that precedes the big soulful chorus of 'It Ain't Easy', to the intimate of defeat in 'Rock 'n' Roll Suicide'. Comparable to Andy Warhol in shifting the whole grammar of pop, Bowie brought a knowing sense of pastiche, parody, playfulness and revivalism to the fore. The would-be rock 'n' roll star, masquerading as a fictitious pop star, who subsequently becomes a star himself, is both a brilliant piece of wish-fulfilment and a chilling metaphor for the ultimate morbidity of rock. It is also a testament to the underlying androgyny of such stars as Iggy Pop. Ziggy's indeterminate sexuality, the spangly costumes, eye shadow and overt theatricality convey a campness that was pivotal to the pop sensibilities of the early 1970s and the world of glam rock, while foreshadowing the deaths of such sexually ambiguous stars as Marc Bolan and Freddie Mercury.[24]

While Ziggy's death is wrapped up in a theatricality that evokes memories of Judy Garland, the pressures of stardom continue to drive the insecure to find escape mechanisms – and drugs are clearly one of the most obvious here in that they both provide the necessary stimulants for an exhausting performance programme, and the means to turn off and relax. It is also apparent that the mythologising of death has situated drugs as the sacraments within the catechism of rock. Its heroes are those whose emotions have broken out of prescribed limits, endowing them with a godlike eminence which is curiously enhanced by their often ignoble deaths – the inhalation of vomit being but one example.

While it is not intended to provide an exhaustive list of dead heroes, the following provide some insights into those who are now venerated as 'gods' and who are, themselves, part of the mythology of rock.

From the rock scene

Brian Jones (rhythm guitar, Rolling Stones; b. Lewis Brian Hopkin-Jones, February 28, 1942, Cheltenham, Gloucestershire, England, d. July 3, 1969) was found dead in the swimming pool of the Sussex house that had once belonged to writer A.A. Milne. The coroner's verdict 'death by misadventure' failed to identify whether it was a heart failure or related to his drug addiction. *He was 27.* A free concert at London's Hyde Park two days after his death was attended by a crowd of 250,000 and became a symbolic wake, so establishing a powerful precedent for the veneration of dead heroes. Jagger released thousands of butterflies and narrated the famous lines from Shelley's elegy for Keats:

> Life, like a dome of many-coloured glass,
> Stains the white radiance of Eternity,
> Until Death tramples it to fragments, – Die
> If thou woulds't be that which thou dost seek.

Three days later, Jagger's girlfriend Marianne Faithful attempted suicide.

Keith Moon (drums, The Who; b. August 23, 1946, Wembley, London, England, d. September 7, 1978) Moon died following an overdose of medication taken to alleviate alcohol addiction. His madcap behaviour and idiosyncratic, exciting drumming had been an integral part of The Who and his death lead to rumours that the band would split. A retrospective film, *The Kids Are Alright*, enhanced the sense of finality but the group resumed recording in 1979, with former Small Faces/Faces drummer Kenny Jones. The same year 11 fans were killed prior to a concert at the Cincinnati Riverfront Colosseum in Ohio during a rush to secure prime vantage points. *Moon was 32 when he died.*

Freddie Mercury (vocalist, Queen; b. Frederick Bulsara, September 5, 1946, Zanzibar, Africa, d. November 24, 1991, London, England) Known for his excessive lifestyle, love of wild parties and theatrical performances, his band 'invented' Concert Rock and are remembered for their memorable hook lines where thousands joined in. Mercury died of AIDS at the *age of 45.*

Michael Hutchence (lead vocals, INXS; b. January 22, 1960, Lain Cove, Sydney, Australia, d. November 22, 1997, Sydney, Australia) Hutchence was found hanged in his hotel room in Sydney. He had been obsessed with pushing sex to an extreme and his 'suicide' at the *age of 37* has been attributed by some to auto-asphyxia.

From the mainstream hard rock scene

Tommy Bolin (guitarist, Deep Purple; b. April 18, 1951, Sioux City, Iowa, USA, d. December 4, 1976, Miami, Florida.)   Died of a heroin overdose, *aged 25*.

John Bonham (drummer, Led Zeppelin; b. May 31, 1948, Birmingham, England, d. September 25, 1980)   Found dead, following a lengthy drinking bout, *aged 32*.

Bon Scott (vocals, AC/DC; b. Ronald Scot, July 9, 1946, Kirriemuir, Scotland, d. February 19, 1980, London, England)   A prison conviction for assault and battery indicated a volatile side to his nature and also resulted in him being rejected for the army. Choked on his own vomit after night of heavy drinking *aged 34*.

Phil Lynott (vocals, bass, Thin Lizzy; b. August 20, 1951, Dublin, Eire, d. January 4, 1986)   Died of heart failure and pneumonia after a drugs overdose *aged 35*.

Steve 'Steamin' Clark (guitarist, Def Leppard; b. April 23, 1960, Sheffield, Yorkshire, England, d. January 8, 1991, London, England)   Found dead in his London flat after consuming a lethal mixture of drugs (prescribed for three broken ribs) and alcohol, *aged 31*.

Punk/retro punk

Sid Vicious (bass, Sex Pistols; b. John Ritchie, May 10, 1957, London, England, d. February 2, 1979, New York, USA)   On October 12, 1978, Nancy Spungen (girlfriend) was found stabbed in their New York hotel room. Vicious was charged with murder. While released on bail, he suffered a fatal overdose of heroin and died in his sleep, *aged 22*.

Ian Curtis (vocalist, Joy Division; b. July 1956, Macclesfield, Cheshire, England, d. 18 May 1980)   Curtis hanged himself, *aged 24*, whilst at the peak of creativity. A note was allegedly found bearing the words: 'At this moment I wish I were dead. I just can't cope anymore'. He had suffered serious epileptic seizures and blackouts and his illness worsened with the group's increasingly demanding schedule.

Richey Edwards (guitarist, Manic Street Preachers, b. December 22, 1966, disappeared, presumed dead, February 1, 1995)   Edwards had cut the words '4 Real' into his forearm when the band's authenticity was called into question by *New Musical Express* critic Steve Lamacq. The haunting '4st 7lb', written by the anorexic Edwards, preceded his temporary admittance to a mental institution. *Age at 'disappearance', 29.*

Grunge

Kurt Cobain (guitar, vocals, Nirvana; b. Kurt Donald Cobain, February 20, 1967, Hoquiam, Seattle, WA, USA, d. April 5, 1994, Seattle, WA, USA)   A failed suicide attempt in Rome, 1994, resulted in a coma induced by a tranquilliser-and-champagne cocktail. Committed suicide in his home in Seattle *aged 27*. Having pumped his veins full of heroin, he wrote a rambling suicide note and shot himself. He did so much damage to his head that police could only identify the body through the fingerprints. Cobain became the ultimate symbol for 'Generation X' (the disaffected twenty nothings) and his death was interpreted as an acknowledgement of the hopelessness and nihilistic apathy that had infected a whole substratum of youth culture.

Responses to the death of Kurt Cobain were diverse, but many agreed with his mother, Wendy, that 'he'd just become a member of "that stupid club" of early rock 'n' roll deaths. Others saw it as a drug-induced tragedy waiting to happen ... Cobain himself stated in the suicide note that it was "better to burn out than just fade away"' (Clarke and Woods, 1999, back cover). His band, Nirvana, was hailed by *Q* (October 2002) as 'the most important band in the world'.

Clearly the death list can be extended. Other dead heroes could well include *Cliff Burton*, bassist for Metallica, who was killed during a freak bus accident in Sweden and who is considered by many to have been the best heavy metal bassist ever. He was *24 years old*; *Nick Drake*, whose desolate songs prefigure his overdose and resultant death at the *age of 26*; *Marc Bolan* (T-Rex) who died in a car crash September 1977, *aged 30*; *Phil Ochs*, who was found hanged at his sister's home at the *age of 36* and who was considered, for a time, Bob Dylan's greatest rival; *Marvin Gaye*, addicted to cocaine and shot, *aged 45*, by his father after a violent disagreement. From the more obscure and extreme metal scene, *'Dead'* – vocalist from the Norwegian black metal band Mayhem – has engendered a cult status and epitomised the bleakness and nihilism of mid-90s Scandinavian underground metal. Then, there's *Van Zandt and Gaines* from Lynyrd Skynyrd whose fans still yell 'Freebird' at one point at every concert, and *Stuart Adamson*, who almost single-handedly saved the guitar in the otherwise synth-drenched 1980s. He is also venerated for his willingness to confront political realities when everyone else seemed to be more interested in trivia. His suicide makes this stand all the more poignant for his many fans. Finally, though by no means least, the recent death of *Chuck Schuldiner* (lead guitarist with Florida's Death) was met with deep grief from underground enthusiasts worldwide. Through his astounding guitar playing and brutal vocal style, Chuck practically single-handedly helped to codify death metal aesthetics and will remain an important source of inspiration for budding death metal musicians and fans alike. *He was 34.*[25]

For many, however, *John Lennon* (b. October 9, 1940, Liverpool, England, d. December 8, 1980, New York, USA) is the ultimate rock hero. While his status is attributable both to his years with the Beatles and his subsequent solo career, his role in educating the young to venerate world peace and his rock anthem 'Give Peace A Chance' (which has been used by various representatives of countries opposed to war, not least during the 1990s Gulf War) were matched only by his espousal of hallucinogenics as a route through to the metaphysical, and his plea for women's rights in 'Woman is the Nigger of the World'. His problems with drugs and alcohol, his love of Yoko Ono (which many believed to have been the cause of the break up of the Beatles) are well documented, and the body of songs created with Paul McCartney remain the finest popular music catalogue ever known. Paradoxically, he was murdered by a man who got his autograph earlier in the day. His death, at the *age of 40*, was greeted by unprecedented mourning worldwide and the airport at Liverpool, England, has now been named in his honour.

Average age at death: 30

Self-destruction – whether drug-related, suicide or the result of severe risk-taking – is, then, curiously related both to the excesses of a rock 'n' roll lifestyle and to much of the litany of its songs. 'From the cute insinuations about shooting smack often imputed to the Mamas and Papas' lyric 'I'm a real straight shooter, if ya know what I mean', through the Stones's 'Sister Morphine' and on to Generation X's 'shooting up for kicks' (Pattison, 1987, 125), rock's infatuation with narcotics is matched only by its fascination with death itself. Other than grand opera, which seems to have several deaths in every performance, it is arguably the case that popular music never dealt adequately with the subject before the advent of rock. Whether rock has helped to break the taboo about death, or whether the incidence of death amongst its young stars gave it a specific status is, of course, conjectural, but over the last 30 years the subject has been covered extensively in songs which range from the deeply moving poetry of, for example, Bob Dylan, through to the extremes of death metal and rap's Death Row Records. The actual names of individual bands such as Dead Boys (first wave punk/no wave band, formed in Cleveland, Ohio, 1976), Dead Can Dance (based in London, but tracing their origins to Australia, 1980s avant garde pop/goth), Dead Kennedys (undoubted kings of US punk and the US underground during 1980s until the advent of Nirvana) also suggest a curious allegiance to the dark romanticism of death that informs not only goth culture[26] and the metal scene[27] but also such cult films as *The Lost Boys* in which vampirism and a Doors-inspired soundtrack provide a ritualistic evocation of rock, Morrison's symbolic role as the Dionysian god and the cult of eternal youth. Death and narcotics, then, is a heady mixture, and thirty years on the 'rock and roll suicide' (David Bowie, *The Rise and Fall of Ziggy Stardust and the Spiders from Mars*) continues to exert a powerful fascination for fans and critics alike.

I am not alone in recognising the significance of death for rock mythology. Having recently reviewed the exhibition 'Air Guitar: Art Reconsidering Rock Music'[28] I was struck by the way in which its powerful images, half-forgotten voices and iconography reflect the relationship between the art world and rock. 'David Byrne of Talking Heads met his fellow band members at Rhode Island School of Design and his first band was aptly titled The Artistics. Freddie Mercury painted pop stars when studying at Ealing College of Art and Malcolm McLaren persuaded Sex Pistols' bassist Glen Matlock to enrol for a foundation course at St. Martins so that he would not have to miss any rehearsals to "sign on" '.[29] Rock also has a powerful conceptual hold over visual artists, due largely to its connotations of rebellion and non-conformism. Significantly, the mantra 'live fast, die young' underpins many of the works which explore the casualties of rock excess, this time from the perspective of the artist as fan.

It is no accident that viewers pause to reflect as they walk around the two mounds of earth, piled onto mirrors, listening to the cassette loops of voices that evoke memories of the utopia of Woodstock and the dystopia of Altamont. Sam Durant's 'Partially Buried 1960s/70s: Utopia Reflected: Partially Buried 1960s/70s: Distopia Revealed' (1998) provides an allegorical representation of the entropic events set in motion by the unprecedented and excessive violence at Altamont. Jagger's voice is heard nervously addressing the crowd: 'Let's just get it together! ... everyone, Hell's Angels, everybody, let's just keep ourselves together'. As the exhibition audience know only too well, his plea was ineffectual and, as Durant's powerful imagery reveals, Altamont can be read as a chilling metaphor for the way in which performance, musical experience and social reality can fuse together: one dead, one murdered, total dead four, two run over, one drowned in a draining ditch, hundreds injured and countless more stoned on acid.

'Taking this "death culture" as his starting point', the artist and graphic designer Scott King pays tribute to gigs that became turning points in rock history: the Hammersmith Odeon where David Bowie 'killed off' Ziggy in 1972; the Stones's concert at Altamont; the last Joy Division gig before Ian Curtis hanged himself; the last Manic Street Preachers concert before Richey Edwards disappeared; the last Sex Pistols gig in San Francisco before Sid Vicious died from an overdose of heroin; The Who's concert in Woodstock, which helped them to break into the American market (Pethick, 2002, 42) and which preceded the death of drummer Keith Moon (1978) from an overdose. The bands, like their audience, are reduced to graphic dots, so reducing their overblown status to the level of their fans (Figure 5).

King's perceptive insight into the often unglamorous and tragic reality of rock suicides and the zombie-like profiteering by their respective record companies is given an appropriate focus in the series *Into the Black 1999* (see Figure 6). Taking his title from Neil Young's 'Hey Hey, My My, Into the

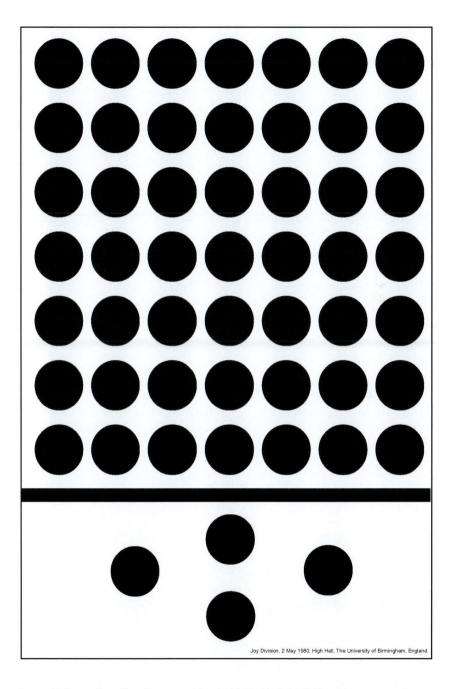

Joy Division, 2 May 1980, High Hall, The University of Birmingham, England.

Figure 5 Scott King 'Joy Division, May 2, 1980, High Hall, The University of Birmingham, England' (courtesy: Magnani, London)

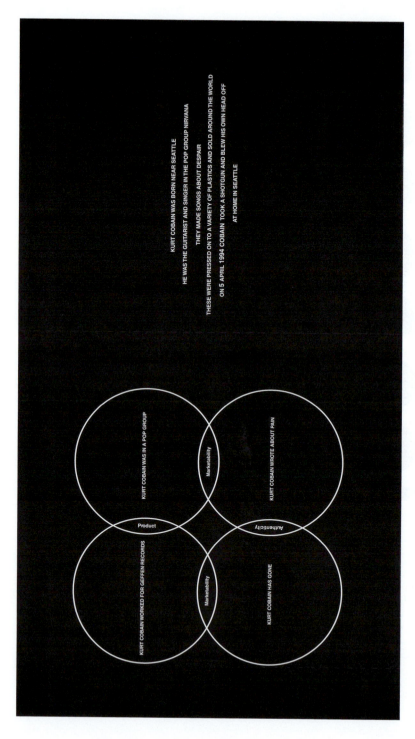

Figure 6 Scott King 'Into the Black' (detail: Kurt Cobain), 2000, bromide print (courtesy: Magnani, London)

Black', the careers of Ian Curtis of Joy Divison, Kurt Cobain of Nirvana and Manic Street Preachers guitarist Richey Edwards are clinically broken down 'into four simplistic but pivotal stages', each occupying one of four interconnecting circles on charts that mimic corporate marketing strategies. 'By reducing their colourful lives and tragic deaths to black and white statistics' (Mahony, 2002, 10), the audience, like King himself, is forced to question the ethics of the record industry who continue to profit from the vulnerability of their young stars.

The 'wild boy' concept instigated by Morrison and Hendrix is a powerful legacy, and its dead heroes constitute a morbid epitaph for rock's continuing obsession with sex, drugs and death. However, for all their notoriety, rock's dead martyrs are also revered musicians who have brought something special to their particular interpretation of the genre, and it is for this reason that they exert such power over successive generations of would-be rock musicians. Does this mean, then, that without a full commitment to its creed, they will never achieve nirvana? To an extent, the answer has to be 'Yes'. But while the heroes of rock have fed on the invisible meals of self-apotheosis and self-annihilation, the average rocker is more likely to make alcohol his eucharist. What is important is the belief rather than the reality. As Robert Pattison observes, 'two hundred years of Romanticism have established the conventions of driving on the road of excess, and the rocker, in the fast lane, observes them scrupulously. He knows the conventions don't permit him to drive sober' (1987, 125).

Boys just wanna be boys

While rock heroes live their lives to the extreme, ostensibly relishing the self-destructive urges inherent in their addiction to drugs and sex and proclaiming their creed through performance and lifestyle, nice boys need to retain a sense of naive purity. Situated within the romantic tradition of popular music, their public image is one of abstinence from sex, narcotics and alcohol – keeping the rules – so allowing for a particular identification with the pubescent and pre-pubescent fan. While their genealogy can be traced back to the clean-cut, boy-next-door image of the early Beatles, and groups such as The Monkees and the Bay City Rollers, individual stars such as Cliff Richard, David Cassidy and, more recently, Robbie Williams (ex-Take That) have also influenced the acceptable image that continues to dominate the 'pop idol' stable. Operating within the romantic tradition of pop, they are characterised as desirable and desiring, boyish and natural. More specifically, the way in which the pop idol is presented to his audience (via the media) and how he performs (on stage, in videos and through the choice of music) produces a different way of being male. Whereas the image of the rock star is readable as potentially dangerous and destructive (so embodying phallic power), the pop idol 'has the look of just being well-kept', and has an apparent 'naturalness' (MacDonald, 1997, 283) that confirms his 'boy-next-door' appeal. Further, while his musical repertoire is 'of its time', and thus crosses over to such phallocentric genres as rock, it is tempered by performance codes which signify enjoyment and fun rather than control and power. Thus, while the pop idol is unlikely to be recognised as authentic within the generic conventions of, for example, rock, his performing ability allows for movement across genres and, hence, the possibility of engaging with different audiences. He is, then, a musical 'actor' whose ability to perform allows him to move from his initial identification with pubescent and pre-pubescent girls to a mainstream audience via a flirtation with films, theatre, cabaret or, in the case of Robbie Williams, big band and swing.

Today's pop charts are dominated by aspiring wannabes who crave fame and whose careers are shaped by such entrepreneurs as Pete Waterman. Image, it seems, is all too often more important than musical ability, and the sense of innovation that characterised the more knowingly ironic groups of the 1980s has been replaced increasingly by the 'anyone can sing' characteristic of karaoke. The question that arises is the extent to which this is a new phenomenon and whether it is the 'stars' or their producers who profit most from this dangerous game. Coping with fame is not easy, as reflected in Part I, and it would seem that pop stars cease to be pop stars at the age of 25. With the emphasis on youthfulness and instant appeal, it is apparent that the hurt to those dumped by what seemed the enduring love of otherwise fickle fans is not confronted. Pop also has its death list, the most recent being Dee Dee, from the 1970s band, the Ramones. Found dead in his home by his wife on June 7, 2002, unconfirmed early reports list the apparent cause of his death as overdosing and choking on his own vomit. Unlike the heroic status conferred on rock stars by drug-related death, fans lament that 'to have lost him this way is devastating ... Dee Dee was my Ramone – he belonged to me. I dressed like him, cut my hair like his and sang his lyrics as if they came from my own heart – because they did'.[30]

Pop, then, is underpinned both by an aesthetic of accessibility and of romanticism. 'It accepts and embraces the requirement to be instantly pleasing and to make a pretty picture of itself' (Hill, 1986, 8). Above all, it has become an 'umbrella name for a special kind of musical product aimed at a teenage market' (Gammond, 1991, 457) which dates back to the 1950s and the emergence of such teen idols as Cliff Richard.

The Young Ones

My earlier observation that 'pop stars who perform in otherwise "authentic" genres are regarded as problematic' is confirmed by the status of Cliff Richard as 'entertainer'. Books on rock (whether academic or general) never mention his name. Somehow, it seems somewhat uncool to set him beside such 'authentic' stars as Elvis Presley and Buddy Holly, and while there is extensive coverage in encyclopedias of popular music, it is his length of service that is celebrated: 'He is British pop's most celebrated survivor'. 'Throughout his forty years in the pop charts, Richard has displayed a valiant longevity' (Larkin, 1999, 1035). Awarded an OBE (January 1, 1980) for 20 years' service to popular music and subsequently knighted in May 1995, his squeaky-clean image clearly situates him outside of the trinity of sex and dope and rock 'n' roll – a point not lost on the critics when he converted to fundamentalist Christianity in 1966 when such top groups as the Beatles and the Stones were en route to Eastern mysticism, transcendentalism and LSD. In retrospect, he is what school reports would damningly identify as 'a good all-rounder'. Small wonder, then, that he is now recognised as successor to Dame Vera Lynn (World War II's 'Forces Favourite') after performing at the 1995 celebrations for VE Day and that his Christmas offerings provide families with the traditional sentiments of peace and goodwill to all men.

Born Harry Roger Webb (October 14, 1940, Lucknow, India), Cliff Richard was the UK's first pop idol, ousting both Tommy Steele and Marty Wilde as Britain's premier rock 'n' roll talent. Like many young boys of his era, his attraction to Elvis Presley inspired to him join a skiffle group[31], subsequently teaming up with drummer Terry Smart and guitarist Ken Payne to form the Drifters. Starting in the suburbs (the Cheshunt/Hoddeston area of Hertfordshire) where they built a strong fan base, they moved to London and Soho's 2 I's coffee bar, previously associated with the early 1950s Beatnik scene and subsequently the mecca for aspiring rock 'n' roll stars. Lead guitarist Ian Samwell then joined the group and in 1958 they secured their first big break 'in the unlikely setting of a Saturday morning talent show at the Gaumont Cinema, Shepherd's Bush' (Larkin, 1999, 1034) where they were discovered by theatrical agent George Canjou. Their demo tape reached the hands of EMI producer Norrie Paramor who gave the group an audition. It was, however, Richard, rather than the group, that appealed. Both recognised his singing ability and, more specifically, his potential appeal to an audience already enamoured by the rock 'n' roll glamour of Presley. 'Teenage Crush', an American teen ballad, was chosen for their debut single, but it was the b-side 'Move It' that attracted the attention of Jack Good, possibly the most influential television producer of his time. Like Canjou and Paramour, he too recognised Richard's vocal ability, but more specifically he picked up on his sexual appeal. Carefully modelled on Presley's performance style, Richard had already developed a strong stage presence and Good promoted his protégé on his TV show *Oh Boy* and secured a full-page review in the music paper, *Disc*. His shrewdness paid off and the popular press moved in, denouncing Richard's 'violent hip swinging' and 'crude exhibitionism' (Larkin, 1999, 1035). Predictably, this only contributed to Richard's emerging status as the British answer to Elvis. It was also apparent to Good that the Drifters contributed little to his appeal and that continuing success depended on finding a backing group who were more attuned to rock 'n' roll. Hank B. Marvin (lead guitar), Bruce Welch (rhythm guitar), Jet Harris (bass) and Tony Meehan (drums) joined Richard in 1958 and, as The Shadows, quickly became established as the UK's premier instrumental group.[32] By 1960 they had ousted Richard's single 'Please Don't Tease' from the top of the charts with their instrumental single 'Apache', firmly establishing themselves as individual artists in their own right.

Meanwhile, it seemed that Richard was changing his image. With management shake-ups and some distinctly average singles he fell back on his boyish good looks and released 'Living Doll' (Lionel Bart) and 'Travellin' Light'. Both reached the UK No. 1 position. As one biographer tellingly observes, 'he matured and transcended his Presley-like beginnings' (in Larkin, 1999, 1035). More accurately, it could be said that he returned to mainstream basics, so demonstrating what seems to be a lasting ability to survive changes in pop fashion, while emphasising the point that true credibility in rock has little to do with mimicking its performance gestures. Conversely, it shows that longevity in pop relies on growing new audiences and engaging with middle-of-the road expectations.

Richard's choice of Presley-inspired music for his initial move into the professional world of popular music relates both to the need for contemporaneity and the fact that in the 1950s and early 1960s rock 'n' roll and pop were perceived as one and the same. What the British music business looked for, at the time, was someone who had the potential to challenge the American domination of teen-based music, and Richard's boyish good looks and engaging stage presence was clearly promising. At the same time, rock 'n' roll itself was perceived as the latest fad and, as such, survival depended on adaptability and a more general appeal. Initially, Richard turned once again to the Elvis model and attempted to extend his audience by starring in two films. The first, *Serious Charge*, was a non-musical drama that dealt with the controversial subject of homosexual blackmail. Although this was banned in some areas, it does provide one particular insight into Richard's appeal. Like Presley, Richard 'looked good' and while his early recordings and performances suggest the 'wild boy' at play image that dominated first-wave rock 'n' roll, his appeal extended beyond the screaming female fans who besieged his live performances. What he possessed was an enigmatic sexuality, one that appealed equally to an emerging gay fan base. The fact that Richard's autobiography denies rumours of homosexuality is, I feel, largely irrelevant. As subsequent generations of pop idols have discovered, denials only fuel interest, and Richard's emerging persona as the eternal 'Bachelor Boy' and his proclaimed lack of sexual relationships with women after his 1966 conversion to Christianity seemed unlikely to dispel the myth that Richard was a closet gay. It should also be noted that the Sexual Offences Act was not passed until 1967 and that homosexuality was previously a criminal offence. Being outed as homosexual was thus a major concern for many artists, but while there is nothing to support the rumours surrounding Richard's sexuality, his attraction for both a straight and gay audience is significant in presaging Robbie Williams's status as a gay icon in an otherwise mainstream musical career, and the observation that a star's sexual attraction is most powerful when there is a mix of male and female physical characteristics and of masculine and feminine behavioural traits (Threadgold and Cranny-Francis, 1996, 230).

Richard's ability as an actor was further developed in *Expresso Bongo*, an adaptation of a Wolf Mankowitz 1958 musical, and a film that evoked the rapacious world of Tin Pan Alley. It marked a cinematic pop landmark and his performance as the aptly named Bongo Herbert demonstrated his ability for both characterisation and humour. Other films followed, most notably *The Young Ones* (1961), *Summer Holiday* (1962), *Wonderful Life* (1964) and *Two A Penny* (1967). Meanwhile, his abandoned black leathers, white tie and sideburns, and increasing reliance on 'respectable' songs led to accusations of emasculation and a growing suspicion that his early career as a rock 'n' roll singer was just another role – a possible reason why he failed to make any impression on the US market. In terms of the UK, however, his move towards mainstream pop led to a string of unbroken hits: 'Please Don't Tease' (1960), 'The Young Ones' (1962), 'The Next Time' (1963), 'Summer Holiday' (1963), 'The Minute You're Gone' (1965) and 'Congratulations' (1968 – the Eurovision Song Contest song)[33]. Tours, summer seasons, regular TV slots and even pantomime performances confirmed his middle-of-the-road status, albeit that the 'showbiz glitz brought a certain homogeneity to his music and image' (Larkin, 1999, 1035). 'The Young Ones', in particular has proved to be a long-standing pop anthem, not least because of Hank Marvin's memorable guitar playing.

Despite Richard's attempt to brave the Beat boom of the early 1960s, his unsuccessful cover version of the Rolling Stones's 'Blue Turns to Grey' (1965) and the rapidly changing cultural climate of the late 1960s marked a decline in his popularity as a performer with teen appeal. Even so, his determination to remain a performer (albeit at the variety level) is significant and presages the change in career of two other pop idols, David Cassidy and Robbie Williams.

Somebody wants to be wanted

Unlike Cliff Richard, who started as a rock 'n' roll performer who moved into film as a way of extending his fan base, David Cassidy (b. April 12, 1950, New York, USA) started his career as a member of the US sitcom. *The Partridge Family* (1970–4). Inspired by the bouncy harmonies of family group, the Cowsills,[34] and with Cassidy's stepmother Shirley Jones (best known for her role in such films as *Carousel*) taking the role of mother, Cassidy, along with Susan Dey and Danny Bonaduce soon attracted attention for their ability to sell records in their own right. The US chart-topper 'I Think I Love You' (1970), with Cassidy as lead singer and Jones on backing vocals, was followed by two more Top 10 hits, 'I'll Meet You Halfway' and 'Somebody Wants To Be Wanted'. It was apparent from the onset that the success of the singles was largely attributable to Cassidy's blue-eyed, blonde hair, boyish appeal. Recognised as classic teen-idol material, he was launched as a solo artist in 1971 and went to US No. 9 with a revival of Association's 'Cherish'. However, as he subsequently revealed in TV interviews, he was not happy with his image, or with the attendant hysteria that accompanied his live performances, and in an attempt to create a more adult, sexual persona he appeared semi-naked on the pages of *Rolling Stone*. While the attendant publicity undermined his image and reputation as the ultra-clean all-American boy, it seemed curiously to fuel his growing popularity in the UK where adolescent adoration for pop stars was, once again, in the ascendant.

It is difficult not to surmise that the Beatles's shift from Beatlemania (characteristic of their early career) to acid-Gurus had left teenagers somewhat bereft of pop idols. By 1967 the chart-toppers included the Rolling Stones, Jimi Hendrix, Cream, Pink Floyd and Procul Harum, and the release of the Beatles's *Sgt. Pepper's Lonely Hearts' Club Band* and the attendant publicity surrounding their espousal of the American west coast's psychedelic philosophy created an attendant moral panic. This was exacerbated in the latter years of the 1960s and early 1970s by the deaths of such iconic figures as Brian Jones, Janis Joplin, Jimi Hendrix and Jim Morrison. While such folk/rock stars as Donovan might have proved a likely attraction for the young teenager, his lyrics ('Sunshine Superman', 'Mellow Yellow') and more specifically his third album, *Sunshine Superman* (1967), which became something of an early acid-head bible, and his double-album *A Gift From A Flower To A Garden* (1968, with its cover pin-up of guru Maharishi Mahesh Yogi) served to undermine the boyish appeal promised by his otherwise whimsical and seemingly naive image, so confirming the old adage that appearances can be deceptive. It is not too surprising, then, that Cassidy seemed an ideal antidote to the problems raised by what the media had termed 'flower power'. Further, the success of The Monkees, whose song 'I'm A Believer' had topped the charts in January 1967,[35] suggested that there was an important market to tap.

The year 1972 is thus significant in seeing both Cassidy and Donny Osmond topping the pop charts, the former reaching No. 1 position in September with 'How Can I Be Sure', the former with 'Puppy Love' (July). Clearly the battle was not won, however, for while this signalled a serious break into the teenage market, August saw Alice Cooper's 'School's Out' at No. 1, a song that was finally ousted in September by Rod Stewart ('You Wear Well') and Slade ('Mama Weer All Crazee Now'). Cassidy and Osmond, however, maintained a steady chart presence between 1972 and 1978 and, in Cassidy's case, this was largely attributable to his non-stop tours. As Barbara Ehrenreich observes (with reference to the early Beatles), 'the star could be loved noninstrumentally, for his own sake, and with complete abandon' (Ehrenreich et *et al.*, 1992, 97), and the mass hysteria that had accompanied their live performances was replicated by the screaming girls who consistently besieged David Cassidy. Their hysteria was equally critical to his marketing, and the status of teenager once again became more than a prelude to adulthood; 'it was a status to be proud of – emotionally and sexually complete in itself' (Ehrenreich et *et al.*, 1992, 98).

Cassidy's songs were carefully chosen to resonate with his appeal to a young audience. In 1972 he had climbed to No. 2 position in the UK charts with 'Could It Be Forever'/'Cherish' and No. 1 with his cover version of the Young Rascals's 'How Can I Be Sure'. 'Rock Me Baby' just failed to reach the Top 10 and in 1973 he was again in the charts with 'I'm A Clown'/'Some Kind of Summer' and his second UK No. 1, 'Daydreamer'/'The Puppy Song'. It is interesting to note that he was already 22 years old when he made his major inroads into the UK charts and that his repertoire largely consisted of songs raided from old catalogues that had already demonstrated an appeal to a teenage audience. These included 'If I Didn't Care' (an Inkspots hit from the 1930s), the Beatles's 'Please Please Me' and the Beach Boys's 'Darlin'. By 1975, however, the demands made by touring were beginning to show and although he just failed to reach the UK Top 10 with 'I Write The Songs'/'Get It Up For Love', he turned increasingly to drugs and alcohol, returning to Los Angeles for what has been described as 'three dark years'.

'I'm a Believer'

While Richard and Cassidy provide two examples of teen pop idols, the fact that the Beatles provided four different fantasy figures (so allowing for a more diverse fan base) had not been lost on the music business. If rock 'n' roll had made mass hysteria probable, then the Beatles had made it inevitable. While it was also evident that not just anyone could be hyped as a suitable object for fandom, it was also apparent that the success of the Beatles had been augmented by their films, *A Hard Day's Night* and *Help!* What America clearly needed at the time was their own group, one that would rival the Beatles and generate their own 'home-grown' appeal. Recognising that an already existing group would cause problems in terms of identification, US TV producers Bob Rafelson and Bert Schneider (NBC-TV), armed with an advance from Columbia's Screen Gems, began auditions for a show about a struggling pop band. An advertisement in *Variety* resulted in 437 applications, including Stephen Stills, Danny Hutton (later of Three Dog Night) and Paul Williams. The final choice paired two musicians, Michael Nesmith (b. Robert Michael Nesmith, December 30, 1942, guitar/vocals) and folk singer Peter Tork (b. Peter Halsten Thorkelson, February 13, 1942, Washington, DC, USA, bass/vocals), with two budding actors and former child stars – Davy Jones (b. December 30, 1945, Manchester, England, vocals) and ex-Circus Boy star Micky Dolenz (b. George Michael Dolenz, March 8, 1945, Los Angeles. CA, USA, drums/vocals) (Kirkpatrick, 1985, 879). On September 12, 1966, the first episode of *The Monkees* appeared on NBC-TV and, despite low initial ratings, the show became hugely popular, a feat mirrored when it was launched in the UK. Attendant singles 'Last Train to Clarksville' and 'I'm a Believer' (US and UK No. 1) and a million-selling debut album confirmed the band as the latest teenage phenomenon.

The success of the Monkeys provided an important precedent for the successful marketing of future 'manufactured' bands. Essentially, the group were personality-driven, with Michael Nesmith being the only 'real' musician. Although he claims that 'he had no real interest in music until he was 20' (Logan and Woffinden, 1976, 167), his ability as a guitarist and songwriter had led to the production of an instrumental album of his own songs *The Wichita Train Whistle Sings* (1968), a reaction against The Monkees's continuous manipulation by NBC – at a press conference in 1967 he had told the world press that they were not allowed to play on their own records (Logan and Woffinden, 1976, 160). While Nesmith's confrontation was a contributory factor to the break-up of The Monkees, it also has a broader significance in highlighting the problem of maintaining a coherent group image. The Monkees were projected as fun-loving individuals who engaged in a string of band-related adventures, and their musical skills were initially considered less significant than their ability to relate to their TV audience. Not least, they were framed by the expectations of 'family viewing' – so inhibiting any real sense of 'authenticity' as an 'on the road' rock band. Group coherence also meant that the individual could not expect to generate a career 'off the set' – and it is interesting to note here that for many teenagers The Monkees were perceived as a 'real band', 'just like the Beatles', hence NBC's restriction on Nesmith who, it seemed, was following John Lennon's example in releasing his own material as an 'individual' artist. The second important precedent lies in the role played by The Monkees's musical director, Don Kirshner and his team of thoroughbred songwriters. Within their two-year 'life span', The Monkees had earned ten gold records, so demonstrating that 'manufactured groups', given the right material and the right coaching, could achieve international success. Finally, it is evident that real musical talent will cause the individual to break away, so leaving the remaining members with a real problem. Nesmith formed his own group, The First National Band, shortly after his confrontation with management. The band was signed by RCA in 1968 and his 1970 album, *Magnetic South*, contained a single, 'Joanne', that was so successful that it attracted cover versions by amongst others Andy Williams and the band Loose Salute. The others were less successful. Tork left The Monkees 'after the disastrous movie, *Head*, which tried so hard to be hip that it alienated the last vestiges of their original pubescent audience' (Logan and Woffinden, 1976, 160). Jones and Dolenz tried to reform the band with Tommy Boyce and Bobby Hart, who had written many of The Monkees's biggest hits. After a US tour they quietly disbanded.

Rollermania

The appeal of image-driven groups continued throughout the 1970s and 1980s. The Bay City Rollers, from Edinburgh, Scotland, were the next in line to be acclaimed as 'the biggest phenomenon to hit the UK pop music scene since the Beatles'. Originally a Beatles cover band, based around two brothers, Derek

Longmuir (b. March 19, 1955, drums) and Alan Longmuir (b. June 20, 1953, bass), they were joined by Les McKeown (b. November 12, 1955, vocals), Stuart 'Woody' Wood (b. February 25, 1957, guitar) and Eric Faulkner (b. October 21, 1955, guitar). Although the line-up of the band was shuffled quite regularly during the early 1970s, their manager Tam Paton drove them relentlessly, overlooking the fact that the band – as it finally evolved – possessed no more than ordinary talent (Kirkpatrick, 1985, 879). Once again, it was the astute management and a succession of carefully chosen singles – mostly by Bill Martin and Phil Coulter (bespoke songwriters for many years and whose repertoire includes Britain's first outright winner of the Eurovision Song Contest, Sandie Shaw's 'Puppet on a String'), that enabled the group to reach the heights they did. Not least, accusations that they didn't play on their records became irrelevant as both their fan-base and media coverage grew. Predictably, all their songs were teen-directed and included such innocuous ditties as 'Summertime Sensation' and 'Shang-A-Lang'. 'Rollermania' (as the press predictably termed the group's almost fanatic girl-fan following) was, however, triggered by their cover version of the Four Seasons's song 'Bye Bye Baby' and daily press coverage of their nationwide tour. It is also significant that the Rollers had originally sewn a tartan stripe onto their cut-off jeans (a cheap way of initially attracting a group identity) and adopted a tartan scarf as part of their image. Fans nationwide quickly followed suit and so triggered the marketing strategy of producing cheap give-aways in the teen-oriented magazines – tartan framed photo-holders with pin up pictures of the band being but one example. However, it was not simply their management that initiated success. The band themselves were determined to conquer the US and a No. 1 success, 'Saturday Night', consolidated their efforts in 1976.

The ages of any teen-based pop band are clearly important. Ideally, they should both instigate worship whilst maintaining an image of 'the boy next door'. As discussed in Nursery Crymes (pp. 56–61), 'Little Girls' (pp. 65–70) and 'Little Boys' (pp. 125–136), the problems associated with 'who is eligible' in terms of appeal is critical to both individual and group success. Today, as the age range for both pop stars and pop idols indicates, it is recognised as lying between the ages of 16 and 25. Reaching the age of 26, then, presents problems – not least when a pre-pubescent fan club relates to the fresh-faced boyishness that accompanied their early years. The first to recognise the problem was Alan Longmuir, whose place was filled by 18-year-old Ian Mitchell, who in turn left to be replaced by Pat McGlynn. Curiously, the change in band membership made little difference to their popularity and Rollermania continued unabated until 1977 when McGlynn also left the group. However, it would be naive to think that a band whose average age is 19 (or 22 prior to Longmuir's departure) would match the squeaky-clean image (virginal and teetotal) promoted by their management. Increasingly the press moved in, and over the next three years their constant surveillance of the group was rewarded. McKeown was charged with reckless driving after hitting and killing a widow aged 73. Eric Faulkner and Alan Longmuir attempted suicide, and Paton was put in jail for committing indecent acts with underage teenagers.[36] Meanwhile, Ian Mitchell starred in a pornographic movie and Billy Lyall died from an AIDS-related illness in 1989.

'Do What U Like'?

The unsavoury end to the Bay City Rollers, arguably one of the most famous teeny-bop groups in British pop history, provided yet another lesson for the managers and members of would-be pop groups. 'Little Boys' must live up to their image – a point not lost on boy-group Wham! (the most successful teen-oriented group of the 1980s), whose founder member George Michael was finally outed in 1998 after years of denial that he was, in fact, a closet gay. The *Daily Mirror*'s jubilant 'Zip Me Up Before You Go Go' (April 8, 1998) is but one example of the pleasure the press seem to get from their relentless pursuit of star-based gossip.[37] It seemed, then, that any new boy group would not only have to have the right image, but also that the management would have to ensure that there was nothing 'nasty in the woodshed' for the press to home in on. By 1990, the advent of Take That provided the perfect image. The boys were all from the north-west and were an all-vocal group, thus setting the precedent for future boy bands. Members were as follows: Gary Barlow (b. January 20, 1971, Frodsham, Cheshire, lead vocalist), Howard Donald (b. April 28, 1968, Droylsden, Manchester), Jason Orange (b. July 10, 1970, Manchester), Mark Owen (b. January 27, 1972, Manchester) and Robbie Williams (b. February 13, 1972, Port Vale). Take That released their debut single 'Do What U Like' on their own Dance UK label in July 1991. Much of the attendant publicity surrounded the risqué video that accompanied it, featuring the band revealing their buttocks. The attendant furore attracted the attention of RCA records who signed the band in September, and 'Promises' reached No. 38 on the UK charts two months later. In February 1992 'Once You've Tasted Love' reached No. 47, coinciding with a 'Safe Sex' club tour undertaken with the support of the Family Planning Association. By June, they had broken through to No. 7 on the UK charts with 'It Only Takes A Minute'. By this time the press were reporting on their clean-cut (with the exception of the bearded Orange) good looks, dance routines and simple, catchy songs. Their popularity was confirmed by the receipt of seven trophies at the *Smash Hits* Poll Winners Party Awards in December, an effective barometer of the prevailing tastes of the UK's teen market. The following year, their debut album was revived and climbed to No. 2 in the British charts, and they finally achieved their first No. 1 chart single with 'Pray' (July 1993). Over the next two years they achieved a total of eight No. 1 singles in Britain (Kirkpatrick, 1985, 1204).

As Paul McDonald observes, much of Take That's success was attributable to their videos which always focused on the spectacle of the male body. For 'Pray' (dir. Greg Masuak), '[t]hey appear from between a line of pillars. First Howard, elegantly curving his arms over his head. Then Robbie, who brings his hands together in prayer. Jason emerges, bends, and arches his back. Gary just sort of stands. Finally, Mark saws the air with his arms. For most of the video the boys will individually occupy separate spaces, each lost in his own world …' (McDonald, 1999, 277). The appeal is arguably voyeuristic. Throughout the video, 'areas of intimate flesh are offered to the viewer by the various states of undress displayed by the boys. Additionally, lighting, colour and make-up contribute to presenting the flesh of these bodies as a smooth, firm, surface … a spectacle to be desired' (MacDonald, 1997, 278–9). Above all, the video signifies a mood of romantic yearning. What is obvious, however, is that this yearning is non-specific in terms of gender and, in common with their other videos, the boys' portrayal of enjoyment results largely from their engagement with male-to-male looking –whether in a gym, a beach, a café bar or a nightclub setting. It is a performance style that is equally recognised in Boyzone and, more recently, Westlife. What is important, however, is that the homoerotic connotations are contained. Seven years after the break-up of Take That, and having established himself as Britain's top pop idol, Robbie Williams continues to deny any rumours that he is gay and the press continues to pick up on any new romance.[38]

Pop idols

The lessons on how to launch, build and maintain a successful boy group is closely related to the attributes of the single pop idol. In both cases they have to be young (between the ages of 16 and 25), clean living, attractive and hetero-sexual. Mixed race has also proved useful in extending the fan base, as instanced in, for example, East 17, but in all instances the emphasis lies on fun and enjoyment, and while there are homoerotic associations these are carefully contained within an often dance and party mode which represents utopian solu-tions and pleasures rather than specific gender-inflected scenarios. It is also apparent that within the pop arena the notion of 'manufactured' no longer attracts derisory comments. Rather, it seems to confirm that the 'boy-next-door' really can be the next big thing, and that the consumer really possesses the power to make him the next 'pop idol'. Clearly, this is largely illusory, and builds on the myth earlier established by the Beatles fan club that they were 'who they were because girls like them had made them that … Fans knew of the Beatles' lowly origins and knew they had risen from working-class obscurity to world fame on the acoustical power of thousands of shrieking fans. Adulation created stars, and stardom, in term, justified adulation' (Ehrenreich et et al., 1992, 103). Reality TV has simply taken that power one step further. Based on the success of Big Brother, a simple phone call can now determine who is to be the next 'pop idol'.

In my earlier discussion of girl/boy groups ('Nursery Crymes', pp. 60–1) I mentioned briefly the growing popularity of ITV's interactive programme Pop Idol. By February 2002, it had become somewhat of a phenomenon, attracting nearly 15 million viewers for its last showing. At a cynical level, it's a fusion concept, taking something from the talent show and the 'drop the loser' vote of reality TV's *Big Brother*. Starting with televised open auditions across the UK, it moved to regional and national finals until just ten hopefuls were left. The 'serious' business of viewers' phone calls then took over and one desperate hopeful was dropped each week until four remained, three boys and one girl, Zoë Birkett, who was then voted off by a largely 'little girl' vote.

Will, Gareth and Darius all appeared to fulfil the established criteria of 'boys your mum would approve of'. They were clonishly bright and good looking without being overtly handsome, and they all sang with what A.A. Gill describes as 'a rather spooky adult-manqué assurance' (2002, 7). Simon Cowell, one of the judges, and Simon Fuller (the man responsible for S Club 7 and the Spice Girls) who came up with original concept, admitted that they were looking 'for someone like David Cassidy (if it was a boy) and Britney Spears (if it was a girl)', so eliminating from the onset the hopefuls who were either 'fat' or Eminem clones. Predictably, Darius was voted out in the run-up to the final heat (but nevertheless topped the pop charts in August 2002), leaving Will Young (aged 22, boyish, with a lop-sided smile and a velvety smooth voice) and Gareth Gates, described as a 'Barbie boy' (Woods, 2002, 12), whose stutter when talking and his determination to overcome this problem when speaking to the judges, to comperes Ant and Dec and to his growing fan-base, had made him the country's favourite contestant.

I was invited to speak on the topic of pop idols prior to the final. The fact that the broadcast was on BBC's *Drive Time* is an indication of its broad-based popularity. My 'agenda' was to predict who would win – and this time I got it wrong, by choosing Gareth – and to talk about the phenomenon itself. While I made the points that this was no new thing (citing such examples as Cliff Richard, David Cassidy and manufactured boy and girl groups), one key point was dropped in the broadcast edit: the fact that my students feel shamed by the fact that their generation will be remembered as 'the generation of manufac-tured groups and pop idols'. While this doesn't infer that those who reach the top of the charts are untalented, it does suggest that the UK has been wooed by karaoke, and that success relies on supplying the most appealing cover version of well-established teen-oriented classic. Will's debut single (a double A-side) was released through BMG records on February 25 and, predictably, went straight to the top of the singles charts. The songs had already been heard during the finals – 'Evergreen' (Westlife) and 'Anything Is Possible' (written by Cathy Dennis)[39] – with Will also 'crooning' 'Light My Fire' (The Doors) and Gareth 'Unchained Melody' (Righteous Brothers).

My interview also gave me an opportunity to ask about 'who votes'. While it was confirmed that young girls are in the majority, I was also told that the 'older' vote was drawn largely from the C2/D viewer. Its successful format is evidenced by its viewing figures which swelled to ten million, with the famous vote registering 8.7 million phone calls and many more complaining of blocked lines. The back-ground of the two would-be pop idols is also interesting: Will Young is a university graduate and the son of a company director from Hungerford, Berkshire; Gareth Gates is a student at a college of technology and son of a postman from Bradford. There is, then, an interesting North–South, rich–poor divide which has been cynically described as 'piquant and perhaps even convenient' (Woods, 2002, 12) in creating distinctive personalities for Will and Gareth. What has driven them both, however, is the lure of fame, and Britain is well experienced in creating celebrities, as evidenced last year by the chart-topping group Hear'Say. For me, the success of *Pop Idol* opened up the old debate of what influences most what we hear – the media, the producer, or the consumer. Ostensibly the consumer has been seen to have some power in voting Will 'Pop Idol', so massaging their perceived power while providing free market research; the media has also demon-strated its very real presence in capitalising on reality TV formats and in attracting viewers. What this signals is that the phenomenon is not based on fame, let alone music, but on people power in a multimedia world. Clearly this is significant in that satellite and digital channels have fragmented audiences and, as such, the potential offered by reality TV is to give viewers active involvement in programmes. It is also apparent that manufactured stars have a built-in obsoles-cence and that there is potential for further contests – as evidenced by the *Fame Academy* auditions (August 2002). As Peter Bazalgette, head of the British company that makes *Big Brother* observes: 'You can vote, you can affect the outcome. Here is fantastic weaponry to let people get involved. We haven't begun to invent all the ways you can do it'.[40] This must also be good news for British Telecom, who reported that more than 57 million calls were made to the two numbers (Will/Gareth). This is equal to one call for every person in Britain. Up to one million people attempted to get through every second on the 28,000 dedi-cated lines, and at 10p a call, this generated £870,000.

Even so, it is surely the producers who gain most. *Pop Idol* may have been made by Thames Television, but 'Simon Fuller and his team have already signed up all 10 finalists with contracts that reportedly give Fuller's company, 19 Management, a 20% cut of future earnings for up to 12 years, and an option on a 10% cut for a further six years. The runners up are also legally prevented from releasing a single within the next three months. Further, the programme's most "hated" judge, Simon Cowell, is a director of the record label BMG, which released the winner's single – a cover version of Westlife song 'Evergreen' (Wood, 2002, 12). If Young proves to be a one-hit wonder, then there's nine others to promote and with the heavily plugged Wembley concert (February 17, 2002) featuring all ten finalists, it would seem a no-losers situation. Gareth Gates and Will Young – despite his being outed – are now confirmed chart-toppers, but is that such a surprise? With 50 years of experience in finding the right face at the right time, producers have simply confirmed the old adage that they are the main creative force behind pop stars and mainstream success.

Even so, pop idols must have more than the right image and the ability to cover teen-oriented songs if they are to survive. They must, above all, toe the line, and that means that 'Little Boys' should be able to engage not only with the targeted fan group but also with the mums and dads, thus ensuring a wider audience base for when they move into the arena of mass entertainment. Robbie Williams provides the latest insight into the transition from pop idol to entertainer. As Mark Edwards cuttingly writes: 'One of the most irritating things about 2001 was the immediate success of Robbie William's 'Swing When You're Winning'. Yes, he's a great pop performer; yes, he's covering great songs; but he does it really badly. The album's rapid sales sadly prove that people still buy the brand name on the cover, not the content of the CD inside' (2002, 7). There is, then, an indication that the general public no longer mind that they are being manipulated and that the star's image is more powerful than the quality of their music. However, as Edwards notes, 'it's a good thing that our manufactured pop, like our processed food, is clearly labelled'.[41] How sad, then, that it took George Harrison's death to remind us what real song-writing talent is about and what the title 'pop star' really means. Perhaps, then, it is time for 'Little Boys' to grow up, and for the record-buying public to expect more than cloned idols and regurgitated oldies.

Postscript

Life after death: Old Girls and Old Boys

As my discussion so far indicates, age is critical to the identity of both performers and musical genres. For teen-directed pop, the dividing line between youthful attraction and being 'over the hill' occurs around the age of 25. For the rock star, the creed of 'live fast, die young' has led to the deaths of many of its most prominent performers. The question is thus raised of what happens to popular music's 'old boys and old girls' when they exit from the fast lane of superstardom and, more specifically, is there any way back?

It would seem, perhaps, somewhat of a truism to observe that stars live on as long as they embody what their fans think they represent. While the enshrining of Morrison and Hendrix provides a particular insight into the cult of dead heroes, the 25th anniversary of Elvis Presley's death, age 42, has shown that he is suddenly once again hip. While his fans may have mourned his somewhat ignoble death, on August 16, 1977, slumped in front of his toilet bowl, his gold pyjamas round his ankles, his face in a puddle of vomit, for the majority he had become little more than a somewhat grotesque has-been who bore little resemblance to the strutting superstar of the 1950s. Addicted to amphetamines, sleeping pills and junk food and working in cabaret in Las Vegas, his misfortune, it seemed, had been to live to middle age and in his last years he was bloated almost beyond recognition. As Philip Norman observes: 'The terrible anti-climax of his final years and ignominy of his death all but blotted out the towering achievement of his life … "Good career move", commented one executive at his record company on hearing of his end' (2002, 20).

As discussed earlier (Little Boys, pp. 127–9), Presley's significance for the image and attitude of rock is undeniable, and his early classics ('Blue Suede Shoes', 'Hound Dog', 'All Shook Up'), which led to his title 'King of Rock 'n' Roll', were such that the Beatles's aim to be 'Bigger than Elvis' seemed, at the time, no mean objective. Nearly 40 years later, the release of his 1968 track 'A Little Less Conversation' (featured earlier in Nike's World Cup TV commercial) gave Presley his 18th UK No. 1, so moving him to top position on 'most sold singles', a position previously shared with the Beatles. All thirty hits – including those not heard by Elvis himself – are featured on a new compilation album (released September 23, 2002) with the expectation of equalling Beatles worldwide sales of their '1' album. The old rivalry, then, still exists – albeit as another shrewd move on the part of the record producers.

The album also stimulated a renewed interest in Presley's thirty-one films. *Love Me Tender* (1956) was produced by David Weisbert, who had previously worked on James Dean's *Rebel Without a Cause*. While the movie received mixed reviews, the title track topped the US charts for five weeks. *Loving You* (1957) was quasi-autobiographical, with Presley playing a truck driver who becomes a pop star. The title track became the B-side of '(Let Me Be Your) Teddy Bear', which was No. 1 on the singles charts for seven weeks. *Jailhouse Rock* (1957) followed, and the Leiber and Stoller track again topped the US charts for seven weeks and made pop history by entering the UK listings at No. 1. While his early films, including *King Creole* (1958) and *Flaming Star* (1960), are remembered more for his magnetic presence than for his acting ability, the post-*Blue Hawaii* (1961) films are characterised by his increasing 'tameness', the somewhat absurd plots and the poor quality of the songs (Larkin, 1999, 991). As John Lennon once observed, 'Elvis died when he joined the army'. Even so, as Joe Queenan writes, 'None of us will ever witness a phenomenon like Elvis Presley's movie career; he could literally get away with murder … No pop star before or since ever achieved what Elvis did: the landscape is littered with the bones of his imitators' (2002, 4).

It is a curious fact that Presley died with a book on the Turin shroud beside him. While this may have related to his own religious beliefs, it also invites a speculative comparison on the mystical power of resurrection and the quasi-religious respect of his fans – 'If you haven't got Elvis in your life, then you haven't got a life'.[1] The jubilee anniversary of his death, when over 30,000 fans visited his home at Gracelands and countless more celebrated his memory worldwide, provides some indication of the continuing reverence in which he is held. Somewhere between a vigil (with candles burning throughout the night) and a belief that his presence lives on through impersonation, the night curiously resembled the grandeur of his original funeral where crowds had lined the two-mile route to the cemetery and the states of Tennessee and Mississippi had each declared a day of mourning.

While the Elvis cult appears somewhat tacky for those not committed to 'the King', the fact that his fans celebrate, through impersonation, all aspects of his career is, at the same time, rather touching. The more youthful appear as the hip-swivelling rock 'n' roller of the 1950s, while the more paunchy Elvis of his later years is evidenced in the countless oldies, resplendent in the white suits characteristic of his cabaret days. The 'parable of how sour sweet music can turn; how horribly wrong genius can go' (Norman, 2002, 23) is forgotten as fans relive the 'feel good' moments when Elvis became part of their lives. For the majority it seems that he will always remain 'the all American boy', one who chose to do his military service whilst at the height of his career, and whose death prompted President Carter to say that something unique had gone out of American life.

Clearly it hasn't. Yet while Elvis provides a specific example of how super-stardom can fall apart, 'his terrible example has pulled many another pop icon back from the brink of self-destruction, notably Elton John, who never forgot meeting the near-death 'King', by then a barely coherent blubber ball with bluish hair dye trickling into his once-mesmeric eyes' (Norman: 2002, 23). John Lennon's 'retirement' in the late 1970s, when he opted out of megastardom to become a family man, was also prompted by his decision to avoid the Elvis trap. It is also evident that his move from rock to family entertainment and his prolific acting career provided a blueprint for other stars confronting the perennial problem of making money when their music was no longer fashionable. For Presley, the principal threat came from the Rolling Stones, the Beatles and Bob Dylan, when the corny *Viva! Las Vegas!* demonstrated, once and for all, that he was no longer a threat to middle America.

The Beatles, Mick Jagger and Bob Dylan also moved into films, but while the former's escapades in *A Hard Day's Night* (1964), *Help!* (1965), *Yellow Submarine* (1968) and *Magical Mystery Tour* (1968) retain their sense of naive commentary on the 1960s and contain many of their best songs, Mick Jagger's impersonation of Ned Kelly, the Australian highwayman, is remembered more for his extraordinary accent and unconvincing performance. Prince and Madonna have also met with less than complimentary reviews, and the closest to Elvis's crossover success are the careers of Cher and Will Smith. Even so, the record of his thirty-one money-making films remains unchallenged, albeit that the majority were badly made and undeniably corny. His success lay, perhaps, in always being Elvis. When he reverted back to a centre-stage position, singing one of his hits as the role-playing momentarily ended, the magic returned.

As discussed in Part III, Cliff Richard was among the first to follow in the 'King's' footsteps and to move into films. He also starred as Heathcliff in the much-maligned musical of the same name, but today it is not simply the star who attracts attention. Rather, the urge to recreate, through musicals, the euphoria attached to stars during the heyday of their careers is, it seems, more successful than a sideways move into cinema. The 13-year run of the Buddy Holly show has led to discussions of a follow-up on Elvis. While there have been other Elvis musicals, this focuses on 'Presley's triumphant return from Hollywood to live performance in 1968, when nobody on the planet was sexier and he still had a thirty-inch waist. Though there will be pointers to the tragedy ahead, it will be essentially a 'feel good' show',[2] a characteristic that is also shared with *Mama Mia!* which helped make Abba Gold a permanent fixture in the compilation charts, and *We Will Rock You* which propelled Queen's Greatest Hits to the Top 3 position. With Boy George's *Taboo* still running (as of August 2002) the 'theatre listings are starting to resemble *Smash Hits* circa 1985' (Paterson, 2002, 21).

It would seem, then, that the earlier trend towards cover versions is now being matched by an increasing number of shows with the aim of kick-starting back-catalogue sales. *Our House*, features Madness and the sliding doors narrative device of showing the two different paths a life can take. Erasure are also developing a show in which Andy Bell will play a man having to deal with his sexuality in the late 1980s. The trend is also evident in the USA with *Signed, Sealed and Delivered: The Stevie Wonder Story* playing in Los Angeles with Chaka Khan(!) in the leading role, and *Movin' Out*, based on twenty-six Billy Joel classics opening on Broadway in October 2002. The extent to which nostalgia can be relied on to compensate for the almost karaoke-like performances of singers playing lost heroes is debatable. What is evident is that the late 1990s and the early years of the twenty-first century have seen an unprecedented number of cover versions of golden hits and a string of TV programmes inviting the viewer to enjoy 'the best of …'.

Celebrating the past, which was arguably accelerated by the turn of the millennium, is one way of triggering a presence in the charts for old heroes. Becoming a celebrity is another, as evidenced by the Queen's Jubilee Gig at Buckingham Palace. While the thought of rock being simply another form of entertainment may well appal those who continue to defend its authenticity, it nevertheless seems that some notorious rebels were more than willing to jeopardise their iconic status by performing for the Queen and her family. Predictably, such establishment figures as Sir Elton John, Sir Paul McCartney and Sir Cliff Richard were there, but three inspiring moments stand out. The first was guitarist Brian May playing the national anthem on the roof of Buckingham Palace. Wearing a suit emblazoned with the words 'Purple Haze', the sense of anticipation was mesmeric. For those who remember Jimi Hendrix's performance of the 'Star Spangled Banner' at Woodstock, where feedback and sustain provided a chilling musical allegory of the war in Vietnam, and which segued into the acid-inspired 'Purple Haze', there was a double irony. 'Star Spangled Banner' was a vision of cultural crisis, an interpretation of history and a commentary on the tragic follies of patriotism which posited the hallucinogenic as a positive way out. In contrast, May played the British national anthem straight, albeit with the odd string-bend, but the question marks remained. Were the celebrations of the Queen's Jubilee another instance of misplaced patriotism as connoted by May's homage to Hendrix? For Queen fans, there was a double irony and a more overt connotation. Mass singing of 'God Save the Queen' became a regular custom at their performances long before the band recorded their version in 1975 for their album, *A Night At The Opera*. The size of audiences at a Queen concert (typically in excess of 70,000) also suggests that the fans enthusiastic singing of the National Anthem turned its more nationalistic connotations into one of camp revelry. Add to that the fact that Freddie Mercury was often seen on tours wearing either jackets emblazoned with the Union Jack, or with the flag draped around his shoulders, and that the UK and the USA banned a special edition CD containing 'We Are the Champions' and 'Another One Bites the Dust' – issued to American troops in the Gulf War (1990) and the ironies compound. Just which Queen was May saluting? The 'White Queen', the 'Black Queen', 'Killer Queen' or HRH Queen Elizabeth? As the rock world might well comment, 'Heavy!'

For the media, the principal attraction, and one which inspired most dread on the part of the establishment, was the appearance of Ozzy Osbourne whose band, Black Sabbath, was notorious for such doom-laden metal as *Paranoid* (1970) and *Sabbath Bloody Sabbath* (1974). Well-known for courting publicity, most famously in 1982 when he had to undergo treatment for rabies following an onstage incident when he bit off the head of a bat, Osbourne's satanic, werewolf image seemed an unlikely choice for the Buck House gig, albeit that his popular MTV series *The Osbournes* has become compulsive viewing in Britain. As a hard rocker who has tried every excess and survived, his arrival on stage, replete with black coat and make-up, was met with a certain nervous anticipation. As ever, his performance was inspiring, albeit de-fanged, but again a question mark remained. Had he become simply another celebrity, a pantomime villain, willing to act out excess for the sake of royal patronage?

My third moment was Queen performing the quintessential rock/pop song 'Bohemian Rhapsody'. Featuring the transvestite look-alike Freddie Mercury, star of their new show *We Will Rock You*, there was a curious sense of *déjà vu*, enhanced by video clips of the original line-up and a staggeringly bravura performance by May. While the overall effect was one of staginess, so showcasing rock as entertainment, the fact Queen had been notorious for Mercury's outrageous camp theatrics and decadent lifestyle, provided an underlying edginess. The pomp and circumstance that had previously attended his performances, and which was still evident in the band's homage to Mercury, effected a curious reflection on the Queen's Jubilee celebration itself. In terms of bravura performance Queen outclassed Her Majesty as she watched with what appeared to be a benign passivity.

In retrospect the Jubilee gig was significant not only in showcasing rock as entertainment, but equally in rock storming the bastion of respectability, Buckingham Palace, in the presence of the Queen and her family. Ending with an unprecedented fireworks display, and with the guests fed and watered by a picnic provided by the Queen, it was, in many ways, a very British affair. Yet, the fact that the evening was dominated by performances by the so-called deviants of the rock world suggests that rebels can now be considered part of the establishment. Being gay, being a casualty of drugs (as evidenced by Brian Wilson's static performance), even being Ozzy Osbourne, is no longer a threat. Rather, their identities are locked in the past. They have become simply celebrities whose rebellious status has been tamed by age and familiarity.

It is also a sad fact that there were no contemporary rock groups performing. Rather, it seems, that the best of British is characterised by past glories. This was also evidenced by Channel 4's *Top Ten Guitar Heroes* (June, 2001). While my agenda was to discuss why there were no women lead guitarists, it did provide an opportunity to discuss with the producers the criteria behind their choice. This was based both on the number of UK top albums (and the average here was ten, with many scoring higher) and research into 'Who is the best?', determined largely through votes by a representative sample of the public. As such, consistently innovative bands like Metallica, with lead guitarist James Hetfield, were notably missing. It was also apparent that copyright affected the end result. I had asked whether Keith Richards, lead guitar of the Rolling Stones, had been considered for the 'Top Ten', but was told that permission could not be obtained for showing their early performances and extracts from their repertoire. As Alan Klein had earlier refused permission for me to reproduce extract lyrics and transcriptions for my chapter on the Stones in *Sexing the Groove*, and is well known in the media for prohibiting TV transmission on histories of famous groups for whom he holds copyright, I could well understand Channel 4's problem. However, it does serve to perpetuate the myth that the Rolling Stones were simply a loud-mouthed group, more famous for their macho performances and lifestyle than their musicality, and Richards is clearly a notable omission from the 'Top Ten' stable.

The final line-up, however, was interesting in that it privileged innovation, transatlantic success and influence rather than the criteria of dexterity and sheer speed that characterises such virtuoso guitarists as Yngwie Malmsteen. At the same time, the list provides one, albeit national, perspective on 'Old Boys' as – with the notable exception of Jimi Hendrix – the nine other guitar heroes are still alive and performing, albeit that their inclusion celebrated past glories. At number 10, *Johnny Marr*'s tough yet tender melodic style coupled with his spring-heeled rhythm had earned his place as defining the style of the 1980s guitar hero, not least for his performances with The Smiths. He later became known as the best-known session musician in the business, playing with, amongst others, Bryan Ferry, Talking Heads, Billy Bragg, Kirsty McColl, the Pet Shop Boys, Stex and Banderas, as well as The Pretenders, The The and Electronic. (*Age at time of transmission 38.*)

Ritchie Blackmore (Deep Purple) was number 9, most notably venerated for 'putting the heavy in metal' and for his unpredictable guitar sound which made Deep Purple a true opponent of Led Zeppelin during the early 1970s. Known equally for shuffling his band members, he is now into the medieval, playing simply 'music that's dear to me'. (*Age at time of transmission,* 56.) *Carlos Santana*'s free-playing, sexy yet spiritual style of guitar playing accounts for his continuing popularity and earned him the number 8 position. Originally the pioneer of Afro-Latin rock, he is noted for being uncommercial (he has turned down invitations to perform from the Pope and Bill Clinton) and is committed to following his personal sense of direction. He appeared at Woodstock II (1994), rekindling memories of the his incendiary performance at the original festival, and has played with such legendary performers as Bob Dylan, Herbie Hancock, Wayne Shorter, Willie Nelson and Booker T. Jones, so demonstrating his thoughtful and versatile musicianship as well as his impressive guitar playing. (*Age at time of transmission,* 54.) In contrast, *Dave Evans* ('The Edge'), in at number 7, is best known for his mercurial guitar style, the continuing success of U2 as Britain's top stadium band and their standing as an international group whose work has been unusually consistent and coherent, not least in their political idealism (Amnesty International, Live Aid, anti-Apartheid and Ireland's religious and political conflicts, especially in the key track 'Sunday Bloody Sunday'). Evans has also composed for films (writing the *Goldeneye* James Bond film theme for Tina Turner). (*Age at time of transmission*, 40.)

Pete Townshend, the Mod-father who didn't die before he got old, was given position number 6 and was considered the best all-round guitar player and song-writer 'ever'. Initially famous for his controversial showmanship ('axe and amp thrashing'), his band, The Who, became one of the biggest in the world and, according to the *Guinness Book of Records*, 'the loudest'. Townshend is also famous for his 'big ideas', and as one of rock's most literate and thoughtful talents has not only written such rock operas as *Tommy* and *Quadrophenia*, but has been a consultant editor for Faber and Faber, and composed a musical adaptation of poet Ted Hughes's famous children's story, the *Iron Man*, which featured cameos from several musicians, including John Lee Hooker. In the 1990s his early hits again became fashionable due to the Mod revival and Blur's top selling album, *Parklife*. Sadly, Who bassist John Entwistle died a year after 'Top Ten' was transmitted (June 29, 2002), the day before the band was due to begin their American tour. Characteristically, Townshend decided that the tour should continue as a tribute; Robert Plant (Led Zeppelin) took his place. (*Age at time of transmission*, 56.) *Brian May* was placed in fifth position, a reminder that while Queen was known for the androgynous strutting of Freddie Mercury, their status within rock was largely attributable to May's intelligent lead guitar playing. (*Age at time of transmission*, 54.)

I don't think I would have predicted *Hank Marvin*'s position at number 4, despite his significance for the early years of British rock 'n' roll. However, as Cliff Richard recalled on the programme, the girls related to him, the boys to Hank, adopting his black-rimmed glasses (albeit without lenses) as a tribute to his extraordinary talent. Richard had bought him a pink Stratocaster guitar (imported from the US) and Marvin built his career around its sound. His recording of 'Apache' changed the world for would-be guitarists in the early 1960s and has subsequently become the most sampled music in rap. Today, he still plays the same repertoire in a style which is remarkable for its economic sound – metallic, echoed picking, with a seeming lack of bravura virtuosity. (*Age at time of transmission*, 60.) *Jimmy Page*, number 3, started, like Marvin before him, in skiffle, learning rock as a session musician with such established performers as Petula Clarke and Tom Jones. He then moved to the Yardbirds, then the New Yardbirds before forming Led Zeppelin. Noted for never tidying up 'bum notes' in his recordings, he instigated death-music ('while I'm killing you, you'll love me'), riffs ('obvious, but you'd wish you'd thought of them') and excess (both musically and in his lifestyle). His virtuoso guitar style continued to attract attention throughout the 1970s and 1980s, not least in 'Stairway to Heaven' (1972), and his stage performances were characterised by his famous double-necked guitar. The death of drummer, John Bonham, and his continuing fascination with the occult and Alistair Crowley contributed towards the break-up of the band and it was not until 1994 that Page and Robert Plant (vocalist) came together with their ironically titled *Unledded*, cementing their relationship with an album of new Page and Plant material in 1998. (*Age at time of transmission*, 55.)

I have to admit that I was curious about who would get the number one position and I had to wait until the transmission to see whether it would be Eric Clapton or Jimi Hendrix (my personal top two contestants). *Clapton*, despite his veneration as The King, came second, albeit dubbed by B.B. King 'this nation's greatest bluesman'. Clapton admitted to 'always wanting to be the best guitar player in the world' and it seemed that he was always a serious player, as evidenced by his earlier performances with super-group Cream (1966–8). He continues to be venerated as a guitarist's-guitarist and his albums, from the onset, have attracted critical acclaim. While he has changed his style of rock music countless times, he has always returned to his first love, the blues, and across his career has contributed to numerous artists' albums, including John Martyn, Phil Collins, Joe Cocker, Bob Dylan, Aretha Franklin, Howlin' Wolf, Sonny Boy Williamson, Alexis Korner, the Mothers of Invention and Stephen Stills amongst many others. He also appeared as the Preacher in Ken Russell's film of Pete Townshend's rock opera, *Tommy*. In 1998 he parted company with his long-time manager Roger Forrester, and spends time working with Crossroads, the drug rehabilitation centre he founded in Antigua, partly funded by the auction sale of over 100 of his personal guitars. It is, perhaps, a salutary reminder that Clapton was also addicted to heroin in the early 1970s and that it was due, in no small measure, to Pete Townshend's organisation of the now famous Eric Clapton At The Rainbow Concert that he booked into Dr Meg Patterson's Harley Street clinic for treatment rather than suffering a similar fate to that of *Jimi Hendrix*, the number 1 'guitar hero' (*Age at time of transmission*, 56.)

As Andy Ellis writes, 'The story of the electric guitar will forever be told in two parts: Before Jimi and After Jimi. Before Jimi, visionary players[3] used the instrument as a powerful voice *within* an accepted musical setting ... But when Jimi exploded on the scene with "Purple Haze", "Manic Depression", and "Third Stone From The Sun", in a flash we understood: Here was a *music* beyond anything ever heard before, conceived and born of electric guitar. The instrument was inseparable from the song' (1995, 200–1). Following Hendrix's death in 1970, it seemed that every guitarist in the public eye was making a personal testament to the beauty of his style (Potash, 1996. 53–80, 175–210). Many of his trademark licks became an immediate addition to every electric guitarist's vocabulary, and his use of effects and artful self-expression provided the means to access both moods and complex feelings. His musicianship and example has led to 'Hendrix-inspired black rock and white noise; Black Flag and white boys; new music and fusion jazz ... "If 60s Were 90s" by Beautiful People put Hendrix samples to an acid house/trance beat. The Kronos Quartet covered 'Purple Haze'. The Chili Peppers's Flea has a Hendrix tattoo covering part of his arm' (Potash, 1998, xviii). More tangentially, his ability as a mercurial guitarist, whose ability to exploit both effects (wah-wah and echo, for example, increasing both the rhythmic complexity of the line and timbral colour), volume (so enabling guitarists to take the leading role in bands) and amplification (so prolonging decay and enhancing long legato lines) provided successive generations of guitarists with a vocabulary that embraced both lyric beauty and demonic fire. Thirty years after his death, his talent and artistic vision continue to be the most influential in the history of electric guitar. Small wonder, then, that Hendrix was awarded first place.

At the most basic level, it would seem that the defining characteristics for top 'lead guitarists' are personal innovation and influence, and while the majority of those *Top Ten Guitar Heroes* have lived their lives in the fast lane, it does provide some initial evidence that not all heroes are dead heroes. Rather, rock's leading practitioners are 'what made the guitar happen'. Provided they can handle the associated lifestyle and its seemingly unavoidable association with drugs, then musicianship prevails and life continues – the average age of the Guitar Heroes, excluding Jimi Hendrix, was 52 at time of transmission. It also goes without saying that the majority composed their own music – or the guitar solos – and while interpretations (rather than cover versions) are also significant in such blues-based guitarists as Eric Clapton, originality, innovation and influence remain the cornerstones of their heroic status and the defining characteristics of authenticity in rock.[4]

With plaudits seemingly centred on past glories, both in terms of nostalgia, celebrity and status (as suggested in my discussion of Elvis, Buck House and Guitar Heroes), the question of maintaining a visible presence in the contemporary world of rock appears problematic. To an extent, success continues to depend largely upon the confirmation of past joys rather than a switch in direction. As such, Bruce Springsteen's latest album, *The Rising*, inspired by the response of New Yorkers to the strikes on the World Trade Centre (September 11, 2001) is an interesting development, albeit relevant to the blue-collar street poet from New Jersey. Acclaimed by his millions of fans as the world's greatest rock 'n' roll star, the 'Boss' (Bruce Springsteen, b. September 23, 1949, Freefold, NJ, USA) has always had the ability to communicate in a language 'ordinary people' understand and his new record displays the virtuosity that earlier characterised *Born to Run* (1975) and *Born in the USA* (1984).

Springsteen's principal motivation came from a bus ride when he saw, first hand, the devastation caused by the air strike. His first song, written shortly after, was about darkness and a lone fire-fighter disappearing upstairs to his death. Called 'Into the Fire' it was originally intended to be sung during a national telethon ten days later, but was not finished in time. It is now the centrepiece of the album and Springsteen's live performance at Asbury Park Convention Hall, New Jersey, July 26, 2002. Beginning with:

> the death rattle of a bagpipe swirl, it builds stealthily, each band member easing themselves into the instrumental backdrop as Springsteen sings, 'I heard you calling me/Then you disappeared into the fire'. By the time the

heart-stopping chorus invokes 'strength, faith, hope and love' people are looking at the fire officers present and tears are falling. It climaxes in a cappella fashion and if Springsteen has written a better song, few here have heard it. Likewise the ominous 'Worlds Apart' which is heralded by a muezzin call and Tyrell's fiddle, before its motif of despair swells into the afternoon's most beautiful moment. He doesn't need to mention 11 September: everybody knows.

(Aizlewood, 2002, 151)

While the memory of September 11 motivated the intentions behind the album, Springsteen's earlier involvement in political causes, such as the anti-apartheid project Sun City and the Human Rights Now! tour for Amnesty International has lent validity to his concern to communicate understanding and compassion – and to keep faith with his fans. 'I didn't set out to write a 9/11 album. I didn't want to write literally about what happened, but the emotion's in the air,[5] so although what happened that day informs all fifteen songs, it's not *about* 11th September per se. Rather, the songs are about loss, optimism and redemption and, significantly, are designed to be sung along to as much as sat down and listened to'. As John Aizlewood comments, 'By the second chorus of all-out rockers "Waitin' On A Sunny Day" and "Mary's Place", the crowd take over, to Springsteen's genuine delight. "That's fantastic!" he coos' (2002, 151).

While Springsteen's concern for human rights has led to politicians such as Bill Clinton expressing a love for his music, and Ronald Reagan appropriating 'Born in the USA' as a patriotic song for the Republicans (despite its sense of bitter disillusionment), his more contemplative side has not always attracted critical acclaim and his stylistic U-turns from hard rock to simple folk music have, in the past, perplexed both critics and fans alike. Rather, it is the more popular image of Springsteen that has been most applauded, the hard-rocker, dressed in jeans and a sweaty bandanna, punching out songs about his job, his motorbike, his girl friend and his hometown.

The Rising is Springsteen's first album in years and, as such, it is too soon to know whether it will be yet another instance of the roller-coasting ups and downs of his career. However, his well-honed feeling for the economically dispossessed, immigrants and other marginalised peoples – as evidenced in his earlier album *The Ghost of Tom Joad* (1995) – remains strongly in evidence and, together with the E Street Band (with saxophonist Clarence Clemons) and fiddler Soozie Tyrell, Springsteen's more contemplative mood does full justice to his feelings. Even, so, disaster themes do not sit easily in today's rock world, as evidenced by Sting's role as an environmentalist supporting the cause of the Amazon rain forests. It is not easy to capture the full depth of disasters, and the first anniversary of the September 11 terrorist attacks were already being capitalised on 'by record companies who are hoping their recordings will play a central role in setting the national mood' (Winnett, 2002, 5). U2 and

Coldplay are among the artists who have written songs about the assault on the World Trade Centre and the Pentagon and, along with Bruce Springsteen's new album, older songs by Sir Paul McCartney and Whitney Houston are likely to be re-released.

While Bono has a well-established reputation for aligning himself with quasi-political causes and has just recorded 'The Hands That Built America' which refers to the New York skyline and 'a day when innocence died', the fact that there appeared to be a competitive edge in finding the most 'fitting' record to top the charts in the weeks preceding the anniversary and which rivalled the traditional Christmas race is nauseating. As one record industry executive said: 'We need to get it right as there could be some really big sales worldwide' (Winnett, 2002, 5). It is hoped that Springsteen's new album will not be tarnished by what has already been termed 'the September 11 chart attack', but having already reached the top of the British album charts (August 2002), it seems that his integrity as the 'Boss' will override what appears to be yet another instance of manipulation by the zombies of the record industry.

What hope, then, for other ageing rock stars when they achieve celebrity status or who simply seem like golden oldies with one foot in the grave? One marketing ploy is the re-release of earlier triumphs, and currently this includes albums by Rick Astley, *Greatest Hits* ('Hits and far superior misses from the Will Young of his day'), Black Sabbath, *Reunion* ('Live at Birmingham NEC, plus two new studio cuts. Ozzy's opening words: "Yeaaah, you fuckaaahs!"'), Marc Bolan and T Rex, *Zinc Allow and the Hidden Riders of Tomorrow, Dandy in the Underworld, 20th Century Superstar Box Set* ('A glittering cache of Bolan treasures on the 25th anniversary of his death'), James Brown, *Original Funk Soul Brother* ('Live James Brown in the '80s – post-Golden Age, pre-prison') and David Axelrod, *Anthology Vol. 2* ('Sexagenarion composer/producer combs the archives again') (Q, October 2002, 122). Another strategy is to make yet another come-back, but once you have been banned by Radio 1 for being too old and your guitarist has had a quadruple heart bypass, is such an option really viable? Status Quo, often dubbed the unhippist band in the history of rock, clearly think so – 'We've got the old Quo vibe back'. They are also against any change in image. 'I can't stick all this Madonna-like reinvent yourself', says Rossi. 'We do what we do. For some reason it works' (Landesman, 2002, 9). Fans seem to agree, and for the first time in 12 years, they've appeared on *Top of the Pops* (their 70th appearance, September 13, 2002) and are back in the charts with their single, 'Jam Side Down', the promo for their album *Heavy Traffic*.

With their heyday in the 1970s, when their albums sold by the millions and they played to packed stadiums worldwide, Rossi's addiction to cocaine (he once confessed to spending £1,200 a week for 10 years) and the band's wild lifestyle were contributory factors in their demise and by the 1980s, as the hits began to dry up, it seemed that they were yet another casualty of rock excess. It appears, however, that their determination not to give in is paying off and that they have chosen the right moment to make their comeback. As Cosmo Landesman observes, 'The return of Status Quo comes at an interesting time. Wrinkly stars are shining brighter than ever before. Bruce Springsteen, 51, has just topped the British album chart with *The Rising* and Phil Spector, 62, has come out of retirement.' (2002, 9)

Most recently (July 2004) I received an e-mail from Paul Taylor (*Manchester Evening News*), raising these self-same issues and asking my thoughts on the never-ending returns of the 'wrinklies'. Writing about the numbers of rock and pop stars reaching what would, in an ordinary job, be retirement age, he drew attention to 'Phil Collins, the Shadows, Meat Loaf and Cher all playing in Manchester on what they say will be their last big tours. Simon and Garfunkel head our way on July 14 for what everyone knows will be their last UK performances. Yet the Stones roll on, James Brown looks mighty fine at 71, Chuck Berry and Lee Lewis play Manchester week beginning 12 July, and Eric Clapton has been touring again three years after saying he would retire from the road … and what are we to make of rock 'n' roll as the music of its best practitioners start to collect pensions and the headline act at Glastonbury this year is 62-year old Paul McCartney ?' At a cynical level, it seems that established performers today keep embarking on their Debut Farewells. 'The last' is followed by 'definitely the last' and so on, it seems *ad infinitum*. However, while the Andrew Ridgeleys of pop retire in their twenties, it does seem also that we continue to value and venerate those artists who made original contributions to the field of popular music, that as an audience (which today often spans the age range from teens to 60 year olds) we want to either hear or relive classic moments. Not least, as the generation that first developed rock we are, perhaps, selfish. We continue to consider it 'ours' and that, it seems, gives us the licence to both revisit the past and to enjoy such new acts as 'The Darkness' or (in my case) to enjoy the occasional visit to Manchester's Rock World.

It does seem, however, that our oldies and goldies are primarily male – with the obvious excpetion of Cher. Does this mean, then, that women in pop and rock are suffering the same fate as their sisters on stage and screen, where maturity all too often equals obscurity? Clearly women in rock do not enjoy the same mythologising as their male counterparts. Wendy O. Williams of Plasmatics, who paved the way for women in punk, was known for her wild stage performances and making the mohawk fashionable. Fearless, rebellious and sexual, she committed suicide on April 7, 1998, aged 48. Mia Zapata of Gits was raped and murdered while on her way home from a Seattle pub on July 7, 1993. Her death prompted friends to start Home Alive, educating women on self-defence and protection. Kristen Pfaff of Hole overdosed on heroin in 1994, two months after Kurt Cobain's death and Hole's heralded album, *Live Through This*. Bianca Halstead of Betty Blowtorch was killed in a car accident in 2001. Her album, *Are You Man Enough?* was released in the same year.[6] With the exception of Hole, there are no biographies in encyclopedias of popular music, and it would seem that the only woman in rock who has been subject to mythologising is Janis Joplin.[7] The rest, it appears, are only missed by their loyal fans.

Of those who have survived, Patti Smith (b. December 31, 1946, Chicago, Illinois) has become somewhat of a shamanic figure for her admirers. Her inspiration, as a rock icon and poet, lies in the synthesis of religious, political and artistic non-conformism, most specifically a sense of romanticism, which she tracks through the Bible, through French poetry (most notably Rimbaud), Native American art, abstract expressionism (de Kooning, Pollock) and rock (Jim Morrison, Jimi Hendrix and Bob Dylan). Above all, her identification with the art and spirituality of William Blake, as a political and religious artist who was often in opposition to his artistic peers and organised society, government and religion, has provided an inspiration for fusing her visionary insights with a politicised and often troubled interpretation of contemporary reality. Her early albums, *Horses* (1975) and *Radio Ethiopia* (1976), for example, provided an important link between the Beat culture of the 1950s and the urban violence of New York proto-punk in the mid-1970s; *Easter* (1978) included the powerful 'Because the Night' (co-written with Bruce Springsteen); *Dream of Life* (1988) embraced both idealism ('People Have The Power') while reflecting her continuing respect for the rock and poetic tradition. Following the death of her husband (MC5 guitarist Fred 'Sonic' Smith) in 1994 she released the intensely melancholic album, *Gone Again*, possibly her finest album. *Peace and Noise* (1997) marked a return to her earlier 'spiky' style of composition and reunited Smith with Lenny Kaye (guitar) and J.D. Daugherty (drums) from the Patti Smith Group. It was dedicated to the memory of William Burroughs.

The seven albums recorded since 1975 all resonate with a questioning energy and often-violent mysticism, which attempts to communicate an idea of God with a living sense of spiritual and religious purpose. She has also written radical rock journalism for *Creem* magazine, culminating in an account of her trip to Jim Morrison's grave in Paris. Entitled 'Jukebox crucifix', it provides a specific insight into the connections between mythic American rock, visionary religious language and her own sense of an artistic calling. Although Patti Smith has been castigated by feminists for her reliance on male colleagues (not least Robert Mapplethorpe, Bruce Springsteen and the musicians in the Patti Smith Group), the visceral tone of her poetry (she had published four books of poetry prior to releasing any records) allied to rock has provided an inspiration for women musicians in foregrounding the relationship between the erotic and the religious, and in refashioning rock through intensely personalised lyrics and compositional style.[8] It is this legacy that relates most specifically to Kate Bush and Tori Amos whose own confrontations with religion, sexuality and mysticism provide personalised insights for their poetic lyrics and fiercely individual compositional styles.

It is considered that any artist who continues to conflate cultural and historical influences with their own inner life will have lasting relevance, regardless of age. While such an introspective vision can result in music that is overly self-indulgent, and all three artists have been criticised across their careers for their lack of integrity – Smith, *Radio Ethiopia*, Bush, *The Dreaming* (1982, her so-called 'she's gone mad' album[9]), Amos, *Boys for Pele* (1996, described as overly dramatic) – their sense of the visionary, their impassioned and often sensuous lyrics, and their individualistic musicianship provides a particular trajectory which enables personal growth and a fascination, on the part of their fans, as to 'what next?' The singer-songwriter, then, is often permitted that sense of transformation (whether in terms of musical style or image) that ensures acceptance and which allows for personal growth as an artist.

Even so, it is a salutary fact that the importance of Carole King (b. Carole Klein, February 9, 1942, Brooklyn, NY) to the world of popular music – where she has been a major influence not only on women singer-songwriters but also on such groups as the Beatles – is attributed largely to her early run of hit singles and her seminal album *Tapestry* (1971), which has now sold over 15 million copies worldwide. In collaboration with her partner/husband Gerry Goffin, early successes included The Shirelles ('Will You Still Love Me Tomorrow'), Bobby Vee ('Take Good Care of My Baby') and The Drifters ('Up on the Roof'), Little Eva ('The Locomotion') and The Cookies ('Chains' and 'Don't Say Nothin' Bad About My Baby'). Her first solo hit, 'It Might As Well Rain Until Tomorrow', came in 1962. During the latter part of the 1960s the Goffin/King partnership produced a number of sophisticated, personalised ballads including 'A Natural Woman' (Aretha Franklin), 'Going Back' (Dusty Springfield and The Byrds) and 'Pleasant Valley Sunday' (The Monkees).

King's solo career started in 1970, after her marriage and partnership with Goffin ended. Having moved from New York to Los Angeles, she demonstrated a new maturity with her solo album, *Tapestry*. Foreshadowing Mitchell's seminal album *Blue*, there is a comparable sense of introspection and incisiveness, with tracks that address adult fears and emotions through instantly memorable melodies and poignant lyrics. 'You've Got a Friend' became a US No. 1 for James Taylor and 'It's Too Late' for King. As James Taylor wrote in the preface to her remastered CD (1999), King 'was a tune-smith, inventing popular music, hammering out songs for any occasion, tailor-made sequels ... very accessible, very personal statements, built from the ground up with a simple, elegant architecture ... We recorded together, shared a band and hung out ... Those were remarkable days in Laurel Canyon. Joni, Jackson, SCNY, The Eagles, Carole King ... exceptional was commonplace'.

While it is easy to attribute Taylor's words to nostalgia, such songs as 'I Feel the Earth Move' and 'Natural Born Woman' have achieved classic status within the world of popular music, but while King continued to produce an album annually throughout the 1970s, with *Music* (1971), *Rhymes and Reasons* (1972) and *Fantasy* (1973) all achieving gold disc status, *Pearls* (1980), which comprised 'classic' Goffin/King songs, was interpreted by many as an artistic impasse, and her live appearances became increasingly restricted to fund-raising concerts. She relocated to Ireland in the early 1990s where she produced *In Concert* in 1994.[10]

It would seem, then, that maturity and personal development can mitigate against the confirmation of past pleasures that relate to key moments in an artist's career. Audiences are notorious for wanting to hear the music that initially attracted them to a particular group or musician – as discussed previously in my investigation into Jim Morrison and Jimi Hendrix – and when this sense of outrage as rock, for example, is seemingly abandoned for the 'higher ground' of jazz, it can create problems. Joni Mitchell (b. Roberta Joan Anderson, November 7, 1943, Fort McLeod, Alberta, Canada) is one such example. Her initial integration of jazz and rock (*Court and Spark* 1974; *Miles of Aisles* 1974, a double-album of her supportive tour with Tom Scott's LA Express; *The Hissing of Summer Lawns* 1975; *Hejira* 1976 and *Don Juan's Reckless Daughter* 1977) had met with mixed receptions that subsequently turned to hostility with the 1979 release of *Mingus*. Recorded with top jazz musicians Charlie Mingus, Herbie Hancock, Wayne Shorter, Peter Erskine and Don Aliaz, the album was considered to be too stylistically hybrid to have any real credibility. As an expatriate from folk and rock/pop, jazz and rock purists alike rejected her. With hindsight, however, it is evident that Mitchell's ability to cross genre boundaries demonstrates a musicality which has proved an inspiration to women musicians who search for creative fulfilment rather than mainstream success, and her more recent releases, such as *Taming the Tiger* (1998), a lush, textured album which echoed the sound of her mid-'70s work, evidence a woman who continues to produce strong and musically challenging ideas. Not least, her compositions encompass the changing concerns and emotions of a generation, from 1960s idealism to adult responsibility, and her musical flair, artistic depth and lyrical consistency has made her one of the finest singer-songwriters of her generation. She is now 61 years of age.[11]

It is also evident that Mitchell's legacy has prompted record companies to find female artists who can be passed off as serious musicians. The pop bubble, it seemed was about to burst as Britney clones were superseded by what has been termed 'the Phoney Joni's' – artists who could sell singles to the kids and albums to the adults. Former ballet dancer and Blue Note discovery Norah Jones is one such example and her *Come Away With Me* album has spent almost two months in the Top 10 UK album charts – initially due to extensive television advertising. As Colin Paterson observed at the time, 'Norah's cred comes from a chill-out jazz sound and being Ravi Shankar's daughter. But closer inspection of the writing credits reveals "singer-songwriter" Norah penned a pitiful two-and-a-half songs out of 14 on her album. These acts may be billed as "for real" but are every bit as cynically manufactured as the teen pop they replace' (Paterson, 2002, 20).

While Paterson's comments highlight the ways in which young artists are promoted and the continuing significance of authorship, there is little doubt that Jones is a fine performer with a nuanced vocal style and an ability to communicate with her audience. Her continuing success evidences both her musicianship and her popularity as an artist who spans pop, country and jazz, as evidenced by her latest album, *feels like home* (Blue Note, Parlaphone, 2004). What is disturbing is the way in which critics and reviewers are so quick to place an emphasis on the sexual appeal (or otherwise) of young artists, rather than listening to the quality of their music. Avril Lavigne's debut CD *Let Go* (2002) for example, was written off as a blend of radio-friendly rock and unrequited love for boys on skateboards. Largely self-written, albeit polished by producers Clif Magness (Celine Dion) and up-and-coming trio, The Matrix, it reached No. 5 in the US, where she attracted the attention of the media, which promoted her as Alanis Morisette Jnr. Image again predominated: 'looking like Gwyeth Paltrow's baby sister means that not all of Lavigne's admirers are interested solely in her music'. (*Q*, October 2002, 32) As Lavigne commented at the time, 'I didn't know too much about the industry when I started so I learned about it and I was like "Whoa!" This is dangerous, it's a slimy business' (*Q*, October 2002, 32). Her cautionary note is further exemplified in the promotion of 21-year-old Vanessa Carlton and her Marc Cohn-like piano anthem 'A Thousand Miles'. Again, her musical credentials are questioned by the discovery that Ron Fair, the producer of her Top 5 US album, *Be Not Nobody*, masterminded her launch and that the cleavage shots on Carlton's single sleeve are remarkably similar to those of his earlier discovery, Christina Aguilera. In contrast, Natalie Imbruglia and Jamie Benson were marketed as credible female rock artists (!) but as Paterson rightly observes, 'although they strap on a Gibson they remain very much from the school of Debbie Gibson' (2002, 20) – a reminder that critics and audiences alike are all too aware of marketing tactics and that 'credibility' depends on personal innovation and artistic integrity and not, simply, the emblematic fronting of a guitar.

It is, as they say, a dirty business and the comparison with artists such as Björk is stark. Few today seem even to share the conviction that characterised her early years in Iceland – 'I won't use music as a whore … I'd rather be in the bravest band in Iceland that no one knows and do two jobs than make music to pay the rent' (Patterson, 1996, 222). Having weathered the imperialistic and arrogant attitudes of the media (where a heritage other than American or British marks you as different/other) and having consistently engaged with musical experimentation, it would be surprising if she suddenly faded from the scene. Rather, her ability to transform her image and engage with musical genres as far apart as techno and chamber music suggests that she will continue to relate to the increasing hybridity of popular music and, like Patti Smith before her, align her mystical insights, spirituality and love of mythology with the evocative colours of her developing compositional style. Her creative attitude involves 'wanting to do 700 exciting things tomorrow, that's the source of creativity. And it's courage as well: to have the courage to stand on top of a hill and take it all in. Funnily enough, there's not that many people who have that kind of courage' (Evans, 1997, 219).

What she dislikes most is middle-of-the-road stagnation (Evans, 1997, 213), and it is here that the contrast between the innovative singer-songwriter and the pop idol once again emerges. Bjork's latest album, *Medulla* is dominated by her voice (with piano and an occasional gong). It is her first political album, remarkable even by the standards of someone who has spent her life making singular records, refusing to 'use music as a whore'. In contrast, pop idols are of their time, and, as such, have to effect a successful transition from a teen-based audience if they are to survive.

While Robbie Williams provides one example of a star who successfully moved from a teen-directed boy group to a solo artist whose current career involves a transition to a Sinatra soundalike, it is apparent that the ability to relate to a broad-based audience is crucial to longevity. When Take That broke up in February 1996, it seemed initially that Williams's success as a solo artist was less likely than his fellow group member Gary Barlow, whose voice, musicianship and marketability suggested that he would be the likely successor to George Michael. Williams, the so-called 'cheeky chappie' of the group, notoriously partied and overindulged in drink and drugs, his every move covered by a some-what censorial press who were already outraged by his vitriolic attacks on Barlow. After a brief spell in a detox clinic he recorded *Life Thru A Lens* (1997), which included the symbolic 'Old Before I Die'. Acclaimed by the public and critics alike, it eclipsed Barlow's debut album *Open Road* and, despite the success of his single 'Stronger' (July 1999), his career is still up and down. In contrast, William's star was in the ascendancy and in December, 1999, his Christmas single 'Angels' stimulated a renewed interest in the album which entered the UK Top 10 for the first time, eventually climbing to the No. 1 position twenty-eight weeks after its release. 'Millennium' entered the UK singles charts at No. 1 in September 1998, and two months later *I've Been Expecting You* topped the album charts. With backing vocals by Neil Tennant (Pet Shop Boys) and Neil Hannon (The Divine Comedy), Williams finally demonstrated that he had moved into the position of Britain's top pop star, a position that has been consolidated by his Albert Hall concert (2002) and the release of his album *Swing When You're Winning*, a big-band epic of songs by Frank Sinatra, Dean Martin and Sammy Davis Junior. Having cut alcohol and drugs out of his life since Christmas 2001, he is now lauded for his gentle charm, continuing 'daft' humour and curious Potteries accent – qualities that seem to confirm his essential 'Englishness' and lack of pretension, despite his jet-set lifestyle. The English, it seems, have a particular affection for the 'return of a prodigal son' and Williams's role as the country's favourite entertainer seems assured. He not only possesses the ability to charm his audience and to give a convincing performance of such Sinatra clas-sics as 'My Way', but he is also blessed with a commanding stage presence – and the credibility to attract substantial monies for his albums. With the lure of more than £500 million-worth of CDs being sold in the UK during the three months leading up to Christmas, it is clear that Williams can't lose.

Williams topped the Christmas charts in 2001 with his album *Swing When You're Winning*, which sold five million copies, and his status as Britain's top recording artist was subsequently reflected in the bidding war 'between Sony, BMG, Warner Universal, Sir Richard Branson's V2 label and EMI for the right to release his new album, entitled *Escapology* ...' EMI initially offered 'Williams

£40 million to re-sign. Rival labels [dangled] a £75 million three-album deal in front of the star, who insisted on a clause giving him financial control over sales from digital downloads' (Sherwin, 2002, 9). Eventually an £80 million contract was signed with EMI in what is probably the UK's biggest record deal ever, and with compilations accounting for 25–30 per cent of album sales in the UK, and with one in every four CDs sold being a compilation, Williams's back catalogue undoubtedly benefitted from his new deal. Being a top entertainer, then, undoubtedly pays off.

While it is difficult to imagine Mick Jagger (b. Michael Philip Jagger, July 26, 1943, Dartford, Kent, England) becoming a figure of the establishment, he shares with Williams the accolade of being one of Britain's favourite sons, albeit one whose rebellious status is not diminished by time. Even so, his notoriety and appetite for sex and drugs that had led earlier to his characterisation as aggressively sexual, insolent and undesirable, made it seem unlikely that he would join the elevated ranks of Sir Paul McCartney and Sir Cliff Richard. As such, his knighthood in the Jubilee Honours list (June 2002) came as somewhat of a surprise to fans and critics alike. It implied that Jagger can also be designated the dubious title of 'first-class celebrity entertainer', and thus rewarded for services to his country. Thankfully, his rock spirit appears to survive intact, as evidenced by the release of the Stones's album, *Licks* (released after years of contractual wrangling with EMI to allow all singles to appear on one album) and their 40th anniversary world tour. Opening in Boston on September 3, 2002, the tickets (£224 for the best seats) cost 'three times as much as the group was paid for its first performance on the tiny stage of London's Marquee Club, in July 1962. And with most dates sold out, second-row seats for Madison Square Gardens later this month are now on sale at TicketsNow.com at £3,457' (Williamson, 2002, 23). The Stones played an estimated 100 concerts, including America, Europe, India and China, and it seems that some 2.5 million people will have paid £200 million to see the band by the end of the tour. Predictably, the opening song 'Street Fighting Man' and the encore numbers 'Sympathy For The Devil' and 'Jumpin' Jack Flash' come from way back, a subtle reminder that the Stones's finest hours were during the late 1960s, albeit that the former was originally banned by American radio for its insurrectionary lyrics and that 'Sympathy …' was dropped from their repertoire for several years following the dystopia of Altamont.[12] As Williamson observes, 'Old devils still give satisfaction' (2002, 23) and the Stones remain, for many, the world's greatest rock 'n' roll band – albeit that they have uncharitably been dubbed the 'Strolling Bones' – a reference, perhaps, to their combined age (at the time) of 235 years.

For their fans, the Stones have acquired the status of veterans and it is apparent that success continues to rely on the confirmation of audience expectations. The most successful of the Stones's 1990s albums, *Stripped* (1995), included energetic acoustic versions of 'Street Fighting Man', 'Wild Horses' and 'Let It Bleed', while *Bridges to Babylon* (1997) confirmed Charlie Watts's exceptional drumming ability, this time mixed to the fore and with a clean, funky sound. It is, however, the band's live performances that are so significant to their continuing success in that they provide access, for old and new fans alike, to the Stones's 40-year repertoire and the exceptional talents of the Jagger/Richards songwriting team. It is also evident that they have always placed great emphasis on being 'entertaining', with elaborate set designs, lighting and provocative screened graphics matched only by Jagger's centre-stage presence as the omnipresent 'Jumping Jack Flash'.

The ability to stay 'on the scene' for 40 years requires not only an outstanding repertoire of songs but also stamina, and any article on the Stones includes a comment on the band's appearance. 'Jagger, approaching 60, seemed more subdued. When he removed his jacket, his muscles suggested he'd been in serious training, but he was careful to preserve his energy, and paced himself throughout the two-hour show. Keith Richards, too, was less flamboyant, in a black leather jacket and blue T-shirt, with only a sash around his waist to add the usual piratical dash' (Williamson, 2002, 23). For a woman, emphasis on appearance is always significant (as discussed previously in Part II on Bush, Amos and Björk), and while jazz and blues singers are accorded a certain licence, pop stars are under constant surveillance. The emphasis on the body beautiful is one that is most apparent in the 40-year career of Cher (b. Cherilyn Sarkisian La Piere, May 20, 1946, El Centro, California). As Alan Jackson writes, 'Never mind Madonna. In a culture shaped by our own fickle-ness and attention-deficit, Cher is a phenomenon. Fashions come and go (she embraces most of them, not always wisely), but she endures. Hippie-chick, Vegas tack, cod-metal, power balladry? She's been there, done all of that and more' (2001, 39). Cher, it seems, has the power of reinvention, and after the personal and professional demise of Sonny and Cher (the husband-and-wife team who first came to international attention in the mid-1960s with their 'groovy true love' singles, 'Just You' and 'I Got You Babe' (1965), their one-hour television show and 1970s hit single 'All I Ever Need Is You'), it became apparent who was the 'real' star. Reasserting her status as a top recording artist with such hits as 'Gypsies, Tramps and Thieves' and 'Dark Lady', Cher moved into modelling with Vogue where she became known as a fashion queen, before returning to her first love, acting, taking a leading role in Come Back to the Five and Dime, Jimmy Dean, Jimmy Dean (1982), Silkwood (1983), The Witches of Eastwick (1987), Suspect (1987) and Moonstruck (1987) for which she won an Oscar for best actress.

She also staged her comeback as a singer with Cher and 'I Found Someone' (US No., 10, November 1987; UK No. 5, December 1987) and in 1989 had three more hits with 'After All', 'If I Could Turn Back Time' and 'Just Like Jesse James'. 'The Shoop Shoop Song (It's In His Kiss)' reached No. 1 in the UK charts in April 1991 and was also the theme song to Mermaids, where she made another screen performance. Her popularity was confirmed by the hit single 'Believe', which topped the UK charts for seven weeks in 1998, resulting in personal appearances on the teen-oriented TV programme *Top of the Pops*. 'Believe' finally climbed to the top of the US *Billboard* Hot 100 in March 1999 (Larkin, 1999, 253).

Despite becoming one of the greatest American pop icons of the 1990s, Cher's glitzy image continues to attract as much, if not more, attention than her ability as a singer, so reinforcing the sad fact that a good voice (and Cher's powerful vocals are significant in terms of delivery) is less important in the pop arena than her often notorious fashion sense. Her outfit for the 1986 Oscars remains one of the most outrageous in the history of fashion. Designed by Bob Mackie, the spider-like, torso-bearing black outfit with its feathered headdress made the front page of almost every newspaper. Mackie's association with Cher began in 1971 when he designed the costumes for *The Sonny and Cher Comedy Hour* TV show where she constantly changed her image, appearing one week as a tramp, another as Olive Oyl, a gypsy and an Indian princess. Arguably, it was Mackie and Cher's influence that accounted for the success of belly-bearing low-cut jeans in the 1970s, and he still continues to design her often freaky, and always flamboyant, costumes. Cher is also famous for her wigs, and in the booklet to her CD *Living Proof* (2001) her style ranged from rag doll-curled brown, Brünnhilde blonde and varying degrees of white, grey and black. At 58 she continues to tour, and despite the media attention given to her plastic surgery and fear of ageing, she exerts a strong appeal that is not confined to her older fans. While this may be partly attributable to successful marketing, it nevertheless demonstrates that the physical status quo remains an intrinsic part of a pop star's appeal, and that Cher's ability to project her youthfulness (whether in global promotions, tours, cable television and TV spin-offs) remains central to her status as 'the singer/actress/icon of indestructibility' (Jackson, 2001, 39).

Cher's 40-year recording career, her ability to identify with contemporary sounds (and hence contemporary audiences), her fright wigs and extraordinary outfits, provide a unique example of how female pop stars can engage with, and continue to excel in, a highly competitive pop market. Madonna (b. Madonna Louise Veronica Ciccone, August 16,1958, Rochester, Michigan) provides another example and, like Cher, has also been notorious for her image – not least her Gaultier-designed conical metal bra, her torn fishnet tights and externally worn undergarments. Now aged 46, her controversial recordings, most specifically *Erotica* (1992), her documentary film *Truth or Dare: On the Band Behind The Scenes, aka In Bed With Madonna* (1991), her notorious book *SEX*, and often outspoken views on female sexuality, initially led to fierce debates as to whether she was a feminist icon or simply a shrewd mover. The Vatican were also alarmed by the way in which she draped her cleavage with rosary beads and religious jewellery, and by such controversial pop videos as *Like A Prayer* (1989) which they condemned for its burning crosses and dancing semi-naked with a black Jesus. Her *Blond Ambition* tour was also castigated as 'one of the most satanic shows in the history of humanity'.[13] In contrast, her teenage fans copied her fingerless gloves, jangly bracelets and armour-plated corsets, defending their idol who, they felt, was acting responsibly in bringing sex to the fore, so forcing the media, schools and parents alike to confront the inconsistencies inherent in the public attitude towards female sexuality.[14] Certainly Madonna's combination of outrageousness and ambiguity has proved a successful strategy in maintaining a consistent media scrutiny. By the mid-1990s, the woman who once declared 'I'm a creamy smooth pop icon goddess' had successfully negotiated several self-reinventions. Her persona as an actress, arguably a contributory factor in her pop performances both on stage and on video, demonstrated a diversity which ranged from the humorous in *Desperately Seeking Susan*, to the do-gooding missionary in *Shanghai Surprise*, to, more characteristically, the bad-girl singer, Breathless Mahoney in *Dick Tracy*. By the early 1990s her ambition was to play Evita, and she wrote a four-page letter to Alan Parker, the director, explaining why she would be perfect for the role. She even persuaded Carlos Menem, the Argentine president, to allow her to sing 'Don't Cry For Me Argentina' on the presidential balcony. Her performance won her a Golden Globe award.

Today, Madonna seems perfectly at home as a mother and a performer. Her tour to promote her 2001 album *Music* was a sell-out and her image as a cowgirl seemed to suggest that, at heart, she was the 'All American Gal'. In contrast, her role as mother led to her putting down her daughter for a top London private school. There is, then, more than a hint that she continues to enjoy her paradoxical image as good girl/bad girl. Her claimed spirituality ('I go to church. I go to the Church of England, I go to Catholic churches, I go to synagogues. I partake in all religions') seems somehow compromised by her somewhat self-indulgent belief in her own importance: 'I won't be happy until I'm as famous as God'.[15] Even so, she does provide another example of how an older woman can continue to enjoy a successful career within the world of popular music; remain newsworthy, remain paradoxical, continue touring and engage with theatre/film as well as popular music.

While Madonna started out in soft-porn movies, Kylie Minogue (b. May 28, 1968, Melbourne, Australia) – possibly Britain's favourite pop star – was, like David Cassidy before her, a TV icon, this time in the Australian soap opera *Neighbours*. Her first recording, a cover version of Little Eva's hit, 'The Locomotion', attracted the attention of hit producers Stock, Aitken and Waterman who moulded Minogue's attractive, wholesome, androgyne image to their distinctive brand of radio-centred pop. Her first UK single, 'I Should Be So Lucky' reached No. 1 in early 1988, presaging an impressive chart run of instantly singalong UK hits, including 'Got To Be Certain' (No. 2), 'Je Ne Sais Pas Pourquoi' (No. 2), 'Hand On Your Heart' (No. 1), 'Wouldn't Change A Thing' (No. 2), 'Never Too Late' (No. 4), 'Tears On My Pillow' (No. 1), 'Better The Devil You Know' (No. 2), 'Step Back In Time' (No. 4), 'What Do I Have To Do' (No. 6) and 'Shocked' (No. 6). Her solo successes were enhanced by hits with former *Neighbours* 'boyfriend', Jason Donovan, including the UK No. 1 'Especially For You' (Larkin, 1999, 869).

Within 3 years, Minogue had emerged as one of the most successful pop stars of the late 1980s/early 1990s but, as suggested earlier, the transition from teen-oriented pop to a more mainstream audience is essential if a star is to achieve any longevity in pop music. Such a transition was undoubtedly helped by her role in the film *Delinquents* (1991), where Kylie metamorphosed from a bubbly, seemingly innocent, pop idol to a more sexual persona. In doing so, she attracted useful media coverage, especially when she became romantically involved with INXS lead singer, Michael Hutchence. Further hit singles included a duet with Keith Washington, 'If You Were With Me Now', and 'Give Me Just A Little More Time' (No. 2), and earned her a new title, 'pop goddess', although it seems, in retrospect, that she was pursuing a more serious career by collaborating with Nick Cave on 'Where The Wild Roses Grow' (1994) and the Manic Street Preachers for her 1997 album *Impossible Princess* (the title was subsequently changed to *Kylie Minogue (Deconstruction)* as it was considered inappropriate given the recent death of Princess Diana).

Her fans did not welcome Minogue's move to a more grunge-driven sound and her affair with Hutchence. In particular, it seemed that 'pop purity' was being desecrated by rock depravity, and the statement by Hutchence that his hobby was 'corrupting Kylie' cunningly exploited the seamier side of their relationship and the fantasies involved. His death, in mysterious, possibly sexual, circumstances seemed to confirm that Minogue had been seriously led astray and, together with the new raunchiness of her music ('I want to sing about sex now'), situated her simply as a naive Madonna clone. Nick Cave, whose heroin addiction and often-inflammatory lyrics – 'She's Hit' and 'Deep In The Woods' which evoke images of a corrupt deity feeding on a depraved appetite for flesh – was seen as another serious threat to Minogue's 'girl-next-door' image. Her recitation of the lyrics to 'I Should Be So Lucky' at the Poetry Olympics held at the Albert Hall, London in 1996 seemed to many a somewhat jaded, if ironic, response to her earlier role as a pop star and, as a reinvented indie star, her career foundered, predictably sneered at by such 'authentic' rock stars as Liam Gallagher from Oasis. Once again, the media stepped in, showing photos in which she looked older, drained and 'past it'.

Then, in 2000, she bounced back with a new No. 1, 'Spinning Around'. As Brian Appleyard enthusiastically reported in his cover story, 'Why Kylie? Why Now?', it appears that 'her simple sexiness is just what we need ... suddenly the girl voted "the most fanciable female of 1989" was the most fanciable of 2000' (2001, 4–5). His opinion was confirmed when, in 2002, she won five Brit awards. Like Robbie Williams before her, it seems once again that the British love the return of their prodigal sons and daughters, and after 11 years' residency in the UK Kylie Minogue has become somewhat of a pop institution, sexy but safe. It is also true to say that the cameras love her, and galleries of Kylie portraits clog the fan sites on the Internet. The fans themselves are adoring and affectionate and include a large proportion of gays. As Appleyard observes, 'Survival is a specifically feminine ideal ... Age withers: this is the

truth women most need to survive' (2001, 5) and while Minogue is not classi-
cally beautiful, her face retains a certain teenage appeal, and her famous 'bum'
continues to inspire hundreds of Internet eulogies. Even so, as Francis Rossi of
Status Quo caustically observed, ' "What's all this fuss about Kylie's bottom, eh?
Look, cover your arse up love," he says, sounding like John Thaw in the
Sweeney' (Landesman, 2002, 9). For him, like many more cynical commentators, she has become yet another instance of 'pop pretenders', but nevertheless
one who has a keen sense of survival.

What is evident, both from my earlier discussions in 'Nursery Crymes', 'Little
Boys' and 'Little Girls' and from this brief survey, is that age and identity are
inextricably linked to popular success. Clearly, I have done little more than
scratch the surface of what is an important study in popular music, and work
continues to be needed within the fields of jazz, soul, rap and so forth to
consider why some continue as respected heroes and heroines, whilst others fall
by the wayside. Not least, there remains the problematic question of how to
combat the tyrannical and seemingly svengali-like powers of the music industry
itself whose control over the destiny of young stars, golden oldies and dead
heroes appears undiminished. To return to my earlier discussion of Elvis Presley,
the JXL remix of 'A Little Less Conversation' clearly enhanced the sales of *Elvis
Presley. 30# Hits*, but 'would the King have approved of a Dutch DJ messin' with
his thang?' One thing we can be sure about is 'that Colonel Tom Parker (a
Dutchman himself, on the quiet) would have watched those sales figures and
approved with all his huckster's heart' (Du Noyer, 2002. 124); RCA/BMG
would clearly agree.

Notes

Introduction

1 The elements which enable us to make links and draw the distinctions (between, e.g. 'pop ballad', 'rock ballad', 'country ballad', 'soul ballad' etc.) are examples of what Philip Tagg (1992) calls 'genre synecoches' and 'style indicators' ('Towards a sign typology of music' in *Studi e Testi 1, Secondo Convegno Europeo di Analisi Musicale*. Ed. Rossana Dalmonte and Mario Baroni [University of Trento], pp. 369–78). A genre synecdoche refers 'from inside one musical style to elements of another ... thence to the genre of which the second style is a part': a style indicator is a 'compositional-structural norm in a musical style (p. 371). What tells us that 'Sailing' (Rod Stewart) is specifically a *rock* ballad, for example, is mostly (I suspect) the type of voice and singing style. These, when originally used in ballads, acted as a genre synecdoche, referring to the 'rock'-style/genre; as they became assimilated, they turned into a style indicator (of 'rock ballad') – so that by the time of Bryan Adams's '(Everything I Do) I Do It For You' (1991), they inform us directly'. My discussion here is informed by Middleton, R. (1997) *Popular Culture: Understanding Pop Music*. Milton Keynes: The Open University, p. 37.

2 The title of this section relates to the retelling of nursery rhymes by the rock group, Genesis (Tony Banks, Michael Rutherford, Peter Gabriel, Steve Hackett, Phil Collins) on their 1971 album *Nursery Cryme* (Charisma) and, in particular, Paul Whitehead's sleeve design.

3 As Bush told *Q* magazine. Quoted in Gaar, G.G. (1992) *She's A Rebel. The History of Women in Rock 'n' Roll*. Seattle: Seal Press, p. 268.

4 The significance of 'my cock' and the emphasis on virility in rock-based music (at its most ironic in the film *Spinal Tap*) has a precedence in the writings of Leonardo da Vinci.

> Perhaps because Leonardo da Vinci had declared his puzzlement as to why men were ashamed of their virility and 'hid their sexual organs when they ought solemnly to decorate them, as they would a high-ranking minister', that year it had become the custom among fashionable men to exhibit and gaudily festoon their genitals. Almost all the guests, except the very elderly, wore light-colored tights that showed off their owner's private parts with ribbons tied to the waist and groin. Those who had larger reasons to be grateful to their Creator, embraced the new fashion wholeheartedly. Those who did not, employed various methods to adapt to the times without needing to feel ashamed. In the Bottega Del Moro, prosthetic devices were sold for placing under the clothes to lend fortune to those less fortunate. Among the many adornments, from diadems in precious stones that ringed the 'minister' to showy nettings of stringed pearls, were ribbons tied to four or five bells that betrayed with their tinkles the moods of 'his lordship'. According to the tinkling of the bells, the

ladies were able to measure their acceptance among the men ... Mona Sofia was greeted by a veritable carillon, the sound of hundreds of masculine bells.

(Andahazi, 1998, 84–6)

5 It is interesting to note that Will Young's outing as gay did not, initially, prevent his first single from going straight to the top of the charts. By the next week, however, it lost its top position to Gareth Gates, the runner-up in *Pop Idol*. Even so, Young has retained his popularity, and it is suggested that this is largely due to his clean, fun-loving persona. While he is no Boy George, both come across as inoffensive and non-transgressive, which accounts for the latter's longevity within the pop world.

Part I: Nursery Crymes

1 Clearly, other issues such as a child's potential delight in sado-masochistic pleasure or cruelty – from the de-winging of flies to the extremes of bullying, for example – are also problematic.

2 Aaliyah died on August 29, 2001 when her private plane crashed in Bermuda upon take off. She was 22 years of age.

3 So described by Red Foley, the country music veteran who sponsored Brenda Lee on his ABC-TV series *Ozark Jubilee* on March 31, 1956. Her performance led to a five-year contract with *Jubilee*'s booking affiliate, 'Top Talent'.

4 Brenda Lee now enjoys a high standing in the country music world and in 1993 she was billed as 'the biggest-selling female star in pop history' (Larkin, 1999, 754). Larkin (1999) also supplied the information on singles.

5 This is beautifully parodied in Van Halen's cover to the eponymous 1984 album, where a cherub with arguably knowing eyes is shown smoking a cigarette.

6 The reform of the Age of Consent for Girls was accelerated by the publicity surrounding the trial of William Stead, editor of the *Pall Mall Gazette*, and Rebecca Jarratt, an ex-prostitute and alcoholic. In order to test how easy it was to procure a young virgin for prostitution, Eliza Armstrong, aged 13, had been bought for £5, ostensibly as a maid; Eliza was taken to a backstreet midwife and confirmed a virgin before being taken to a brothel in Regent Street. Dosed with chloroform, she had been made ready for a 'libertine rapist'. Stead himself visited the young child and subsequently published his 'shocking findings' over one week. While the initial reaction was outrage, retaliation by Cavendish Bendick and other members of the establishment focused on Stead's framing of his argument – the implicit assumption that all poor working-class families sold their children into prostitution. The mother of thirteen-year-old Eliza, who was presented in the article as a drunk, went to find her daughter and her story was picked up by the right-wing paper *Lloyd's Weekly*. Although Eliza was unharmed, public opinion turned against Stead. His article was considered as having affected the country's national reputation, as an affront to Victorian morality. In retrospect, it appeared that those who speak out are perceived as bigger villains than those who perpetrate immoral acts. Stead was imprisoned for three months; Jarratt for six. Source: Channel 4, *Victorians Uncensored*, May 2001.

7 Transcribed from Adrian Lyne's film version of *Lolita*.

8 Police investigations into the recent murders of Holly Wells and Jessica Chapman (August, 2002) drew attention to problems inherent in WWW chat rooms. Although there was no evidence of interaction on the Web, the case highlighted the potential dangers of unfettered Internet access, where there are hundreds of thousands of electronic meeting rooms. They allow any number of computer users to communicate simultaneously in anonymity and are hugely popular with children and teenagers. One child in five is estimated to have entered a chatroom, with one in

ten going on to arrange a meeting in real life ('IRL' in chatroom jargon). A recent survey found that a third of children were unaware of the risks associated with meeting people face-to-face. A new criminal offence of 'online grooming' may be introduced by Home Secretary David Blunkett, under the aegis of which police could prosecute paedophiles for 'cultivating' children on the Web. At present such activity is not a criminal offence. Information from Paul Kelso, 'Danger lurking in the chatrooms', *Guardian*, August 10, 2002, p. 8.

9 *The Times Magazine Fashion Special*, Autumn/Winter 2001, p. 13, provides a specific example here in 'Girls and boys come out to play', with an emphasis on the childlike appeal of fluffy pink garments.

10 Wham! (George Michael, Andrew Ridgeley) are generally acknowledged as the most commercially successful English pop group of the 1980s, but it was the success of Take That (Gary Barlow, Mark Owen, Howard Donald, Jason Orange and Robbie Williams, formed September 1990) that arguably triggered the craze for young boy groups, with their string of chart-topping singles over a five-year career.

11 The record was withdrawn due to legal complications, but nevertheless won Jackson another Grammy Award.

12 My discussion, and quotes, are informed by Pattison, R. (1987) *The Triumph of Vulgarity. Rock Music in the Mirror of Romanticism*. Oxford: Oxford University Press, pp. 142–4.

13 These were at their most brutal during the investigations surrounding accusations of paedophilic activity.

14 Taken from Michael Jackson's speech to the Oxford Union, March, 2001.

15 Manzarek invited Morrison to join his R & B band Rick and the Ravens after hearing his rudimentary composition 'Moonlight Drive'. The band included the organist's two brothers. John Densmore (b. December 1, 1945) was recruited as drummer and the group recorded six Morrison songs at the World Pacific studios. These included 'Summers Almost Gone' and 'End of the Night'. Manzarek's brothers disliked the new material and dropped out of the group to be replaced by Robbie Krieger (b. January 8, 1946), an inventive guitarist, and with Morrison as lead singer the quartet moved to their first residency at Whiskey-A-Go-Go.

16 George Morrison's career – from active service in the Pacific during World War II, through to his appointment in Washington, his subsequent posts in Clearwater (FL), Claremont, LA, Los Altos and San Francisco (CA) – was a destablising influence on the young Morrison and as biographs reveal he was both resentful and angry about his father's control over him. Morrison Snr was finally promoted to the rank of Rear Admiral.

17 As exemplified when his father vetoed Morrison's transfer to UCLA, a matter which he took into his own hands, studying appropriate courses and ensuring his acceptance on the degree programme.

18 As Ray Manzarek recalls when Morrison was studying at UCLA: 'He certainly had a substantial investment in books. They filled an entire wall of his apartment. His reading was very eclectic. It was typical of the early- to mid-sixties hipster student. Classics – both Greek and Roman – French Symbolist poets, German romantics, modern novels – Hemingway, Faulkner, Fitzgerald – existentialists – Camus, Sartre, Genet – contemporary literature – Norman Mailer, especially *The Deer Park*, Jim's favourite. He identified with the character Marion Fay. And lots of Beatniks. We wanted to *be* beatniks. But we were too young. We came a little too late, but we were worshippers of the Beat Generation. All the Beat writers filled Morrison's shelves, along with James Joyce and Celine. All the antecedents to the Beat Generation … That is what influenced and inspired Jim Morrison' (Manzarek 1999, 77).

19 Francis Ford Coppola opened and closed his movie *Apocalypse Now* with 'The End' and had remixed it to bring up the vocal part which Rothchild had originally mixed down to the threshold of inaudibility.

20 Frankie Lymon (and the Teenagers) provides another example of a child star whose enjoyment of the excesses of stardom (smoking cigars, drinking and under-age sex with a woman old enough to be his mother) subsequently led to drug-addiction. His career foundered at the age of 15 when his voice broke. It is a fear that was shared by Michael Jackson, whose sister LaToya recalls 'Michael doesn't want to let go of his voice. He doesn't want it to change. He believes his fans want to keep him as he was with Jackson Five'. While Jackson survived (and maintained a vocal range from low E in the bass clef to A flat above middle C), Lymon became increasingly addicted to drugs and after three broken marriages he died of a heroin overdose in February 1968. He was 26.

21 Their punk burlesque reached its height in the cover of their 1979 Island debut *Cut*, where they were pictured topless, wearing loincloths and daubed in mud as a ridicule of typical girls.

22 McLaren had briefly managed the New York Dolls and was attracted to their sense of danger, the torn t-shirts that suggested sexuality and violence. As Jon Savage observes: 'If such a thing is possible to identify, it was the origin of what would become the Punk style ... He copied the New York groups (Richard Hell and the Voidoids, Television, the Ramones and Patti Smith)' (Savage, 1991, 91–2, provides a full discussion.).

23 It is interesting to note that Goddard, together with a new set of Ants, effectively reinvented himself and, abandoning his earlier punk riffs and bondage, incorporated a sound influenced by Burundi Black drummers. He had three UK hits in 1980, culminating in the No. 2 hit 'Ant Music'. 1981 was 'the year of Adam and the Ants' and, in effect, he successfully dismissed his rivals, Bow Wow Wow.

24 McLaren had first come across the Situationists through some of his more radical friends and had obtained his magazines from Compendium Books during the late 1960s. Situationist art was largely seen as an update on Pop Art in Britain and was interpreted as gimmicky, witty, sexy and young. By 1966, interpretation was transmitted globally by the Beatles, the Rolling Stones and the Kinks.

25 Julia O'Connell Davidson (1998, 35) cites the list of physical injuries and illnesses suffered by child prostitutes in Thailand compiled in August 1985 by the United Nations Group of Experts on Slavery. The list included 'rectal fissures, lesions, poor sphincter control, lacerated vaginas, foreign bodies in the anus or vagina, perforated anal and vagina walls, death by asphyxiation, chronic choking from gonorrhoeal tonsillitis, ruptured uteruses, bodily mutilation and death in childbirth'.

26 Annabella and Leigh Gorman (bass) resurrected Bow Wow Wow in 1997 and together with guitarist Dave Calbourn and Drummer Eshan Khadaroo went on a four-month tour of America.

Part II: Little Girls

1 For the majority of early feminist theorists (radical, liberal, socialist and Marxist) there was a consensus that differences between the sexes were 'man-made' and more rigid, absolute and inflexible than the gradations of 'natural' difference on which sex distinctions were ostensibly grounded.

2 A brief review entitled 'Britney and the 90s' provides some indication of media attitude.

> Little Brit's main purpose was to embody perfection in mind, deed and complicated choreography and charting prowess. The main delusion of the 90s,

politically and culturally, was that, with a personal trainer, a protein-rich diet, a very emphatic tone of voice and a plucky determination to be innocent in the face of all evidence to the contrary, you too could be a flawless individual. We were duped. Only Britney is perfect.

(Williams, 2001, 37)

3 Having made her film debut in 1980 in a low-budget softcore film, *Certain Sacrifice*, it is not too surprising that her first video, *Like A Virgin* (1985), with musical director Patrick Leonard, exhibits a professional confidence in its play on pornographic imagery and metaphor against a lightweight disco pop format.

4 So conforming to discussions surrounding cultural feminism, which often highlights the specificity of female (and male) bodies.

5 For a detailed discussion of Joplin, Madonna, k.d. lang and the girl-group Spice Girls, see Whiteley, S. (2000) *Women and Popular Music: Sexuality, Identity and Subjectivity*. London: Routledge.

6 A fuller discussion of the Stones and issues surrounding gender can be found in Whiteley, S. (ed.) (1997) *Sexing the Groove: Popular Music and Gender*. London: Routledge, pp. 67–99.

7 For example, Motley Crue's 'She Goes Down' and Extreme's 'Suzi (Wants Her All Day What?)'.

8 As described by Wayne and Garth of *Saturday Night Live* and *Wayne's World*. For a more detailed discussion, see Sloat, Lisa J. (1998) 'Incubus: Male songwriters' portrayal of women's sexuality in pop metal music' in Epstein, J. (ed.) *Youth Culture: Identity in a Postmodern World*. Blackwell: Malden, Massachusetts and Oxford.

9 Marianne Faithfull also comments on such songs as 'Yesterday's Papers', which she recognised as a 'horrible public humiliation' for Chrissie Shrimpton with whom Jagger was living when he began his affair with Faithfull. '"Who wants yesterday's papers, who wants yesterday's girl ...". "Under My Thumb" was also about Chrissie. You see, when he got her where he wanted her, he didn't want her any more' (Hotchner, 1990, p. 39).

10 For a more detailed discussion of the Beatles and issues surrounding gender see Whiteley, S. (1992) *The Space Between the Notes: Rock and the Counter-Culture*. London: Routledge and Whiteley, S. (2002) 'Love is all and love is everyone: A discussion of four musical portraits' in Reising, R. (ed.) *'Every Sound There Is'. The Beatles' Revolver and the Transformation of Rock and Roll*: London: Ashgate.

11 Sloat, L. (1995) 'From playthings to fatal flowers: The image of women's sexuality in hard rock/heavy metal music 1980–1995. Unpublished independent study.

12 Identity politics refers to the practice of basing one's politics on a sense of personal identity – as female, gay, etc. It focuses either upon the affirmation of common identities by groups of mobilising individuals or on the deconstruction of those identities as socially constructed and therefore open to refusal.

13 This is not intended to suggest that Courtney Love failed. Her reception by fans and by such feminist commentators as Amy Raphael (1995) show her to be one of the most significant female artists of the early 1990s, not least in her awareness of feminism and the problems surrounding the male gaze and its relation to women as sex objects.

14 See my earlier discussion in 'Nursery Crymes', p. 42.

15 Sleevenotes to *Lionheart*.

16 As executive Bob Mercer comments, 'EMI is like another family for her ... she was the company's daughter for a few years' (in O'Brien, 1995, 188).

17 As Bush told *Q* magazine (in Gaar, 1992, 268).

18 Lou Reed, Iggy Pop, David Bowie, the Sex Pistols and others all shared a fascination with pre-war Germany. Liza Minelli's role in the film *Cabaret* was a particular influence

on Siouxsie Sioux and the white shirt, black tie and cropped black hair informed her own *Weimar* image.

19 The song title 'Get Out Of My House' appeared nearly ten years later as a line in 'Teenage Whore' on Hole's *Pretty on the Inside*, where the body becomes a battlefield for a struggle between degradation and control.

20 Gale Colson, who met Bush when managing Peter Gabriel, explained that after *The Dreaming* EMI had said that they wanted her to have a producer, that she could no longer produce herself. Kate was so angry that she went home and built a studio and produced *Hounds of Love* (Gaar, 1992, 268).

21 Thanks to Emma Mayhew for her permission to use these examples from her PhD research and for her reflections on Kate Bush's role in the studio.

22 Bush's music has never achieved significant US commercial status. *Hounds of Love* reached No. 30 in the Top 40 and 'Running Up That Hill (A Deal With God)' also hit No. 30, but Gale Colson of EMI A&R considered that she would never make it big. She remains, largely, a cult artist with a strong following on the alternative/college radio (Gaar, 1992, 388–9).

23 Copyright permission was denied.

24 1989 interview with *Melody Maker* (in Reynolds and Press, 1995, 380).

25 Julia Kristeva locates the semiotic with the *chora*, a non-geometrical space where both positive and negative, creative and destructive, activities are 'primarily' located. Sounds (speech acts, timbre, rhythm, gesture) draw attention to the semiotic pre-symbolic in language through exaggeration. As such, the chora is mobile and is analogous to vocal or kinetic rhythm which, in turn, constitutes the pre-symbolic *significance*. See Lechte, J. (1990) *Julia Kristeva*. London: Routledge, pp. 127–32.

26 She was voted one of the Top Ten 'Pop Princesses' for her performance of 'Babooshka' on Channel 4's *Top Ten* series (2001).

27 Ian McEwan (author of *First Love, Last Rites*) on Angela Carter (1979) *The Bloody Chamber*. London: Penguin, back cover.

28 Tori Amos was often derided as the poor man's Kate Bush, and her producers at Atlantic Records were accused of marketing her specifically to cater to Kate Bush's fans.

29 Joni Mitchell is noted for her individualistic tuning of the guitar, for example; Amos for her individualistic and often tempestuous piano playing.

30 On a personal note, he kindly gave permission for me to quote from *Little Earthquakes* for discussion of Tori Amos in *Women and Popular Music* (2000). I will always be grateful.

31 The album, *Y Kant Tori Read*, was released in 1988, together with singles 'The Big Picture' and 'Cool On Your Island', and a video for 'The Big Picture'. Compared with *Streets of Fire* 'without the nifty soundstage and silly villains' and Amos 'tottering away in her plastic thigh-high boots' by Charles Aaron in the October 1994 issue of *SPIN* magazine, it was considered a weak, rock-chick version of metal star, Lita Ford.

32 'Me And A Gun' was inspired by the rape scene in the film *Thelma and Louise*. It suddenly brought back memories of her own horrifying experience and she wrote the song just a few hours before her gig at the Mean Fiddler in North London, singing it for the first time that night (*Tori Amos, All These Years*. 1994. Authorised illustrated biography. London/New York: Omnibus, p. 47).

33 The Aeolian, or natural minor, is most often found in the death motifs of heavy metal.

34 Amos donated the proceeds from the concert and the single to the Rape, Abuse and Incest National Network.

35 Amos's personal notes on her compositions on the sleevenotes to *Little Earthquakes*.

36 Amos, quoted in *Tori Amos, Silent All These Years*, p. 55.

37 Both these songs are discussed in Whiteley (2000), p. 202.

38 Bloodletting, or self-mutilation, is common amongst psychiatric patients, not least the young, who feel that the cutting and sight of their own blood releases pent-up tension.

39 Amos's sleevenotes to 'Leather'.

40 'WEIRD CHICK – On the Couch with Tori Amos'. Q cover, February 1992.

41 So providing a comparison with Eric Clapton, whose 'At the Rainbow' concert (1971) marked part of his rehabilitation from drugs, so breaking two years of silence, and 'Tears In Heaven', a poignant song about the death of his son, Conor, in 1991, which became a worldwide hit.

42 Amos had earlier considered giving her album the title, 'God with a capital G'.

43 Amos had written the song after receiving a letter from fans who wanted to tell her about their girl friends. 'I wrote this song to help them overcome their self-pity' (St Michael, 1996, 94).

44 From personal e-mail correspondence with Thomas Crayton Harrison who, like me, is a member of the Rocklist.

45 Amos believes strongly that Richard III was one of the most misunderstood characters in history and always defended him.

46 By 1996 Underworld's computer-aided sounds had become the bedrock of House.

47 Early in 1987 the London-based DJ Tim Simenon, making music under the name Bomb the Bass, copied artwork from a record by Miama act Maggotron for the initial pressings of his first single 'Beat Dis'. 'Beat Dis' was a sampler-aided record made just as dancefloors were often dressed up to look like American dance records. The man behind Maggotron, James McCauley, was immersed in mid-1980s electro sounds and went on to play a central role in what would soon be labelled 'Miami Bass' (Haslam, 2000, 205).

48 David Morales was an American DJ who went on to earn thousands of pounds guesting at big clubs all over Europe. He was one of the first Americans to benefit from the demand for guest DJs in the early 1990s (Haslam, 2000, 205).

49 Justin Robertson was a DJ during the early days of the Hacienda, Manchester scene which was to become the epicentre of the so-called 'House Nation' in the late 1980s.

50 Björk had supported hardcore industrial band Einstürzende Neubauten in Germany aged 20.

51 The Hacienda (Manchester, England) was at the epicentre of rave and had been transformed from an old yacht warehouse into what was later considered the best House club in the UK. Sadly, it has now been pulled down as part of the City's regeneration project.

52 Sleeve notes to Debut.

53 Dante Alighieri ascribes this phenomenon to the Wood of Suicides in his journey through the Inferno.

54 It is also possible that the image was a subconscious response to her experience in Bankok in 1996. Accompanied by her son Sindri, she was approached by TN news reporter Julie Kaufman and camera crew, broadcasting live, wanting an interview. As Björk explains, 'there were 40 people following us. When my son is there, I just don't go into interview mode. I just don't. That's work.' Kaufman persisted and 'Then she went for my son, live on air, on TV, and she said "Isn't it difficult to be the son of a woman who is a pop star and is so self-important that she won't give us an interview?" She could do it to me, but not to him, I just snapped.' It was the third time in her life that Björk had hit someone and she acknowledges the fact that 'a lot of shit comes with my job. I'm willing to take that on, but I'd be lying if I said it didn't piss me off when it spills over to my friends and family'. Information from Lindsay Baker, 'Norse Code', Guardian Weekend, September 27, 1997, pp. 14–15.

55 Björk had written the soundtrack for the film.

56 The cover of Q, February 1992.

Part III: Little Boys

1 Useful perspectives on style and genre have been developed from Mikhail Bakhtin's 'dialogical' theory of languages. His application to music can be found in Hirschkop, Ken (1989), 'The classical and the popular: musical form and social context', in Norris, C. (ed.) *Music and the Politics of Culture*. London: Lawrence & Wishart, pp. 283–304.

2 See, for example, papers originating from the Centre for Contemporary Cultural Studies, Birmingham University; Epstein, J.S. (ed.) (1998) *Youth Culture. Identity in a Postmodern World*. Malden, Massachusetts and Oxford: Blackwell.

3

> In the early 1950s it was by no means an obvious move for a hillbilly bandleader to start fooling around with black r & b songs, and it is to Haley's credit that he saw the change coming, and moved in the right direction. His first r & b cover version 'Rocket 88' was recorded in 1951, and by 1953 he had renamed his band the Comets, and enjoyed his first national hit with his own song, 'Crazy Man Crazy', an obvious example of capitalising on a current catchphrase. In 1954 he recorded 'Rock Around the Clock', an international success when re-released to tie in with the classroom rebellion movie 'The Blackboard Jungle' which featured the song. In Britain, every record from then until 1957 reached the Top Twenty, and 'Clock' has been a hit half-a-dozen times over the years.
>
> (Collis, 1980, 25–6)

4 Little Richard moved to Speciality Records in 1955 after an unsuccessful career as a blues artist (with RCA, 1951–2 and Peacock, 1952–5). His hits continued throughout the 1950s, including 'Long Tall Sally', 'The Girl Can't Help It', 'Lucille' and 'Good Golly Miss Molly'. They were all in the same style: a pounding twelve-bar chord progression, with a solid persistent riff and wild piano decorations (usually by Hey Smith).

5 However, as Sanjek (1997, 138) observes, in the heyday of rockabilly, many men probably shared Clarence Worly's view that Elvis was prettier than most women and that 'if I had to fuck a guy – *had to* if my life depended on it – I'd fuck Elvis' (*True Romance*, 1993, directed by Tony Scott with a script by Quentin Tarantino). Clearly, the urge to perform Elvis's music exceeded this fantasy, as evidenced in the world-wide fascination with the 'King' and the look-alike performers that today compete for the most credible performance of his songs.

6 for a detailed discussion of the Pet Shop Boys see Hawkins, S. (1997) 'The Pet Shop Boys: Musicology, masculinity and banality' in Whiteley (1997), pp. 118–133, and Hawkins, S. (2002) *Settling the Pop Score. Pop Texts and Identity Politics*. London: Ashgate, pp. 130–58.

7

> When the Serbian-Montenegrin forces in the Balkans war cursed the women they raped that they would bear children who would forever be their enemies and fight against their mother and her people, they were behaving according to a particular complex of inherited social beliefs, they were speaking out of commitment to military values, paternal lineage and a cult of male heroism.
>
> (Warner, 1994b, 28–9).

8 The idiolectology described by Barthes (1977, 168).

9 This was enhanced by subsequent performances, most notably at Chet Helm's psychedelic ballroom, the Avalon (San Francisco, January 1967), where the walls of the auditorium and stage moved and pulsated with light moving through coloured liquid.

10 William Blake, 'Satan Rousing His Legions', from the Liverpool set of Blake's illustrations for *Paradise Lost* (1807). The Henry E. Huntington Library and Art Gallery.

11 John Densmore is now a disciple of Robert Bly's Men's Movement.

12 This was composed as a performance piece for the rock stage and includes songs, poetry, sound effects, music and, to a certain degree, audience participation.

13 Morrison's debt to a Romantic Symbolist literary movement is well documented and his citations of Burroughs/Kerouac have been interpreted as suppressed homoerotic desire. See Ortiz, R.L. (1999) 'L.A. Women. Jim Morrison and John Rechy' in Smith, P.J. (ed.) *The Queer Sixties*, London: Routledge, pp. 164–86.

14 Evidence from his notebooks suggests many drafts of 'Celebration'. See Morrison, J. (1991) *The American Night. The Writings of Jim Morrison.* London: Viking Penguin, p. 206.

15 Morrison's alleged stage exposure led to a court case in Miami in 1971. Offered in evidence were 150 photos, but not a single one showed Morrison's penis. The charge read in court, however, stated that 'He did lewdly and lasciviously expose his penis, place his hands upon his penis, and shake it. And further, the said defendant did simulate masturbation upon himself and oral sex upon another'. Again, there were no photos to support this, but Morrison was sentenced to six months' hard labour at Dade County Jail and had to pay a fine of $500. The case was heard in Florida and Morrison left the country from Los Angeles prior to the appeal. There were no computerised CIS criminal checks at airports in 1971 (Manzarek, 1999, 315).

16 Morrison's addiction to alcohol fitted with his particular slant on the Dionysian myth – getting drunk and picking up (or being picked up by) women. His macho code was influenced by Norman Mailer: 'Night after night he trundled from bar to bar along Sunset Strip, sometimes picking up a girl, sometimes befriending a group of drunks before stripping naked in the street and maybe scaling a hotel wall, or playing the matador with cars on the freeway. And he slept where he fell. God help anyone who tried to help him' (Jones, 1990, 68).

17 Morrison's addiction spiralled out of control after the Miami trial and accounts partly for the change in his image from Morrison the boy god to Morrison the bear. 'He was practically dead at this point. He'd aged ten years, his hair, which was matted and greasy, was starting to recede, and he'd gotten really fat' (Jones, 1990, 169).

18 In doing so he draws on his philosophical mentor's dictum that 'the death instinct is reconciled with the life instinct only in a life which is not repressed, which leaves no "unlived lives" in the human body, the death instinct then being affirmed in a body willing to die' (Norman O. Brown cited in Roszak, 1970, 115).

19 It is also interesting to note that the owner of the hotel refuses to let guests know the number of the room in which Morrison died. It is probable that the more extreme of his fans would take advantage of this and follow Morrison's example.

20 *Are You Experienced?* (1967) used the building up of multiple tracks on four-track equipment, the manipulation of tape speeds, the mixing down of some material played backwards, the use of controlled feedback, phaze shifting, Fuzz Face and Cry Baby sound-effects pedals, and special effects achieved through the manipulation of the tremolo arm and the toggle switch controlling the selection and combination of pickups (Piccarella, 1986, 47).

21 Hendrix was arrested on May 3, 1969 at Toronto International Airport when a custom's officer found six small packages inside a glass bottle at the top of his bag. CFRB, a Toronto radio station, reported that the chemical was heroin.

22 Hendrix actually said he used his gums, rather than his teeth.

23 As Germaine Greer noted in her obituary for Hendrix in *OZ* (subsequently reprinted in her 1986 collection *The Madwoman's Underclothes*), Hendrix's grandstand play for Marianne Faithfull was, as much as anything else, a calculated slap at Jagger's own

status as the king-pin of the London scene. Jagger had his revenge a couple of years later, when Devon Wilson – the new York super-groupie who was the model for Hendrix's song 'Dolly Dagger', and one of the most important women in his life – walked out of Hendrix's 27th birthday party with Jagger on her arm (Shaar Murray, 1989, 70).

24 From 'Ziggy first played guitar 30 years ago', a Radio 3 discussion on Ziggy Stardust and the Spiders from Mars ('Nighwaves', June 6, 2002) with Sheila Whiteley, Nicola King (University of Salford), Mark Petress and Martin Newall.

25 I am indebted to fellow contributors to Rocklist (Academic discussion of popular music) for their very helpful response to my e-mail on 'dead heroes': Albert Bell, Jonathan Epstein, Timothy Lynch, Jonathan Millen, Jason, sugar-mouse, Marjorie Preston, Luis Pulgar Aleman, Louie and Steve Court. Biographic details were obtained from Larkin, C. (ed.) (1999) *The Virgin Encyclopedia of Popular Music.* Concise 3rd edn. London: Virgin Books.

26 Goth, or gothic rock is a musical genre influenced by the proto-punk music of American band The Velvet Underground and the sound experiments of the rock avant-garde. It was first applied to such bands as Joy Division, Southern Death Cult, Sisters of Mercy and Bauhaus, whose debut record *Bela Lugosi's Dead* (Small Wonder Records 1979) introduced the genre to the UK. The nine-and-a-half minute title track became a cult anthem. The music is characterised by a low bass sound, electronic sound effects, pounding drumbeats and low pitched-vocals, often spoken rather than sung. Elements of psychedelia (usually associated with the darker sides of tripping) were also evident in Joy Division ('Love Will Tear Us Apart'). Goth style was characterised by black clothes, the heavy use of dark eye and face make up and pointy boots. Above all, it is associated with the mysticism of death and the Dracula cult inspired by Tod Browning's 1931 film, *Dracula.*

27 Death metal is a sub-genre of metal and is characterised by a grating vocal, although the music itself ranges from hardcore to mellow. The names of bands reflect the thanatic: Death, Pestilence, etc. It should also be noted that the originators of metal (Black Sabbath) were named after a cult horror movie of the same title.

28 Milton Keynes Art Gallery, Preview, July 11, 2002.

29 from 'Anyone Can Play Guitar', Emma Mahony, curator of 'Air Guitar: Art Reconsidering Rock', catalogue, p. 7.

30 Gaines, D. (2002) 'An open letter to the Ramones family worldwide' on *www.ofical-ramones.com*, June 7.

31 Skiffle, a musical genre that developed out of traditional jazz, was more significant as a catalyst than a musical style. Characterised by a DIY ethic, and comprising a simple rhythm section of homemade string bass and washboard, augmented by banjo and guitars, it was popularised in Britain during the 1950s by Lonnie Donegan whose style drew on American blues and folk, most specifically the work of Woody Guthrie and Leadbelly. By the early 1960s skiffle had developed into beat. It was an influential training ground for John Lennon's group, The Quarrymen.

32 Their success is largely attributable to their 1960 recording 'Apache', which was voted single of the year in numerous music papers. Unlike Richard, The Shadows feature in books on rock, and Marvin's status was confirmed when he featured in Channel 4's choice of *Top Ten Lead Guitarists*, November 2001.

33 In a Granada News interview (February 22, 2002), Richard discussed his forthcoming national tour – a possible prelude to his next Christmas release, by now a yearly occurrence. Fans were also interviewed in the street and two middle-aged women sang the first verse of 'Summer Holiday'. Shown regularly on TV, it seems to confirm his eternal status as a youthful pop star whose appeal (to a largely middle-aged audience) never diminishes.

34 The Cowsills were billed as 'America's First Family of Music' and were all born in Newport, Rhode Island, USA. Featuring Bill (b. January 1948, guitar/vocals), Bob (b. August 26, 1949, guitar/vocals), Paul (b. November 11, 1952, bass/vocals), John (b. March 2, 1956, drums) and Susan (b. May 20, 1960, vocals), they came to attention of writer/producer Artie Kornfeld who co-wrote and produced their debut single 'The Rain, The Park and Other Things' which reached No. 2 in the US charts in December 1967. Occasionally augmented by their mother Barbara (b. 1928, vocals), their happy, bouncy harmonies and family atmosphere inspired the NBC US television series *The Partridge Family* (Larkin, 1999, 315).

35 Chart ratings have all been taken from Rice, T., Gambaccini, P. and Read, M. (eds) (1985) *The Guinness Book of British Hit Singles*. London: GRRR Books Ltd and Guinness Superlatives Ltd, pp. 292–9.

36 During a recent Channel 4 programme on the Bay City Rollers (January 26, 2002), Paton pointed out that underage (at the time) meant under 16 for a girl and 21 for a boy and that his so-termed indecent acts would not have resulted in a prison sentence today.

37 On April 7, 1998, George Michael was arrested for 'lewd behaviour' in a toilet cubicle at the Will Rogers Memorial Park in Beverley Hills, CA. He later confirmed his long-rumoured homosexuality and was sentenced to perform community service. He bounced back with an excellent single, 'Outside', which entered in the UK charts at No. 2 in October 1998. The *Ladies and Gentlemen* compilation was a best-seller, topping the UK charts for eight weeks.

38 In an interview in *The Sunday Times Magazine* (November 18, 2001) Robbie Williams remained evasive on the nature of his relationships. On previous girlfriend Geri Halliwell, he admitted that 'we slept together but we didn't find each other physically attractive. It wasn't really a sex thing', while Nicole Kidman has 'an ethereal quality to her aura'. 'Kiss-and-tells' ensures that we his general public 'don't forget that he has had considerably more sex than most men on the planet'. Meanwhile, he continues to share a house with Jonathan Wilkes.

39 Cathy Dennis's biggest hit as an artist, 'Touch Me (All Night Long), made No. 5 in May 1991. She also works with S Club and co-wrote Kylie Minogue's recent No. 1, 'Can't Get You Out Of My Head'.

40 As Woods reports, 'His company is now working on a programme where football fans would have a say in running a real team. Such interactive voting allows ordinary viewers to have an active part in fulfilling a dream that for Britain's new pop idols has become a reality' (2002, 12).

41 Edwards also notes that 'the consoling high was the subsequent upswing in sales of Frank Sinatra's catalogue, as discerning punters reminded themselves of how the songs on *Swing* were supposed to sound' (2002, 7). Having seen the concert I find this overly critical – as did his fans at the packed Albert Hall.

Postscript: Life after death – Old Girls and Old Boys

1 Interview with a fan from the BBC1 programme *There's Only One Elvis*, August 11, 2002.

2 The script is by Philip Norman in partnership with producer Laurie Mansfield. Norman, P. (2002) 'The King and I'. *The Sunday Times Magazine*, August 18, p. 23.

3 Early pioneers identified by Ellis (1995, 200–1) include Charlie Christian, T-Bone Walker, Les Paul, B.B. King, Chuck Berry, Jimmy Bryant, Jimmy Nolen, Wes Montgomery, Dick Dale, Jeff Beck and Pete Townshend, all of whom 'pushed the boundaries in the context of their chosen genre'.

4 Authenticity has become an important defining factor in rock music since the late 1960s and distinguishes it from early rock 'n' roll. Returning briefly to Elvis Presley, it is clear that his early success owed much to Otis Blackwell, the legendary song-writer who died of a heart attack on May 8, 2002. Born in Brooklyn in 1931, the African-American Blackwell grew up idolising such 'singing cowboys' as Tex Ritter before being attracted to the newer R & B styles that grew out of Jump Blues after World War II. Blackwell not only wrote 'Don't Be Cruel', 'Return to Sender', 'All Shook Up' and 'One Broken Heart for Sale' for Presley (and it is reported that the singer also closely copied Blackwell's singing on the demos), but was also responsible for Jerry Lee Lewis's big hits, 'Great Balls of Fire' and 'Breathless'. The Who later covered one of his first original songs, 'Daddy Rolling Stone', and 'Fever' (written under the pseudonym John Davenport) became a hit for Peggy Lee. Other artists who bought Blackwell's songs included the Drifters, Gene Vincent and Bobby Darin. It is a salutary fact that he is seldom mentioned in biographies of Presley, whose early success is more generally attributed to the guiding influence of Sun Records owner/producer Sam Phillips and Colonel Tom Parker.

   Information is taken from William E. Harris, Bernard C. Harris Publishing Company, Norfolk, VA and circulated via the Rocklist.

5 Information from 'Born-again patriot rocks back in 9/11 time'. Profile on Bruce Springsteen. *The Sunday Times*, July 21, 2002, p. 13.

6 Thanks to Jeannefury from Rocklist for her thoughts on rock casualties.

7 See Whiteley, S. (2000) 'Try just a little bit harder: Janis Joplin and the search for personal identity' in *Women and Popular Music: Sexuality, Identity and Subjectivity*. London: Routledge, pp. 51–71.

8 See Whiteley, S. (2000) 'Daughters of chaos: Patti Smith, Siouxsie Sioux and the feminisation of rock' in *Women and Popular Music*, pp. 95–107.

9 As told by Bush to *Q* magazine (in Gaar, 1992, p. 268).

10 Factual information from Larkin (1999, 722).

11 See Whiteley, S. (2000) 'The lonely road: Joni Mitchell, *Blue* and female subjectivity' in *Women and Popular Music*, pp. 78–94.

12 See Whiteley, S. (1997) 'Little Red Rooster v. The Honky Tonk Woman. Mick Jagger, sexuality, style and image' in *Sexing the Groove*, pp. 67–99.

13 From 'Modesty? It's just a phase she's going through'. Profile, Madonna. *The Sunday Times*, July 23, 2000, p. 19.

14 See Whiteley, S. (2000) 'Madonna, eroticism, autoeroticism and desire' in *Women and Popular Music*, pp. 136–51.

15 From 'Modesty? It's just a phase she's going through', p. 19.

Bibliography

Aizlewood, J. (2002) 'Working Class Hero'. Q, October.

Andahazi, F. (1998) *The Anatomist*. Trans. Manguel, Alberto. London: Transworld Publishers Ltd.

Appleyard, B. (2001) 'Why Kylie? Why Now?' *The Sunday Times Magazine*, October 21.

Baker, L. (1997) 'Norse Code'. *Guardian Weekend*, September 27.

Baker, S. L. (2003) *Rock On, Baby! An Exploration of Pre-teen Girls' Negotations of Popular Music and Identity in Adelaide, Australia*. (unpublished PhD Thesis)

Barthes, B. (1990) in Gaines, J. and Herzog., C. (eds) *Fabrications, Costume and the Female Body*. London: Routledge.

Barthes, R. (1957) *Mythologies*. Trans. Heath, S. London: Fontana.

Barthes, R. (1977) *Image, Music, Text*. Trans. Heath, S. London: Fontana.

Best, S. and Kellner, D. (1998) 'Beavis and Butt-Head: No future for postmodern youth' in Epstein, J. (ed.) *Youth Culture: Identity in a Postmodern World*. Malden, Massachusetts and Oxford: Blackwell.

Black, F. (2004) 'Too Much, Tatu Young' in Bruce, I.S. *The Sunday Herald*, February 2, 2004

Bloustien, G. (1996) 'Striking a Pose! Girls, cameras and deflecting the gaze', *Youth Studies Australia*, vol.15, no.3, Sept: 26–32

Bloustien, G. (1999a) 'On not dancing like a "try hard"' in *Musical Visions: Selected Conference Proceedings from 6th National Australian, New Zealand IASPM and Inaugural Arnhem Land Performance Conference*, ed. G. Bloustien, Wakefield Press, Kent Town: 8–20.

Bloustien, G. (1999b) 'The consequences of being a gift', *The Australian Journal of Anthropology*, vol.10, no.1, April: 77–93.

Bly, R. (1991) *Iron John: A Book About Men*. Dorset: Element.

Bradby, B. (1990) 'Do-talk and don't talk: the division of the subject in girl-group music' in Frith, S. and Goodwin, A. (eds) *On Record: Rock, Pop and the Written Word*. London: Routledge.

Bristow, J. (1997) *Sexuality*. London: Routledge.

Burroughs, W. (1963) *Dead Fingers Talk*. London: Tandem.

Burroughs, W. (1988) *The Naked Lunch*. London: Paladin.

Butler, J. (1990) *Gender Trouble. Feminism and the Subversion of Identity*. London: Routledge.

Butler, J. (1990) 'Performative acts and gender constitution: An essay in phenomenology and feminist theory' in Case, Sue-Ellen (ed.) *Performing Feminisms: Feminist Critical Theory and Theatre*. Baltimore: Johns Hopkins University Press, p. 270.

Byatt, A.S. (1991) *Possession*. London: Vintage.

Byatt, A.S. (1997) *Babel Tower*. London: Vintage.

Cairns, D. (2002) Cover story on Ms Dynamite, *Telegraph Magazine*, September 5.

Caplan, P. (ed.) (1987) *The Cultural Construction of Sexuality*. London: Routledge.

Carter, A. (1979) 'The Company of Wolves', 'The Tiger's Bride' and 'The Courtship of Mr Lyon' in *The Bloody Chamber*. London: Penguin Books.

Carter, A. (1981) *The Magic Toyshop*. London: Virago.

Carter, A. (2000) *The Sadeian Woman. An Exercise in Cultural History*. London: Virago.

Chester, A. (1990) 'Second thoughts on a rock aesthetic: The band', pp. 315–19, in Frith, S. and Goodwin, A. (eds) *On Record: Rock, Pop and the Written Word*. London: Routledge.

Chodorow, N. (1974) 'Family structure and feminine personality' in Rosaldo, M.Z. and Lamphere, L. (eds) *Women, Culture and Society*. Stanford: Stanford University Press.

Cixous, H. (1981) 'The Laugh of the Medusa' in Marks, E. and de Courivron, I. (eds.) *New French Feminisms*, New York: Schocken Books.

Clarke, M. and Woods, P. (eds) (1999) *Kurt Cobain: The Cobain Dossier*. London: Plexus.

Collis, J. (ed.) (1980) *The Rock Primer*. Harmondsworth, Middlesex: Penguin Books.

Connolly, P. (2001) 'Off the wall ?' *Play. The Times*, August 18.

Crowley, V. (1989) *Wicca: The Old Religion in the New Age*. Wellingborough: Aquarian.

De Beauvoir, S. (1974) *The Second Sex*. Trans. and ed. Parshley, H.M. New York: Vintage.

Densmore, J. (1991) *Riders on the Storm. My Life with Jim Morrison and The Doors*. London: Arrow Books.

Dijkstra, B. (1986) *Idols of Perversity: Fantasies of Feminine Evil in Fin-de-Siècle Culture*. Oxford: Oxford University Press.

Dubecki, L. (2000) 'the knowledge: Five things you didn't know about … young people and music', *The Age Today*, 16 August: 2000.

Duff, L.S. (1988) 'Jim and the Monkees', *Guitar World*, March, in Potash, C. (ed.) (1996) *The Jimi Hendrix Companion. Four Decades of Commentary*. New York: Schirmer.

Du Noyer (2002) 'Conversation Killer'. *Q*, October: 124.

Easthope, A. (1990) *What a Man's Gotta Do. The Masculine Myth in Popular Culture*. Boston: Unwin Hyman.

Edwards, M. (2002) 'Pop'. *The Sunday Times Magazine*, January.

Ehrenriech, B., Hess, E. and Jacobs, G. (1992) 'Beatlemania: girls just want to have fun' in Lewis, L. (ed.) *The Adoring Audience. Fan Culture and Popular Music*. London: Routledge.

Eliezer, C. (2001) 'Pre-teens rule the pop world', *Business Review Weekly*, vol.23, No.2: 42–43.

Elliott, P. (1997) 'Who the hell does Bjork think she is?' *Q*, November, no. 134.

Ellis, A. 'Still reigning, still dreaming', *Guitar Player*, September 1995, in Potash, C. (ed.) (1996) 'Introduction'. *The Jimi Hendrix Companion. Three Decades of Commentary*. New York: Schirmer.

Epstein, J.S. (ed.) (1998) *Youth Culture. Identity in a Postmodern World*. Malden, Massachusetts and Oxford: Blackwell.

Evans, L. (1997) *Girls Will Be Boys. Women Report on Rock*. London: Pandora.

Fort. J. (1969) *The Pleasure Seekers: The Drug Crisis, Youth and Society*. New York: Grove Press.

Freud, S. (1920) *Beyond the Pleasure Principle* in Bristow, J. (1997) *Sexuality*. London: Routledge.

Freud, S. (1968) 'The Passing of the Oedipus Complex' in *Sexuality and the Psychology of Love*, ed. Philip Rieff, pp.176–82. New York: Collier Books.

Frith, S. (1988) *Music for Pleasure: Essays in the Sociology of Pop*. Cambridge: Polity Press.

Frith, S. and McRobbie, A. (1990) 'Rock and sexuality' in Frith, S. and Goodwin, A. (eds) *On Record: Rock, Pop and the Written Word*. London: Routledge.

Gaar, G.G. (1992) *She's A Rebel. The History of Women in Rock 'n' Roll*. Seattle: Seal Press.

Gaines, J. and Herzog, C. (eds) (1990) *Fabrications, Costume and the Female Body*. London: Routledge.

Gammond, P. (ed.) (1991) *The Oxford Companion to Popular Music*. Oxford: Oxford University Press.

Gill, A.A. (2002) *The Sunday Times News Review*, February 3.

Giroux, H. (1998) 'Teenage sexuality' in Epstein, J. (ed.) *Youth Culture: Identity in a Post-modern World*. Malden, Massachusetts and Oxford: Blackwell.

Gledhill, C. (1991) *Stardom: Industry of Desire*. London: Routledge.

Glover, D. and Kaplan, C. (2000) *Genders*. London: Routledge.

Goertzel, B. (1991) 'From "The Rock Guitar Solo: From Expression to Simulation"', *Popular Music and Society*, Spring, in Potash, C. (ed.) (1996) *The Jimi Hendrix Companion. Four Decades of Commentary*. New York: Schirmer.

Greer, G. (1999) *The Whole Woman*. London: Transworld Publications.

Grosz, E. and Probyn, E. (eds) (1995) *Sexy bodies: the strange carnalities of feminism*. London, New York: Routledge

Guralnick, P. (1989) *Feel Like Going Home*. London: Omnibus Press.

Haslam, D. (2000) *Manchester, England. The Story of the Pop Cult City*. London: Fourth Estate.

Hasted, N. (1998) 'Playing with the devil within'. *Eye on Friday, Guardian*, May 8.

Hawkins, S. (1997) 'The Pet Shop Boys: Musicology, masculinity and banality' in Whiteley, S. (ed.) *Sexing the Groove. Popular Music and Gender*. London: Routledge.

Hawkins, S. (2002) *Settling the Pop Score. Pop Texts and Identity Politics*. London: Ashgate.

Henderson, D. (1978) *The Life of Jimi Hendrix: 'scuse me while I kiss the sky*. London: Omnibus Press.

Hicks, B. (1970) 'Jimi Hendrix: A memorial'. *Northwest Passage*, September 29, in Potash, C. (ed.) (1996) *The Jimi Hendrix Companion. Four Decades of Commentary*. New York: Schirmer.

Hill, D. (1986) *Designer Boys and Material Girls: Manufacturing the 80's Pop Dream*. London: Blandford Press.

Hirschkop, (1989) 'The classical and the popular: Musical form and social context', in Norris, C. (ed.) *Music and the Politics of Culture*. London: Lawrence & Wishart, pp. 283–304.

Hopkins, J. and Sugerman, D. (1991) *No One Here Gets Out Alive. The Biography of Jim Morrison*. London: Plexus.

Hotchner, A.E. (1990) *Blow Away: The Rolling Stones and the Death of the Sixties*. New York: Simon & Schuster.

Jackson, A. (2001) 'She will survive'. *The Times Magazine*, November 3.

Johnson, K. (2001) 'Child porn ring busted. Children as young as 4 were abused'. *USA Today*, August 9.

Jones, D. (1990) *Jim Morrison. Dark Star*. London: Bloomsbury.

Keil, C. (1966) 'Motion and feeling through music'. *Journal of Aesthetics and Art Criticism*, 24.

Kirkpatrick, E.M. (ed.) (1985) *Chambers 20th Century Dictionary*. Edinburgh: Chambers.

Kitzinger, J. (1997) 'Who are you kidding? Children, power, and the struggle against sexual abuse', in *Constructing and Reconstructing Childhood: Contemporary Issues in the Sociological Study of Childhood*, eds. A. James and A. Prout, London: Falmer Press, 165–89.

Koha, N.T. (1999) 'All in a whirl for Britney', *The Advertiser*, 27

MayLacan, J. (1977) *Ecrits: A Selection* Trans. Alan Sheridan. London: Tavistock.

Landesman, C. (2002) 'Sex, no drugs and suburbia'. *The Sunday Times News Review*, August 18.

Larkin, C. (ed.) (1999) *The Virgin Encyclopedia of Popular Music*. Concise 3rd edn. London: Virgin Books.

Lechte, J. (1990) *Julia Kristeva*. London: Routledge.

Lewis, L.S. (ed.) (1992) *The Adoring Audience. Fan Culture and Popular Media*. London: Routledge.

Le Vay, L. (2001) 'Scars in their eyes'.*The Guardian Guide*, April 7, 13.

Lockard, J. (2001) 'Britney Spears, Victorian chastity and brand-name virginity', *Bad Subjects*, no. 57, October. (Online: URL:http://eserver.org/bs/57/lockardB.html)

Logan, N. and Woffinden, B. (eds) (1976) *The Illustrated 'New Musical Express' Encyclopaedia of Rock*. London: Salamander Books.

Macdonald, M. (1995) *Representing Women. Myths of Femininity in the Popular Media*. London: Arnold.

MacDonald, P. (1997) 'Feeling and fun. romance, dance the performing male body in the Take That videos' in Whiteley, S. (ed.) *Sexing the Groove. Popular Music and Gender*. London: Routledge.

Mahony, E. (2002) 'Anyone can play guitar'. *Air Guitar: Art Reconsidering Rock Music*. Catalogue : Milton Keynes Gallery.

Maitland, S. (ed.) (1993) *Women Fly When Men Aren't Watching*. London: Virago.

Malins, S. (1994) 'Tori Amos'. *Vox*, May.

Manzarek, R. (1999) *Light My Fire. My Life With The Doors*. London: Arrow Books.

Marcus, G. (1982) *Mystery Train. Images of America in Rock 'n' Roll*. Revised and expanded edition. New York: Dutton.

Marcus, G. (1992) 'Anarchy in the UK', in DeCurtis, A. and Henke, J. (eds) *The Rolling Stone Illustrated History of Rock and Roll*. 3rd edition. New York: Random House.

Maslin, J. (1982) 'Bloodbaths debase movies and audiences'. *New York Times*, November 11.

McCormack, N. (2002) 'Britney, goddess of virginity', *The Age*, 25 Feb. <http://www.theage.com.au/articles/2002/02/24/2225britney-mj-sb.htm>

Mellers, W. (1946) *Music and Society*. London: Denis Dobson.

Mercer, K. (1991) 'Monster metaphors. Notes on Michael Jackson's *Thriller*' in Gledhill, C. (ed.) *Stardom, Industry of Desire*. London: Routledge.

Middleton, R. (1993) *Studying Popular Music*. Buckingham: Open University Press.

Middleton, R. (1997) *Popular Culture: Understanding Pop Music*. Milton Keynes: Open University Press.

Middleton, R. (ed.) (2000) *Reading Pop: Approaches to Textual Analysis in Popular Music*. Oxford: Oxford University Press.

Miller, J. (1968) 'Jimi Hendrix: Axis: Bold As Love', *Rolling Stone*, April 6, in Potash, C. (ed.) (1996) *The Jimi Hendrix Companion. Four Decades of Commentary*. New York: Schirmer.

Minsky, R. (ed.) (1996) *Psychoanalysis and Gender. An Introductory Reader*. London: Routledge.

Mirza, H.S. (1997) *Black British Feminism. A Reader*. London: Routledge.

Mitchell, J. (1974) *Psychoanalysis and Feminism*. New York: Vintage Books.

Mockus, M. (1994) 'Queer thoughts on country music and k.d. lang' in Brett, P., Wood, E. and Thomas, G.C. (eds) *Queering the Pitch. The New Gay and Lesbian Musicology*. New York: Routledge.

Moi, T. (1985) *Sexual/Textual Politics*. London: Routledge.

Morrison, J. (1991) *The American Night. The Writings of Jim Morrison*. London: Viking Penguin.

Mort, F. (1988) 'Boys own? Masculinity, style and popular culture' in Chapman, R. and Rutherford, J. (eds) *Male Order*. London: Lawrence & Wishart.

Mundy, C. (1995) 'Tori Amos'. *Rolling Stone*, February, issue 506.

Nabokov, V. (1959) *Lolita*. London: Shenval Press.

Negus, K. (1992) *Producing Pop. Culture and Conflict in the Popular Music Industry*. London: Edward Arnold.

Norman, P. (2002) 'The King and I'. *The Sunday Times Magazine*, August 18.

Norris, C. (ed.) (1989) *Music and the Politics of Culture*. London: Lawrence & Wishart.

O'Brien, L. (1995) *She Bop. The Definitive History of Women in Rock, Pop and Soul*. London: Penguin Books.

O'Connell Davidson, J. (1998) *Prostitution, Power and Freedom*. Cambridge: Polity Press.

Ortiz, R.L. (1999) 'L.A. Women. Jim Morrison and John Rechy' in Smith, P.J. (ed.) *The Queer Sixties*. London: Routledge.

Palmer, G. Gareth (1997) 'Springsteen and authentic masculinity' in Whiteley, S. (ed.) *Sexing the Groove. Popular Music and Gender*. London: Routledge.

Paterson, C. (2002a) 'Music'.*The Guardian Guide*, June 22.

Paterson, C. (2002b) 'Can they be serious ?' *The Guardian Guide*, August 10.

Patterson, S. (1996) 'Lunatic fringe', *NME* July 20, in Evans, L. (1997) *Girls Will Be Boys. Women Report on Rock*. London: Pandora.

Pattison, R. (1987) *The Triumph of Vulgarity. Rock Music in the Mirror of Romanticism*. Oxford: Oxford University Press.

Pethick, E. (2002) 'Scott King'. *Air Guitar: Art Reconsidering Rock Music*. Catalogue: Milton Keynes Gallery, p. 42.

Philips, C. (1991) 'Experiencing Jimi Hendrix', *Los Angeles Times*, November 26, in Potash, C. (ed.) (1996) *The Jimi Hendrix Companion. Four Decades of Commentary*. New York: Schirmer.

Piccarella, J. (1986) *The New Grove Dictionary of American Music*, p.47, in Potash, C. (ed.) (1996) *The Jimi Hendrix Companion. Four Decades of Commentary*. New York: Schirmer.

Queenan, J. (2002) 'Rockin' Roles'.*The Guardian Guide*, August 10.

Raphael, A. (1995) *Never Mind the Bollocks. Women Rewrite Rock*. London: Virago.

Reising, R. (ed.) (2002) *'Every Sound There Is'. The Beatles' Revolver and the Transformation of Rock and Roll*: London: Ashgate.

Reynolds, S. and Press. J. (1995) *The Sex Revolts. Gender, Rebellion and Rock 'n' Roll*. London: Serpents Tail.

Rice, T., Gambaccini, P. and Read, M. (eds) (1985) *The Guinness Book of British Hit Singles*. London: GRRR Books Ltd and Guinness Superlatives Ltd.

Riordan, J. and Prochnicky, J. (1991) *Break On Through: The Life and Death of Jim Morrison*. New York: William Morrow.

Rogers, K. (1994) *Tori Amos, All These Years*. Authorized illustrated biography. London and New York: Omnibus Press.

Roszak, T. (1970) *The Making of a Counter Culture: Reflections on the Technocratic Society and Its Youthful Opposition*. London: Faber & Faber.

Rowbotham, S. (1993) 'Dreams and dilemma' in Maitland, S. (ed.) *Women Fly When Men Aren't Watching*. London: Virago.

St. Michael, M. (1996) *Tori Amos*. CD and text. London: Cariton Books.

Sanjek, D. (1997) 'Can a Fujiama mama be the female Elvis' in Whiteley, S. (ed.) *Sexing the Groove. Popular Music and Gender*. London: Routledge.

Savage, J. (1991) *England's Dreaming. Sex Pistols and Punk Rock*. London: Faber & Faber.

Seidler, V.J. (1995) 'Reason, desire and male sexuality' in Caplan, P. (ed.) *The Cultural Construction of Sexuality*. London: Routledge.

Shaar Murray, C. (1989) *Crosstown Traffic. Jimi Hendrix and Post-War Pop*. London: Faber & Faber.

Sherwin, A. (2002) 'Labels bid £40 for Robbie at Christmas', *The Times News*, September 5.

Showalter, E. (1991) *Sexual Anarchy. Gender and Culture at the Fin de Siècle*. London: Bloomsbury.

Shuker, R. (1998) *Key Concepts in Popular Music*. London: Routledge.

Sloat, L. (1995) 'From playthings to fatal flowers: The image of women's sexuality in hard rock/heavy metal music 1980–1995'. Unpublished independent study.

Sloat, L.J. (1998) 'Incubus: Male songwriters' portrayal of women's sexuality in pop metal music' in Epstein, J. (ed.) *Youth Culture: Identity in a Postmodern World*. Blackwell: Malden, Massachusetts and Oxford

Smith, D.J. (2000) 'Elf risk'. *The Sunday Times Magazine*, September 10.

Sontag, S. (2000) 'Ameirikas dotre'. *Henne*, no. 10, September/October.

Stanley, L. (ed.) (1990) *Feminist Praxis. Research, Theory and Epistemology in Feminist Sociology*. London: Routledge.

Sugerman, D. (1989) *Wonderland Avenue. Tales of Glamour and Excess*. London: Abacus.

Tagg, P. (1992) 'Towards a sign typology of music' in *Studi e Testi 1, Secondo Convegno Europeo di Analisi Musicale*. Ed. Rossana Dalmonte and Mario Baroni. University of Trento, pp.369–78

Taraborrelli, J. (1992) *Michael Jackson. The Magic and the Madness*. London: Headline.

Thornham, S. (2000) *Feminist Theory and Cultural Studies. Stories of Unsettled Relations*. London: Arnold.

Threadgold, T. and Cranny-Francis, A. (eds) (1996) *Feminism and Masculine Representation*. London: Allen & Unwin.

Tobler, J. and Doe, A. (1987) *The Doors*. London: Bobcat Books (a division of Book Sales Ltd.).

Tong, R. (1992) *Feminist Thought: A Comprehensive Guide*. London: Routledge.

Tosche, N. (1980) in Carr, P. (ed.) *The Illustrated History of Country Music*. Garden City, NY: Doubleday.

Tucker, B. (1989) '"Tell Tchaikovsky the news": post modernism and the emergence of rock and roll'. *Black Music Research Journal* 9 (2), Fall.

Walkerdine, V. (1993) 'Girlhood Through the Looking Glass', in *Girls, Girlhood and Girls' Studies in Transition*, eds. M.de Ras and M. Lunenberg, Het Sphihuis, Amsterdam: 9–24.

Walkerdine, V. (1997) *Daddy's Girl: Young Girls and Popular Culture*. Houndmills: MacMillan.

Warhol, A. and Colacello, B. (1982) 'Michael Jackson'. *Interview* magazine, October.

Warner, M. (1994a) *From the Beast to the Blonde. On Fairy Tales and their Tellers*. London: Chatto & Windus.

Warner, M. (1994b) *Six Myths of Our Time. Managing Monsters. The Reith Lectures 1994*. London: Vintage.

Warner, M. (1996a) *Monuments and Maidens. The Allegory of the Female Form*. London: Vintage.

Warner, M. (1996b) *Wonder Tales. Six Stories of Enchantment*. London: Vintage.

Whiteley, S. (1992) *The Space Between the Notes. Rock and the Counter-Culture*. London: Routledge.

Whiteley, S. (ed.) (1997) *Sexing the Groove. Popular Music and Gender*. London: Routledge.

Whiteley, S. (2000) *Women and Popular Music. Sexuality, Identity and Subjectivity*. London: Routledge.

Whiteley, S. (2002) 'Love is all and love is everyone: A discussion of four musical portraits' in Reising, R. (ed.) *'Every Sound There Is'. The Beatles' Revolver and the Transformation of Rock and Roll*. London: Ashgate.

Wilde, J. (1992) Review of *Little Earthquakes*. *Melody Maker*, January 4.

Williams, Z. (2001) 'Bad Girls Inc'. *Guardian Weekend*, July 28.

Williamson, N. (2002) 'Old devils still give satisfaction', *The Times*, September 5.

Winnett, R. (2002) 'Rock giants tune up for a September 11 chart attack'. *The Sunday Times*, July 21.

Wollstonecraft, M. (1975) *A Vindication of the Rights of Women*. Ed. Carol H. Poston. New York: W.W. Norton.

Woods, R. (2002) 'Pop idols or puppets'. *The Sunday Times*, Focus, February 10.

Selected discography

Tori Amos

Y Kant Tori Read (Atlantic 1988)
Little Earthquakes (East West 1992)
Under the Pink (East West 1994)
Boys for Pele (East West 1996)
from the Choirgirl Hotel (East West 1998)

Bay City Rollers

Rollin' (Bell 1974)
Once Upon A Star (Bell 1975)
Wouldn't You Like It (Bell 1975)
Dedication (Bell 1976)
It's A Game (Arista 1977)
Strangers in the Wind (Arista 1978)
Richocet (Epic 1981)

Björk

Björk (Falkinn 1977)
With Trio Gudmunder Gling-Glon (Smekkleysa 1990)
Debut (One Little Indian 1993)
Post (One Little Indian 1995)
Telegram (One Little Indian 1996)
Homogenic (One Little Indian 1997)
Vespertine (One Little Indian 2001)

Black Sabbath

Black Sabbath (Vertigo 1970)
Paranoid (Vertigo 1970)
Master of Reality (Vertigo 1971)
Black Sabbath Vol. 4 (Vertigo 1972)
Sabbath, Bloody Sabbath (World Wide Artists 1974)
Sabotage (NEMS 1975)
Technical Ecstasy Vertigo 1976)

Never Say Die! (Vertigo 1978)
Heaven and Hell (Vertigo 1980)
Live at Last (NEMS 1980)
Mob Rules (Vertigo 1981)
Live Evil (Vertigo 1982)
Born Again (Vertigo 1983)
Seventh Star (Vertigo 1986)
The Eternal Idol (Vertigo 1987)
Headless Cross (IRS 1989)
TYR (RS 1990)
Dehumanizer (IRS 1992)
Cross Purposes (EMI 1994)
Forbidden (IRS 1995)
Reunion (Epic 1998)

Bow Wow Wow

Your Cassette Pet. Cassette only (EMI 1980)
See Jungle! Go Join Your Gang, Yeh, City All Over! Go Ape/Crazy! (RCA 1981)
I Want Candy (RCA 1982)
When The Going Gets Tough, The Tough Get Going (RCA 1983)
Wild in he USA (Cleopatra 1999)

Kate Bush

The Kick Inside (EMI 1978)
Lionheart (EMI 1978)
Never For Ever (EMI 1980)
The Dreaming (EMI 1982)
Hounds of Love (EMI 1985)
The Sensual World (EMI 1989)
The Red Shoes (EMI 1993)

David Cassidy

Cherish (Bell 1972)
Could It Be Forever (Bell 1972)
Rock Me Baby (Bell 1973)
Dreams are Nothin' More Than Wishes (Bell 1973)
Cassidy Live (Bell 1974)
The Higher They Climb The Harder They Fall (RCA 1975)
Home Is Where The Heart Is (RCA 1976)
Romance (Arista 1985)

Cher

All I Really Want To Do (Liberty 1965)
The Sonny Side of Cher (Liberty 1966)

Cher (Imperial 1966)
With Love, Cher (Imperial 1968)
3614 Jackson Highway (Atcol 1969)
Gypsies, Tramps and Thieves (Kapp 1971)
Foxy Lady (Kapp 1972)
Half Breed (MCA 1973)
Dark Lady (MCA 1974)
Bittersweet White Light (MCA 1974)
Stars (Warners 1975)
with Gregg Allman as *Allman and Woman. Two The Hard Way* (Warners 1977)
Take Me Home (Cassablanca 1979)
Prisoner (Cassablanca 1980)
I Paralyze (Columbia 1982)
Cher (Geffen 1987)
Heart of Stone (Geffen 1989)
Love Hurts Geffen 1991)
It's a Man's World (Warners 1995)
Believe (Warners 1996)
Living Proof (Warners 2002)

Eric Clapton (inc. Cream)

Fresh Cream (Polydor 1966)
Three tracks as the Powerhouse with Steve Winwood, Jack Bruce, Pete York, Paul Jones,
     What's Shakin'? (Elektra 1966)
Disraeli Gears (Polydor 1967)
Wheels of Fire (Polydor 1968)
Goodbye (Polydor 1969)
Live Cream (Polydor 1970)
Live Cream, Vol. 2 (Polydor 1972)
Eric Clapton (Polydor 1970)
Eric Clapton's Rainbow Concert (RSO 1973)
461 Ocean Boulevard (RSO 1974)
There's One In Every Crowd (RSO 1974)
E.C. Was Here (RSO 1975)
No Reason To Cry (RSO 1976)
Slowhand (RSO 1977)
Backless (RSO 1978)
Just One Night (RSO 1980)
Another Ticket (RSO 1981)
Money and Cigarettes (Duck 1983)
Behind the Sun (Duck 1985)
August (Duck 1986)
Journeyman (Duck 1989)
24 Nights (Duck 1991)
MTV Unplugged (Sony 1992)
From The Cradle To The Grave (Duck 1994)
Pilgrim (Warners 1998)

Deep Purple

Shades of Deep Purple (Parlophone 1968)
The Book of Taliesyn (Harvest 1969)
Deep Purple (Harvest 1969)
Concerto for Group and Orchestra (Harvest 1970)
Deep Purple in Rock (Harvest 1970)
Fireball (Harvest 1971)
Machine Head (Purple 1972)
Made in Japan (Purple 1973)
Who Do We Think We Are! (Purple 1973)
Burn (Purple 1974)
Stormbringer (Purple 1974)
Come Taste the Band (Purple 1975)
Deep Purple Live (UK), *Made in Europe* (US) (Purple/Warners 1976)
Deep Purple Live in London. Recorded 1974 (Harvest 1982)
Perfect Strangers (Polydor 1984)
The House of Blue Light (Polydor 1987)
Nobody's Perfect (Polydor 1988)
Slaves and Masters (RCA 1990)
Knebworth '85 (Connoisseur 1991)
The Battle Rages On (RCA 1993)
The Final Battle (RCA 1994)
Come Hell or High Water (RCA 1994)
On the Wings of a Russian Foxbat (Live in California 1976) (Connoisseur 1995)
Live at the California Jam (Mausoleum 1996)
Deep Purple in Concert on the King Biscuit Flower Hour (King Biscuit 1996)
Purpendicular (RCA 1996)
Mark III, The Final Concerts (Connoisseur 1996)
Live at the Olympia '96 (Thames 1997)
Abandon (EMI 1998)

Jimi Hendrix

Are You Experienced (Track 1967)
Axis: Bold as Love (Track 1967)
Electric Ladyland (Track 1968)
Cry of Love (Polydor 1971)
Experience (Ember 1971)
Isle of Wight (Polydor 1971)
Rainbow Bridge (Reprise 1971)
Hendrix in the West (Polydor 1971)
More Experience (Ember 1972)
War Heroes (Polydor 1972)
Loose Ends (Polydor 1974)
Crash Landing (Polydor 1974)
Midnight Lightnin' (Polydor 1975)
Nine to the Universe (Polydor 1980)
The Jimi Hendrix Concerts (Columbia 1982)

Jimi Plays Monterey (Polydor 1986)
Live at Winterland (Polydor 1987)
Radio One (Castle 1988)
Live and Unreleased (Castle 1989)
First Rays of the New Rising Sun (Experience/MCA 1997)
South Southern Delta (Experience 1997)

Michael Jackson

Got To Be There (Motown 1972)
Ben (Motown 1972)
Music and Me (Motown 1973)
Forever, Michael (Motown 1975)
Off The Wall (Epic 1979)
One Day In Your Life (Motown 1981)
Thriller (Epic 1982)
E-T – the Extra-Terrestrial (MCA 1983)
Farewell My Summer Love 1973 Recording (Motown 1984)
Looking Back To Yesterday (Motown 1986)
Bad (Epic 1987)
Dangerous (Epic 1991)
HIStory – Past, Present and Future – Book 1 (Epic 1995)
Blood On The Dance Floor – History in the Mix (Epic 1997)

Carole King

Writer (Ode 1970)
Tapestry (Ode 1971)
Music (Ode 1971)
Rhymes and Reasons (Ode 1972)
Fantasy (Ode 1973)
Rap Around Joy (Ode 1974)
Really Rosie (Ode 1975)
Thoroughbred (Ode 1976)
Simple Things (Capitol 1977)
Welcome Home (Avatar 1978)
Pearls (Songs of Goffin and King) (Capitol 1980)
Touch The Sky (Capitol 1979)
One to One (Atlantic 1982)
Speeding Time (Atlantic 1984)
City Streets (Capitol 1989)
In Concert (Quality 1994)

Led Zeppelin

Led Zeppelin (Atlantic 1969)
Led Zeppelin II (Atlantic 1969)
Led Zeppelin III (Atlantic 1970)

Led Zeppelin IV (Atlantic 1971)
Houses of the Holy (Atlantic 1973)
Physical Graffitti (Swansong 1975)
Presence (Swansong 1976)
The Song Remains the Same. Film Sountrack (Swansong 1976)
BBC Sessions (Atlantic 1977)
In Through the Out Door (Swansong 1979)
Coda (Swansong 1982)

Brenda Lee

Grandma, What Great Songs You Sang (Decca 1959)
Brenda Lee (Decca 1960)
This Is ... Brenda (Decca 1960)
Miss Dynamite (Brunswick 1961)
Emotions (Decca 1961)
All The Way (Decca 1961)
Sincerely Brenda Lee (Decca 1962)
Brenda, That's All (Decca 1962)
All Alone Am I (Decca 1963)
Let Me Sing (Decca 1963)
Sings Songs Everbody Knows (Decca 1964)
By Request (Decca 1964)
Merry Christmas from Brenda Lee (Decca 1964)
Top Teen Hits (Decca 1964)
The Versatile Brenda Lee (Decca 1965)
Two Many Rivers (Decca 1965)
Bye Bye Blues (Decca 1965)
Coming On Strong (Decca 1966)
Call Me Brenda (Decca 1967)
Reflections in Blue (Decca 1967)
Good Life (Decca 1967)
with Tennessee Ernie Ford *The Chauffeur Christmas Seals* (Decca 1968)
with Pete Fountain *For the First Time* (Decca 1968)
Johnny One Time (Decca 1969)
Memphis Portrait (Decca 1970)
Let It Be Me (Vorcalion 1970)
A Whole Lotta (MCA 1972)
Brenda (MCA 1973)
New Sunrise (MCA 1974)
Brenda Lee Now (MCA 1975)
The LA Sessions (MCA 1977)
Even Better (MCA 1980)
Take Me Back (MCA 1981)
Only When I Laugh (MCA 1982)
With Dolly Parton, Chris Kristofferson and Willy Nelson *The Winning Hand* (Monument 1983)

Feels So Right (MCA 1985)
Brenda Lee (Warners 1991)
A Brenda Lee Christmas (Warners 1991)
Greatest Hits Live (MCA 1992)
Coming On Strong (Muskateer 1995)

Madonna

Madonna (Sire 1983)
Like a Virgin (Sire 1984)
True Blue (Sire 1986)
You Can Dance (Sire 1987)
Like A Prayer (Sire 1989)
I'm Breathless (Sire 1990)
Erotica (Maverick 1992)
Bedtime Stories (Warners 1994)
Something to Remember (Sire 1995)
Evita (Warners 1996)
Ray of Light (Maverick/Warners 1998)

Hank Marvin (The Shadows)

The Shadows (Columbia 1961)
Out of the Shadows (Columbia 1962)
Dance with the Shadows (Columbia 1964)
The Sound of the Shadows (Columbia 1965)
Shadow Music (Columbia 1966)
Jigsaw (Columbia 1967)
From Hank, Bruce, Brian and John (Columbia 1967)
with Cliff Richard Established 1958 (Columbia 1968)
Shades of Rock (Columbia 1970)
Rockin' with Curly Leads (EMI 1973)
Specs Appeal (EMI 1975)
Live at the Paris Olympia (EMI 1975)
Tasty (EMI 1977)
With Richard Thank You Very Much (EMI 1979)
Change of Address (Polydor 1980)
Hits Right Up Your Street (Polydor 1981)
Life in the Jungle/Live at Abbey Road (Polydor 1982)
XXV (Polydor 1983)
Guardian Angel (Polydor 1984)
Moonlight Shadows (Polydor 1986)
Simply Shadows (Polydor 1987)
Steppin' to the Shadows (Roll Over Records 1989)
Reflections (Polydor 1991)

Kylie Minogue

Kylie (PWL 1988)
Enjoy Yourself (PWL 1989)
Rhythm of Love (PWL 1990)
Let's Get To It (PWL 1991)
Kyile Minogue (Deconstruction 1994)
Kylie Minogue (Deconstruction 1997)

Joni Mitchell

Joni Mitchell aka Song to a Seagull (Reprise 1968)
Clouds (Reprise 1969)
Ladies of the Canyon (Reprise 1970)
Blue (Reprise 1971)
For the Roses (Asylum 1972)
Court and Spark (Asylum 1974)
Miles of Aisles (Asylum 1974)
The Hissing of Summer Lawns (Asylum 1975)
Hejira (Asylum 1976)
Don Juan's Reckless Daughter (Asylum 1977)
Mingus (Asylum 1979)
Shadows and Light (Asylum 1980)
Wild Things Run Fast (Geffen 1982)
Dog Eat Dog (Geffen 1985)
Chalk Mark in a Rainstorm (Geffen 1988)
Night Ride Home (Geffen 1991)
Turbulent Indigo (Warners 1994)
Taming the Tiger (Warners 1998)

Jim Morrison (The Doors)

The Doors (Elektra 1967)
Strange Days (Elektra 1967)
Waiting for the Sun (Elektra 1968)
The Soft Parade (Elektra 1969)
Morrison Hotel (Elektra 1970)
Absolutely Live (Elektra 1970)
LA Woman (Elektra 1971)
Other Voices (Elektra 1971)
Full Circle (Elektra 1972)
An American Prayer (Elektra 1978)
Alive, She Cried (Elektra 1983)
The Doors Live at the Hollywood Bowl (Elektra 1987)
In Concert (Elektra 1991)

Elvis Presley

Elvis Presley (RCA Victor 1956)

Elvis (RCA Victor 1956)
Rock 'n' Roll Release (HMV 1956)
Rock 'n' Roll No. 2. UK Release (HMV 1957)
Loving You. Film soundtrack (RCA Victor 1957)
Elvis' Christmas Album (RCA Victor 1957)
King Creole. Film soundtrack (RCA Victor 1958)
For LP Fans Only (RCA Victor 1959)
A Date with Elvis (RCA Victor 1959)
Elvis is Back! (RCA Victor 1960)
G.I. Blues. Film soundtrack (RCA Victor 1960)
His Hand in Mine (RCA Victor 1961)
Something for Everybody (RCA Victor 1961)
Blue Hawaii (RCA Victor 1961)
Pot Luck (RCA Victor 1962)
Girls! Girls! Girls!. Film soundtrack (RCA Victor 1963)
Fun in Acapulco. Film soundtrack (RCA Victor 1963)
Kissin' Cousins. Film soundtrack (RCA Victor 1964)
Girl Happy. Film soundtrack (RCA Victor 1965)
Harum Scarum. Film soundtrack (RCA Victor 1965)
Frankie and Johnny. Film soundtrack (RCA Victor 1966)
Paradise Blue Hawiian Style. Film soundtrack (RCA Victor 1966)
Elvis: The First Live Recordings (Music Works, 1984)
Elvis Presley '56 (RCA 1996)
Essential Elvis, Volume 4: A Hundred Years from Now (RCA 1996)
Essential Elvis, Volume 5: Rhythm and Country (RCA 1998)

Queen

Queen (EMI 1973)
Queen II (EMI 1974)
Sheer Heart Attack (EMI 1974)
A Night At The Opera (EMI 1975)
A Day at the Races (EMI 1976)
News of the World (EMI 1977)
Jazz (EMI 1978)
Live Killers (EMI 1979)
The Game (EMI 1980)
Flash Gordon. Film soundtrack (EMI 1980)
Hot Space (EMI 1982)
The Works (EMI 1984)
A Kind of Magic (EMI 1986)
Live Magic (EMI 1986)
The Miracle (EMI 1989)
Queen at the Beeb (Band of Joy 1989)
Innuendo (EMI 1991)
Live at Wembley (EMI 1992)
Made in Heaven (EMI 1995)

Cliff Richard

Cliff (Columbia 1959)
Cliff Sings (Columbia 1959)
Me and my Shadows (Columbia 1960)
Listen to Cliff (Columbia 1961)
21 Today (Columbia 1961)
The Young Ones (Columbia 1961)
32 Minutes 17 Seconds with Cliff Richard (Columbia 1962)
Summer Holiday (Columbia 1963)
Cliff's Hit Album (Columbia 1963)
When in Spain (Columbia 1963)
Wonderful Life (Columbia 1964)
Aladdin and his Wonderful Lamp (Columbia 1964)
Cliff Richard (Columbia 1965)
More Hits by Cliff (Columbia 1965)
When in Rome (Columbia 1965)
Live is Forever (Columbia 1965)
Kinda Latin (Columbia 1966)
Finders Keepers (Columbia 1966)
Cinderella (Columbia 1967)
Don't Stop Me Now (Columbia 1967)
Good News (Columbia 1967)
Cliff in Japan (Columbia 1968)
Two a Penny (Columbia 1968)

Rolling Stones

The Rolling Stones (London/Decca 1964)
The Rolling Stones (London/Decca 1965)
The Rolling Stones Now (London 1965)
December's Children (and Everybodies) (London 1965)
Out of our Heads (Decca/London 1965)
Aftermath (Decca/London 1966)
Got Live If You Want It (London 1966)
Between the Buttons (London/Decca 1967)
Their Satanic Majesties Request (Decca/London 1967)
Flowers (London 1967)
Beggar's Banquet (London 1968)
Let It Bleed (London/Decca 1969)
Get Yer Ya-Ya's Out! (London/Decca 1970)
Sticky Fingers (Rolling Stones 1971)
Exile on Main Street (Rolling Stones 1972)
Goat's Head Soup (Rolling Stones 1973)
It's Only Rock 'n' Roll (Rolling Stones 1974)
Black and Blue (Rolling Stones 1976)
Love You Live (Rolling Stones 1977)
Some Girls (Rolling Stones 1978)
Emotional Rescue (Rolling Stones 1980)

Tattoo You (Rolling Stones 1981)
Still Life (American Concerts 1981) (Rolling Stones 1982)
Undercover (Rolling Stones 1983)
Dirty Work (Rolling Stones 1986)
Steel Wheels (Rolling Stones 1989)
Flash Point (Rolling Stones 1991)
Voodoo Lounge (Virgin 1994)
Stripped (Virgin 1995)
Bridges to Babylon (Virgin 1997)
No Security (Virgin 1998)
Forty Licks (Virgin 2002)

Santana

Santana (Columbia 1969)
Abraxas (Columbia 1970)
Santana III (Columbia 1971)
Caravanserai (Columbia 1972)
Carlos Santana and Buddy Miles! Live! (Columbia 1972)
Love Devotion Surrender (Columbia 1973)
Welcome (Columbia 1973)
Borboletta (Columbia 1974)
Illuminations (Columbia 1974)
Lotus (Columbia 1975)
Amigos (Columbia 1976)
Festival (Columbia 1977)
Moonflower (Columbia 1977)
Inner Secrets (Columbia 1978)
Marathon (Columbia 1979)
Oneness Silver Dreams, Golden Reality (Columbia 1979)
The Swing of Delight (Columbia 1980)
Zebop! (Columbia 1981)
Shango (Columbia 1982)
Havana Moon (Columbia 1983)
Beyond Appearances (Columbia 1985)
La Bamba (Columbia 1986)
Freedom (Columbia 1987)
Blues for Salvador (Columbia 1987)
Persuasion (Thunderbolt 1989)
Spirits Dancing in the Flesh (Columbia 1990)
Milagro (Polydor 1992)
Sacred Fire, Live in South America (Columbia 1993)
With the Santa Brothers: Santana Brothers (Island 1994)
Live at the Fillmore 1968 (Columbia/Legacy 1997)
Supernatural (Arista 1999)

Patti Smith

Horses (Arista 1975)
Radio Ethiopia (Arista 1976)
Easter (Arista 1978)
Wave (Arista 1979)
Dream Of Life (Arista 1988)
Gone Again (Arista 1996)
Peace and Noise (Arista 1997)

The Smiths

The Smiths (Rough Trade 1984)
Meat is Murder (Rough Trade 1985)
The Queen is Dead (Rough Trade 1986)
Strangeways, Here We Come (Rough Trade 1987)
'Rank' (Rough Trade 1988)

Bruce Springsteen

Greetings from Asbury Park, NJ (Columbia 1973)
The Wild, the Innocent and the E Street Shuffle (Columbia 1973)
Born to Run (Columbia 1975)
Darkness on the Edge of Town (Columbia 1978)
The River (Columbia 1980)
Nebraska (Columbia 1982)
Born in the USA (Columbia 1984)
Live 1975–85 (Columbia 1986)
Tunnel of Love (Columbia 1987)
Human Touch (Columbia 1992)
Lucky Town (Columbia 1992)
The Ghost of Tom Joad (Columbia 1995)
The Rising (Columbia 2002)

Status Quo

Picturesque Matchskickable Messages (Pye 1968)
Spare Parts (Pye 1969)
Ma Kelly's Greasy Spoon (Pye 1970)
Dog of Two Head (Pye 1971)
PileDriver (Vertigo 1972)
Hello! (Vertigo 1973)
Quo (Vertigo 1974)
On the Level (Vertigo 1975)
Blue for You (Vertigo 1976)
Status Quo Live (Vertigo 1977)
Rockin' all Over the World (Vertigo 1977)
If You Can't Stand the Heat (Vertigo 1978)
Whatever You Want (Vertigo 1979)

Just Supposin' (Vertigo 1980)
Never Too Late (Vertigo 1982)
1 + 9 + 8 + 2 (Vertigo 1982)
Back to Back (Vertigo 1983)
In the Army Now (Vertigo 1986)
Ain't Complaining (Vertigo 1988)
Perfect Remedy (Vertigo 1989)
Rock 'til You Drop (Vertigo 1991)
Live Alive Quo (Vertigo 1992)
Thirsty Work (Polydor 1994)
Don't Stop (Polygram 1996)

U2

Boy (Island 1980)
October (Island 1981)
War (Island 1983)
Under a Blood Red Sky (Island 1983)
The Unforgettable Fire (Island 1984)
Wide Awake in America (Island 1985)
The Joshua Tree (Island 1987)
The Joshua Tree Singles (Island 1988)
Rattle and Hum (Island 1988)
Achtung Baby (Island 1991)
Zooropa (Island 1993)
Pop (Island 1997)

The Who

My Generation (Brunswick 1965)
The Who Sings My Generation (Decca 1966)
A Quick One (Reaction 1966)
The Who Sell Out (Track 1967)
Happy Jack (Decca 1967)
Magic Bus – the Who on Tour (Decca 1968)
Tommy (Track 1969)
Live at Leeds (Track 1970)
Who's Next (Track 1971)
Quadrophenia (MCA 1973)
The Who By Numbers (Polydor 1975)
Who Are You? (Polydor 1978)
The Kids Are Alright. Film soundtrack (Polydor 1979)
Quadrophenia. Film soundtrack (Polydor 1979)
Face Dances (Polydor 1981)
It's Hard (Polydor 1982)
Join Together (Virgin 1990)
Live at the Isle of Wight Festival 1970 (Essential 1996)

Robbie Williams (inc. Take That)

Take That and Party (RCA 1992)
Everything Changes (RCA 1993)
Nobody Else (RCA 1995)
Life Thru A Lens (EMI 1997)
I've Been Expecting You (Chrysalis 1998)
The Ego has Landed (US only) (EMI 1999)
Swing When You're Winning (EMI 2001)

Note

UK cataloguing data has been used in the compiling of this list.

Index

eBooks – at www.eBookstore.tandf.co.uk

A library at your fingertips!

eBooks are electronic versions of printed books. You can store them on your PC/laptop or browse them online.

They have advantages for anyone needing rapid access to a wide variety of published, copyright information.

eBooks can help your research by enabling you to bookmark chapters, annotate text and use instant searches to find specific words or phrases. Several eBook files would fit on even a small laptop or PDA.

NEW: Save money by eSubscribing: cheap, online access to any eBook for as long as you need it.

Annual subscription packages

We now offer special low-cost bulk subscriptions to packages of eBooks in certain subject areas. These are available to libraries or to individuals.

For more information please contact webmaster.ebooks@tandf.co.uk

We're continually developing the eBook concept, so keep up to date by visiting the website.

www.eBookstore.tandf.co.uk